COWLES FOUNDATION
for Research in Economics at Yale University

MONOGRAPH 21

COWLES FOUNDATION

For Research in Economics at Yale University

The Cowles Foundation for Research in Economics at Yale University, established as an activity of the Department of Economics in 1955, has as its purpose the conduct and encouragement of research in economics, finance, commerce, industry, and technology, including problems of the organization of these activities. The Cowles Foundation seeks to foster the development of logical, mathematical, and statistical methods of analysis for application in economics and related social sciences. The professional research staff are, as a rule, faculty members with appointments and teaching responsibilities in the Department of Economics and other departments.

The Cowles Foundation continues the work of the Cowles Commission for Research in Economics founded in 1932 by Alfred Cowles at Colorado Springs, Colorado. The Commission moved to Chicago in 1939 and was affiliated with the University of Chicago until 1955. In 1955 the professional research staff of the Commission accepted appointments at Yale and, along with other members of the Yale Department of Economics, formed the research staff of the newly established Cowles Foundation.

A list of Cowles Foundation Monographs appears at the end of this volume.

FINANCIAL MARKETS AND
ECONOMIC ACTIVITY

Edited by

DONALD D. HESTER AND JAMES TOBIN

Contributors
WILLIAM C. BRAINARD
ARTHUR M. OKUN
RICHARD C. PORTER
PETER E. SLOANE
JAMES TOBIN

NEW HAVEN AND LONDON, YALE UNIVERSITY PRESS

162686

Printed in the United States of America by
The Carl Purington Rollins Printing-Office
of the Yale University Press.

Distributed in Great Britain, Europe, and Africa by
Yale University Press, Ltd., London; in Canada by
McGill-Queen's University Press, Montreal; in Latin America by Kaiman
& Polon, Inc., New York City; in Australasia by
Australia and New Zealand Book Co., Pty., Ltd.,
Artarmon, New South Wales; in India by UBS Publishers'
Distributors Pvt., Ltd., Delhi; in Japan by John
Weatherhill, Inc., Tokyo.

Contents

Foreword

This monograph is one of three (Monographs 19, 20, and 21) that bring together nineteen essays on theoretical and empirical monetary economics written by recent Yale graduate students and staff members of the Cowles Foundation. Seven of these are based on doctoral dissertations approved by the Yale Economics Department, supervised by Cowles Foundation staff members and other members of the Department.

The sixteen authors do not necessarily have common views about monetary theory and policy or about empirical methods and findings. Their contributions do not fit together in any prearranged master research plan; the idea that they would make a coherent collection is a product of afterthought, not forethought. But the essays do have a certain unity, the result of a common intellectual climate which suggested many of the questions to be asked and many of the theoretical and empirical approaches to finding the answers.

The conception of "monetary" economics underlying this collection of essays is a very broad one. Monetary phenomena are not confined to those involving the quantity of currency and demand deposits, and commercial banks are not the only financial intermediary considered to be of monetary interest. There is no sharp dividing line between assets which are "money" and those which are not or between institutions that emit "money" and those that do not. The emphasis is on differences of degree, not differences in kind. To justify this emphasis, it is only necessary to recall the great difficulty which economists who stress the sovereign importance of the "quantity of money" have in drawing the dividing line to define money.

Monetary theory broadly conceived is simply the theory of portfolio management by economic units: households, businesses, financial institutions, and governments. It takes as its subject matter stocks of assets and debts (including money proper) and their values and yields; its accounting framework is the balance sheet. It can be distinguished from branches of economic theory which take the income statement as their accounting framework and flows of income, saving, expenditure, and production as their subject matter.

Of course, separation of the theory of stocks from the theory of flows is artificial and tentative. Economists work toward the synthesis of the two, and many attempts at combining them have been made, with varying degrees of simplification and success. Nevertheless, the artificial distinction seems a useful one, especially for the development of monetary economics. The processes which determine why one balance sheet or portfolio is chosen in preference to another are just beginning to be studied and understood. In studying these processes it helps to keep the links between capital account and income account as simple as possible. At any rate, that is the approach of most of the essays in this collection.

Like other branches of economic theory, monetary theory has both a microeconomic and a macroeconomic side. Monetary microeconomics concerns the balance sheet or portfolio choices of individual units—households, businesses, or financial institutions. The choices are constrained by the wealth of the unit and by its opportunities to buy and sell assets and to incur or retire debt. Within these constraints, the choices are affected by the objectives, expectations, and uncertainties of the unit. Monetary macroeconomics concerns the general equilibrium of the capital accounts in the economy as a whole, the way in which asset prices and yields adjust to equate the demands to the supplies of the various assets and debts.

Monetary economics is as old as any branch of economics, but until fairly recently it lacked a solid microeconomic foundation. Elsewhere in economic theory this foundation is supplied by some assumption of optimizing behavior, for example, maximization of utility by consumers or of profits by firms. But the usual assumptions of pure economic theory—perfect certainty, perfect markets, no transactions costs or other frictions—provide no rationale for the holding of diversified portfolios and balance sheets (much less for the holding of money and other low-yield assets) or for the existence of financial institutions. Monetary theory was therefore based for the most part on *ad hoc* generalizations about capital account behavior, based on common sense or empirical observation rather than on any logically developed notion of optimal behavior.

During the last twenty years, economic theory, stimulated in part by the upsurge of interest in management science and operations research, has tackled directly the problem of defining optimal behavior in situations involving market imperfections, transactions costs and other "frictions," and uncertainties about future prospects. The tools developed have proved to have some fruitful applications to monetary behavior. For example, the theory of optimal inventory policy gave solid theoretical explanations of the transactions and precautionary demands for cash—phenomena that have long played a central role in traditional monetary economics.[1]

Another theoretical tool with important uses in monetary analysis originated in the general study of decision-making under uncertainty. It became possible to give a precise expression to the common-sense observation that distaste for risk leads investors to diversify portfolios and to hold assets with widely differing expected yields simultaneously. In an earlier Cowles Foundation Monograph, Harry Markowitz proposed a way in which the risk and expected yield of a portfolio could be defined and calculated from the subjective probabilities assigned by an investor to the various future prospects of the assets included in the portfolio.[2] He showed further how to compute *efficient* portfolios; an efficient portfolio is one whose expected return could not be raised by altering its composition without also increasing risk. Markowitz's interest was mainly normative; that is, his objective was to show investors how to be rational. However, if it is assumed that investors are in fact behaving rationally, the same approach can be fruitfully applied in positive monetary analysis. An early application of this kind to the famous question of the "speculative" demand for money was made in the article reprinted here as Chapter 1 of Monograph 19.

The seven essays in Monograph 19, *Risk Aversion and Portfolio Choice*, have both normative implications, as pieces of advice to investors, and positive implications, as descriptions of the economy. They are partly theoretical and partly empirical. They concern, on the one hand, the *attitudes* of investors toward risk and average return and, on the other, the *opportunities* which the market and the tax laws afford investors for purchasing less risk at the expense of expected return.

Monograph 20, *Studies of Portfolio Behavior*, is institutionally oriented. The six essays draw on the theoretical developments mentioned above and seek to apply them to the particular circumstances and objectives of

---

[1] See William J. Baumol, "The Transactions Demand for Cash: An Inventory Theoretic Approach," *Quarterly Journal of Economics*, Vol. LXVI, No. 4 (November 1952), pp. 545–56; James Tobin, "The Interest-Elasticity of Transactions Demand for Cash," *The Review of Economics and Statistics*, Vol. XXXVIII, No. 3 (August, 1956), pp. 241–8; and Don Patinkin, *Money, Interest and Prices* (Evanston, Ill.: Row, Peterson and Company, 1956), Chap. 7.

[2] Harry M. Markowitz, *Portfolio Selection: Efficient Diversification of Investments* (New York: John Wiley and Sons, 1959).

various kinds of economic units·: households, nonfinancial corporations, banks, and life insurance companies. It is our hope that the analytical tools contribute to the interpretation of the statistical data available on balance sheets and capital accounts.

The subjects of Monograph 21, *Financial Markets and Economic Activity*, are macroeconomic. They concern the conditions of equilibrium in economy-wide financial markets. The microeconomic principles discussed in the first two monographs are assumed to guide the behavior of individual economic units, including financial intermediaries, in demanding and supplying assets and debts in these markets. But the main focus is on the adjustment of interest rates and other yields to create equilibrium in various financial markets simultaneously. From this standpoint, the quantity of money as conventionally defined is not an autonomous variable controlled by governmental authority but an endogenous or "inside" quantity reflecting the economic behavior of banks and other private economic units. Commercial banks are seen to differ from other financial intermediaries less basically in the nature of their liabilities than in the controls over reserves and interest rates to which they are legally subject. Models of financial market equilibrium can be used to analyze a wide variety of questions about the behavior of financial markets. The theoretical studies in Monograph 21 apply this framework to investigate the consequences of various institutions and regulations for the effectiveness of monetary control. In addition some empirical findings on the structure of interest rates by maturity and by risk category are reported.

Some of the essays were, as indicated in footnotes, written under a grant from the National Science Foundation. We are grateful for their continuing support of research in this area at the Cowles Foundation. The staff of the Cowles Foundation—secretaries, librarians, and research assistants—has contributed efficiently and cheerfully to the original preparation of the papers and to their assembly into Monographs 19, 20, and 21. Particular gratitude is due Miss Althea Strauss, whose loyal and indefatigable service as administrative assistant provides important continuity at the Foundation, and to Mrs. Amanda Slowen, on whom fell the exacting task of retyping some of the material. Finally, the editors and all the authors are in greater debt than they may realize to Karen Hester, who painstakingly and skillfully edited the papers for inclusion in the monograph. She improved them both in English and in economics, but she is not responsible for the defects that remain.

New Haven, Connecticut   DONALD D. HESTER
October, 1966   JAMES TOBIN

1

Commercial Banks as Creators of "Money"*

JAMES TOBIN

THE OLD VIEW

Perhaps the greatest moment of triumph for the elementary economics teacher is his exposition of the multiple creation of bank credit and bank deposits. Before the admiring eyes of freshmen he puts to rout the practical banker who is so sure that he "lends only the money depositors entrust to him." The banker is shown to have a worm's-eye view, and his error stands as an introductory object lesson in the fallacy of composition. From the Olympian vantage of the teacher and the textbook it appears that the banker's dictum must be reversed: depositors entrust to bankers whatever amounts the bankers lend. To be sure, this is not true of a single bank; one bank's loan may wind up as another bank's deposit. But it is, as the arithmetic of successive rounds of deposit creation makes clear, true of the banking system as a whole. Whatever their other errors, a long line of financial heretics have been right in speaking of "fountain pen money"—money created by the stroke of the bank president's pen when he approves a loan and credits the proceeds to the borrower's checking account.

In this time-honored exposition two characteristics of commercial banks—both of which are alleged to differentiate them sharply from other

---

* SOURCE: Reprinted from *Banking and Monetary Studies*, edited by Deane Carson, for the Comptroller of the Currency, U.S. Treasury (Homewood, Ill.: Richard D. Irwin, Inc., 1963), pp. 408–419.

financial intermediaries—are intertwined. One is that their liabilities—well, at least their demand deposit liabilities—serve as widely acceptable means of payment. Thus, they count, along with coin and currency in public circulation, as "money." The other is that the preferences of the public normally play no role in determining the total volume of deposits or the total quantity of money. For it is the beginning of wisdom in monetary economics to observe that money is like the "hot potato" of a children's game: one individual may pass it to another, but the group as a whole cannot get rid of it. If the economy and the supply of money are out of adjustment, it is the economy that must do the adjusting. This is as true, evidently, of money created by bankers' fountain pens as of money created by public printing presses. On the other hand, financial intermediaries other than banks do not create money, and the scale of their assets is limited by their liabilities, i.e., by the savings the public entrusts to them. They cannot count on receiving "deposits" to match every extension of their lending.

The commercial banks and only the commercial banks, in other words, possess the widow's cruse. And because they possess this key to unlimited expansion, they have to be restrained by reserve requirements. Once this is done, determination of the aggregate volume of bank deposits is just a matter of accounting and arithmetic: simply divide the available supply of bank reserves by the required reserve ratio.

The foregoing is admittedly a caricature, but I believe it is not a great exaggeration of the impressions conveyed by economics teaching concerning the roles of commercial banks and other financial institutions in the monetary system. In conveying this mélange of propositions, economics has replaced the naive fallacy of composition of the banker with other half-truths perhaps equally misleading. These have their root in the mystique of "money"—the tradition of distinguishing sharply between those assets which are and those which are not "money," and accordingly between those institutions which emit "money" and those whose liabilities are not "money." The persistent strength of this tradition is remarkable given the uncertainty and controversy over where to draw the dividing line between money and other assets. Time was when only currency was regarded as money, and the use of bank deposits was regarded as a way of economizing currency and increasing the velocity of money. Today scholars and statisticians wonder and argue whether to count commercial bank time and savings deposits in the money supply. If so, why not similar accounts in other institutions? Nevertheless, once the arbitrary line is drawn, assets on the money side of the line are assumed to possess to the full properties which assets on the other side completely lack. For example, an eminent monetary economist, more candid than many of his colleagues, admits that we do not really know what money is, but proceeds to argue that, whatever it is, its supply should grow regularly at a rate of the order of 3 to 4 per cent per year.[1]

THE "NEW VIEW"

A more recent development in monetary economics tends to blur the sharp traditional distinctions between money and other assets and between commercial banks and other financial intermediaries; to focus on demands for and supplies of the whole spectrum of assets rather than on the quantity and velocity of "money"; and to regard the structure of interest rates, asset yields, and credit availabilities rather than the quantity of money as the linkage between monetary and financial institutions and policies on the one hand and the real economy on the other.[2]   In this chapter I propose to look briefly at the implications of this "new view" for the theory of deposit creation, of which I have above described or caricatured the traditional version.   One of the incidental advantages of this theoretical development is to effect something of a reconciliation between the economics teacher and the practical banker.

According to the "new view," the essential function of financial intermediaries, including commercial banks, is to satisfy simultaneously the portfolio preferences of two types of individuals or firms.[3]   On one side are borrowers, who wish to expand their holdings of real assets—inventories, residential real estate, productive plant and equipment, etc.—beyond the limits of their own net worth.   On the other side are lenders, who wish to hold part or all of their net worth in assets of stable money value with negligible risk of default.   The assets of financial intermediaries are obligations of the borrowers—promissory notes, bonds, mortgages. The

---

[1] E. S. Shaw, "Money Supply and Stable Economic Growth," in *United States Monetary Policy* (New York: American Assembly, 1958), pp. 49–71.

[2] For a review of this development and for references to its protagonists, see Harry Johnson's survey article, "Monetary Theory and Policy," *American Economic Review*, Vol. LII (June, 1962), pp. 335–84.   I will confine myself to mentioning the importance, in originating and contributing to the "new view," of John Gurley and E. S. Shaw (yes, the very same Shaw cited in the previous footnote, but presumably in a different incarnation). Their viewpoint is summarized in *Money in a Theory of Finance* (Washington, D.C.: The Brookings Institution, 1960).

[3] This paragraph and the three following are adapted with minor changes from the author's paper with William Brainard, "Financial Intermediaries and the Effectiveness of Monetary Controls," reprinted in this volume, Chapter 3.

liabilities of financial intermediaries are the assets of the lenders—bank deposits, insurance policies, pension rights.

Financial intermediaries typically assume liabilities of smaller default risk and greater predictability of value than their assets. The principal kinds of institutions take on liabilities of greater liquidity too; thus, bank depositors can require payment on demand, while bank loans become due only on specified dates. The reasons that the intermediation of financial institutions can accomplish these transformations between the nature of the obligation of the borrower and the nature of the asset of the ultimate lender are these: (1) administrative economy and expertise in negotiating, accounting, appraising, and collecting; (2) reduction of risk per dollar of lending by the pooling of independent risks, with respect both to loan default and to deposit withdrawal; (3) governmental guarantees of the liabilities of the institutions and other provisions (bank examination, investment regulations, supervision of insurance companies, last-resort lending) designed to assure the solvency and liquidity of the institutions.

For these reasons, intermediation permits borrowers who wish to expand their investments in real assets to be accommodated at lower rates and easier terms than if they had to borrow directly from the lenders. If the creditors of financial intermediaries had to hold instead the kinds of obligations that private borrowers are capable of providing, they would certainly insist on higher rates and stricter terms. Therefore, any autonomous increase—for example, improvements in the efficiency of financial institutions or the creation of new types of intermediaries—in the amount of financial intermediation in the economy can be expected to be, *ceteris paribus*, an expansionary influence. This is true whether the growth occurs in intermediaries with monetary liabilities, i.e., commercial banks, or in other intermediaries.

Financial institutions fall fairly easily into distinct categories, each industry or "intermediary" offering a differentiated product to its customers, both lenders and borrowers. From the point of view of lenders, the obligations of the various intermediaries are more or less close, but not perfect, substitutes. For example, savings deposits share most of the attributes of demand deposits; but they are not means of payment, and the institution has the right, seldom exercised, to require notice of withdrawal. Similarly there is differentiation in the kinds of credit offered borrowers. Each intermediary has its specialty, e.g., the commercial loan for banks, the real-estate mortgage for the savings and loan association. But the borrowers' market is not completely compartmentalized. The same credit instruments are handled by more than one intermediary, and many borrowers have flexibility in the type of debt they incur. Thus, there is some substitutability, in the demand for credit by borrowers, between the assets of the various intermediaries.[4]

The special attention given commercial banks in economic analysis is usually justified by the observation that, alone among intermediaries, banks "create" means of payment. This rationale is on its face far from convincing. The means-of-payment characteristic of demand deposits is indeed a feature differentiating bank liabilities from those of other intermediaries. Insurance against death is equally a feature differentiating life insurance policies from the obligations of other intermediaries, including banks. It is not obvious that one kind of differentiation should be singled out for special analytical treatment. Like other differentia, the means-of-payment attribute has its price. Savings deposits, for example, are perfect substitutes for demand deposits in every respect except as a medium of exchange. This advantage of checking accounts does not give banks absolute immunity from the competition of savings banks; it is a limited advantage that can be, at least in some part for many depositors, overcome by differences in yield. It follows that the community's demand for bank deposits is not indefinite, even though demand deposits do serve as means of payment.

THE WIDOW'S CRUSE

Neither individually nor collectively do commercial banks possess a widow's cruse. Quite apart from legal reserve requirements, commercial banks are limited in scale by the same kinds of economic processes that determine the aggregate size of other intermediaries.

One often cited difference between commercial banks and other intermediaries must be quickly dismissed as superficial and irrelevant. This is the fact that a bank can make a loan by "writing up" its deposit liabilities, while a savings and loan association, for example, cannot satisfy a mortgage borrower by crediting him with a share account. The association must transfer means of payment to the borrower; its total liabilities do not rise along with its assets. True enough, but neither do the bank's, for more than a fleeting moment. Borrowers do not incur debt in order to hold idle deposits, any more than savings and loan shares. The borrower pays out the money, and there is of course no guarantee that any of it stays in the lending bank. Whether or not it stays in the banking

---

[4] These features of the market structure of intermediaries, and their implications for the supposed uniqueness of banks, have been emphasized by Gurley and Shaw, *op. cit.* An example of substitutability on the deposit side is analyzed by David and Charlotte Alhadeff, "The Struggle for Commercial Bank Savings," *Quarterly Journal of Economics*, Vol. LXXII (February, 1958), pp. 1–22.

system as a whole is another question, about to be discussed. But the answer clearly does not depend on the way the loan was initially made. It depends on whether somewhere in the chain of transactions initiated by the borrower's outlays are found depositors who wish to hold new deposits equal in amount to the new loan. Similarly, the outcome for the savings and loan industry depends on whether in the chain of transactions initiated by the mortgage are found individuals who wish to acquire additional savings and loan shares.

The banking system can expand its assets either (*a*) by purchasing, or lending against, existing assets; or (*b*) by lending to finance new private investment in inventories or capital goods, or buying government securities financing new public deficits. In case (*a*) no increase in private wealth occurs in conjunction with the banks' expansion. There is no new private saving and investment. In case (*b*), new private saving occurs, matching dollar for dollar the private investments or government deficits financed by the banking system. In neither case will there automatically be an increase in savers' demand for bank deposits equal to the expansion in bank assets.

In the second case, it is true, there is an increase in private wealth. But even if we assume a closed economy in order to abstract from leakages of capital abroad, the community will not ordinarily wish to put 100 per cent of its new saving into bank deposits. Bank deposits are, after all, only about 15 per cent of total private wealth in the United States; other things equal, savers cannot be expected greatly to exceed this proportion in allocating new saving. So, if *all* new saving is to take the form of bank deposits, other things cannot stay equal. Specifically, the yields and other advantages of the competing assets into which new saving would otherwise flow will have to fall enough so that savers prefer bank deposits.

This is *a fortiori* true in case (*a*) where there is no new saving and the generation of bank liabilities to match the assumed expansion of bank assets entails a reshuffling of existing portfolios in favor of bank deposits. In effect the banking system has to induce the public to swap loans and securities for bank deposits. This can happen only if the price is right.

Clearly, then, there is at any moment a natural economic limit to the scale of the commercial banking industry. Given the wealth and the asset preferences of the community, the demand for bank deposits can increase only if the yields of other assets fall. The fall in these yields is bound to restrict the profitable lending and investment opportunities available to the banks themselves. Eventually the marginal returns on lending and investing, account taken of the risks and administrative costs involved, will not exceed the marginal cost to the banks of attracting and holding additional deposits. At this point the widow's cruse has run dry.

BANKS AND OTHER INTERMEDIARIES COMPARED

In this respect the commercial banking industry is not qualitatively different from any other financial intermediary system. The same process limits the collective expansion of savings and loan associations, or savings banks, or life insurance companies. At some point the returns from additional loans or security holdings are not worth the cost of obtaining the funds from the public.

There are of course some differences. First, it may well be true that commercial banks benefit from a larger share of additions to private savings than other intermediaries. Second, according to modern American legal practice, commercial banks are subject to ceilings on the rates payable to their depositors—zero in the case of demand deposits. Unlike competing financial industries, commercial banks cannot seek funds by raising rates. They can and do offer other inducements to depositors, but these substitutes for interest are imperfect and uneven in their incidence. In these circumstances the major readjustment of the interest rate structure necessary to increase the relative demand for bank deposits is a decline in other rates. Note that neither of these differences has to do with the quality of bank deposits as "money."

In a world without reserve requirements the preferences of depositors, as well as those of borrowers, would be very relevant in determining the volume of bank deposits. The volume of assets and liabilities of every intermediary, both nonbanks and banks, would be determined in a competitive equilibrium, where the rate of interest charged borrowers by each kind of institution just balances at the margin the rate of interest paid its creditors. Suppose that such an equilibrium is disturbed by a shift in savers' preferences. At prevailing rates they decide to hold more savings accounts and other nonbank liabilities and less demand deposits. They transfer demand deposits to the credit of nonbank financial institutions, providing these intermediaries with the means to seek additional earning assets. These institutions, finding themselves able to attract more funds from the public even with some reduction in the rates they pay, offer better terms to borrowers and bid up the prices of existing earning assets. Consequently commercial banks release some earning assets—they no longer yield enough to pay the going rate on the banks' deposit liabilities. Bank deposits decline with bank assets. In effect, the nonbank intermediaries favored by the shift in public preferences simply swap the deposits transferred to them for a corresponding quantity of bank assets.

FOUNTAIN PENS AND PRINTING PRESSES

Evidently the fountain pens of commercial bankers are essentially different from the printing presses of governments. Confusion results from concluding that because bank deposits are like currency in one respect—both serve as media of exchange—they are like currency in every respect. Unlike governments, bankers cannot create means of payment to finance their own purchases of goods and services. Bank-created "money" is a liability, which must be matched on the other side of the balance sheet. And banks, as businesses, must earn money from their middleman's role. Once created, printing press money cannot be extinguished, except by reversal of the budget policies which led to its birth. The community cannot get rid of its currency supply; the economy must adjust until it is willingly absorbed. The "hot potato" analogy truly applies. For bank-created money, however, there is an economic mechanism of extinction as well as creation, contraction as well as expansion. If bank deposits are excessive relative to public preferences, they will tend to decline; otherwise banks will lose income. The burden of adaptation is not placed entirely on the rest of the economy.

THE ROLE OF RESERVE REQUIREMENTS

Without reserve requirements, expansion of credit and deposits by the commercial banking system would be limited by the availability of assets at yields sufficient to compensate banks for the costs of attracting and holding the corresponding deposits. In a régime of reserve requirements, the limit which they impose normally cuts the expansion short of this competitive equilibrium. When reserve requirements and deposit interest rate ceilings are effective, the marginal yield of bank loans and investments exceeds the marginal cost of deposits to the banking system. In these circumstances additional reserves make it possible and profitable for banks to acquire additional earning assets. The expansion process lowers interest rates generally—enough to induce the public to hold additional deposits but ordinarily not enough to wipe out the banks' margin between the value and cost of additional deposits.

It is the existence of this margin—not the monetary nature of bank liabilities—which makes it possible for the economics teacher to say that additional loans permitted by new reserves will generate their own deposits. The same proposition would be true of any other system of financial institutions subject to similar reserve constraints and similar interest rate ceilings. In this sense it is more accurate to attribute the special place of banks among intermediaries to the legal restrictions to which banks alone are subjected than to attribute these restrictions to the special character of bank liabilities.

But the textbook description of multiple expansion of credit and deposits on a given reserve base is misleading even for a régime of reserve requirements. There is more to the determination of the volume of bank deposits than the arithmetic of reserve supplies and reserve ratios. The redundant reserves of the thirties are a dramatic reminder that economic opportunities sometimes prevail over reserve calculations. But the significance of that experience is not correctly appreciated if it is regarded simply as an aberration from a normal state of affairs in which banks are fully "loaned up" and total deposits are tightly linked to the volume of reserves. The thirties exemplify in extreme form a phenomenon which is always in some degree present; the use to which commercial banks put the reserves made available to the system is an economic variable depending on lending opportunities and interest rates.

An individual bank is not constrained by any fixed quantum of reserves. It can obtain additional reserves to meet requirements by borrowing from the Federal Reserve, by buying "Federal Funds" from other banks, by selling or "running off" short-term securities. In short, reserves are available at the discount window and in the money market, at a price. This cost the bank must compare with available yields on loans and investments. If those yields are low relative to the cost of reserves, the bank will seek to avoid borrowing reserves and perhaps hold excess reserves instead. If those yields are high relative to the cost of borrowing reserves, the bank will shun excess reserves and borrow reserves occasionally or even regularly. For the banking system as a whole the Federal Reserve's quantitative controls determine the supply of unborrowed reserves. But the extent to which this supply is left unused, or supplemented by borrowing at the discount window, depends on the economic circumstances confronting the banks—on available lending opportunities and on the whole structure of interest rates from the Federal Reserve's discount rate through the rates on mortgages and long-term securities.

The range of variation in net free reserves in recent years has been from −5 per cent to +5 per cent of required reserves. This indicates a much looser linkage between reserves and deposits than is suggested by the textbook exposition of multiple expansion for a system which is always precisely and fully "loaned up." (It does not mean, however, that actual monetary authorities have any less control than textbook monetary authorities. Indeed the net free reserve position is one of their more useful instruments and barometers. Anyway, they are after bigger game than the quantity of "money"!)

Two consequences of this analysis deserve special notice because of their relation to the issues raised earlier in this chapter. First, an increase—of, say, a billion dollars—in the supply of unborrowed reserves will, in general, result in less than a billion-dollar increase in required reserves. Net free reserves will rise (algebraically) by some fraction of the billion dollars—a very large fraction in periods like the thirties, a much smaller one in tight money periods like those of the fifties. Loans and deposits will expand by less than their textbook multiples. The reason is simple. The open-market operations which bring about the increased supply of reserves tend to lower interest rates. So do the operations of the commercial banks in trying to invest their new reserves. The result is to diminish the incentives of banks to keep fully loaned up or to borrow reserves, and to make banks content to hold on the average higher excess reserves.

Second, depositor preferences do matter, even in a régime of fractional reserve banking. Suppose, for example, that the public decides to switch new or old savings from other assets and institutions into commercial banks. This switch makes earning assets available to banks at attractive yields—assets that otherwise would have been lodged either directly with the public or with the competing financial institutions previously favored with the public's savings. These improved opportunities for profitable lending and investing will make the banks content to hold smaller net free reserves. Both their deposits and their assets will rise as a result of this shift in public preferences, even though the base of unborrowed reserves remains unchanged. Something of this kind has occurred in recent years when commercial banks have been permitted to raise the interest rates they offer for time and savings deposits.

CONCLUDING REMARKS

The implications of the "new view" may be summarized as follows:

1. The distinction between commercial banks and other financial intermediaries has been too sharply drawn. The differences are of degree, not of kind.

2. In particular, the differences which do exist have little intrinsically to do with the monetary nature of bank liabilities.

3. The differences are more importantly related to the special reserve requirements and interest rate ceilings to which banks are subject. Any other financial industry subject to the same kind of regulations would behave in much the same way.

4. Commercial banks do not possess, either individually or collectively,

a widow's cruse which guarantees that any expansion of assets will generate a corresponding expansion of deposit liabilities. Certainly this happy state of affairs would not exist in an unregulated competitive financial world. Marshall's scissors of supply and demand apply to the "output" of the banking industry, no less than to other financial and nonfinancial industries.

5. Reserve requirements and interest ceilings give the widow's cruse myth somewhat greater plausibility. But even in these circumstances, the scale of bank deposits and assets is affected by depositor preferences and by the lending and investing opportunities available to banks.

I draw no policy morals from these observations. That is quite another story, to which analysis of the type presented here is only the preface. The reader will misunderstand my purpose if he jumps to attribute to me the conclusion that existing differences in the regulatory treatment of banks and competing intermediaries should be diminished, either by relaxing constraints on the one or by tightening controls on the other.

2

A Model of Bank Portfolio Selection*

RICHARD C. PORTER

INTRODUCTION

Over the course of the last century, the implications of the assumption of profit maximization for the behavior of the firm have been tracked down in ever greater detail. Curiously, however, this firm has almost always been a seller of non-financial goods; banking has been studiously exempted from the application of such theory. The exemption is curious because the commercial bank seems in many respects more likely to fit the conditions of such static theory than the product manufacturer. The "method" of production and the "product" itself do not change, and hence the unpleasant necessity of neglecting some of the most interesting features of markets in order to devise marginal conditions does not arise. Even the proverbial conservatism of bankers is a prop to such theory, for it may well make banking less prone to upsetting expectational factors than other markets.

The reason for this neglect of banking probably lies in the implication of straightforward profit maximization: that the bank should acquire a portfolio consisting entirely of the asset whose yield (less any costs of maintenance or acquisition) is greatest.[1] But this procedure misses the very essence of banking, which is to "borrow short and lend long." Thus,

---

* SOURCE: reprinted from *Yale Economic Essays*, Vol. 1, No. 2 (Fall 1961), pp. 323–359.
[1] Diversification can be explained only if the bank is a monopsonist in the market of the highest-yield asset or if it is required by law to carry reserves of low-yield assets.

the "profit" which a bank derives from its portfolio must be interpreted in terms of not only the money return but also the liquidity and capital certainty which the portfolio offers. There is no reason why the concepts of profit maximization cannot be applied to bank operations, provided that "profit" is conceived in this broader sense.

The crux of bank operations is uncertainty, and hence any reference to profits must be in a probabilistic sense. In this chapter, it will be assumed that the bank considers the expected value of its profits (i.e., additions to surplus during the planning period) under various conditions of risk,[2] principally that of change in size of deposits. The problem is somewhat analogous to recent demand-risk-inventory theory for the selling firm,[3] where cash (and other assets readily convertible into cash) represents inventories, the carrying cost of these "inventories" is the surrender of earning power, and various penalties are incurred for insufficient "inventories."

This approach to commercial bank operations is not new, having been first indicated by Edgeworth in 1888,[4] although at that time bankers still considered loans to be liquid (in the sense of self-liquidating) and securities frozen, a view which lingered into the 1920's.[5] Edgeworth indicated the importance of probability to banking through the device of a simple game:

> I have imagined a new game of chance, which is played in this manner: each player receives a disposable fund of 100 counters, part of which he may invest in securities not immediately realizable, bearing say 5 per cent per ten minutes; another portion of the 100 may be held at call, bearing interest at 2 per cent per ten minutes; the remainder is kept in the hands of the player as a reserve against certain liabilities . . . . [22 digits are drawn at random every two minutes, and the difference between their sum and their expected sum, 99, is calculated.] The special object of the reserve above mentioned is to provide against demands which exceed that average. If the player can meet the excess of demand with his funds in hand, well; but if not he must call in part, or all, of the sum placed at call, incurring a forfeit of 10 per cent on the amount called in. But if the demand is so great that he cannot even thus meet it, then he incurs an enormous forfeit, 100 £ or 1000 £.[6]

---

[2] In deference to received literature, the word "risk" is used rather than "uncertainty" since the bank is assumed to know, with certainty, the probability distributions.

[3] *Cf.* pp. 256–259 of K. J. Arrow, T. Harris, and J. Marschak, "Optimal Inventory Policy," *Econometrica*, Vol. 19, No. 3 (July 1951), pp. 250–272.

[4] F. Y. Edgeworth, "The Mathematical Theory of Banking," *Journal of the Royal Statistical Society*, Vol. 51, Part 1 (March 1888), pp. 113–127.

[5] For a review of this revolution in bankers' ordering of relative liquidities, whereby securities became "secondary reserves" and loans frozen assets, *cf.* B. Suviranta, "The Shiftability Theory of Bank Liquidity," *Economic Essays in Honor of Gustav Cassel* (London: George Allen and Unwin, Ltd., 1933), pp. 623–635.

[6] Edgeworth, *op. cit.*, p. 120.

Unfortunately, Edgeworth then proceeded to solve for the optimum portfolio by a kind of enlightened common sense, claiming that "the calculus cannot indeed, I think, by itself determine what chance of great disaster it might be prudent to incur for the probability of a moderate gain."[7] If however, values can be placed upon the various aspects of this "great disaster," the calculus can do just that.

ASSUMPTIONS

It is uncertainty, in its various guises, far more than anything else which makes the banker's job a difficult one. The important areas of this uncertainty arise because the bank cannot know exactly:

1. How large will be its deposit liabilities at any moment of the future.
2. The market value of the non-matured securities in its portfolio at any moment of the future.
3. What proportion of its borrowers will default the loans which the bank has extended to them.[8]
4. The degree of "frozen-ness" of the loan portfolio at any moment of the future, where this degree depends upon the ability (and, to a certain extent, willingness) of customers to accept refusal of loan renewals.[9]

While the first element of uncertainty is particularly critical to the bank, the last three areas are clearly not unimportant. If bonds were always marketable at par and loans callable on demand, without possibility of default, the bank could never become illiquid no matter how erratic the behavior of its deposits. The greater the extent to which any or all of these latter three uncertainties exist, the greater becomes the bank's first concern for the future course of deposits. Thus, no one of these four aspects may be properly neglected in a model of bank operations.

The assets which the bank can hold may be divided into three general categories: cash assets, securities, and loans. Since the problem of diversification within each of these portfolios (that is, what *types* of securities and loans are held) will not be of concern in this chapter, each

---

[7] *Ibid.*, p. 121.

[8] There is also the possibility of default on securities, but Government obligations comprise so large a part of banks' portfolios that this area of uncertainty may be neglected.

[9] The nominal maturity distribution of the bank's loan portfolio may have little to do with the actual degree of "frozen-ness" of its loans. A study by the Federal Reserve Bank of Cleveland indicated that continuous borrowing through renewal of short-term loans was quite widespread. While only six per cent of the loans of banks in that district matured in five years or more, 25 per cent of the total dollar amount of loans had been made to borrowers who had been in debt continuously to the same bank for over five years. Federal Reserve Bank of Cleveland, *Monthly Review*, September 1956.

of these categories will be assumed internally homogeneous. "Cash" assets in fact consist of Federal Reserve Bank reserves, vault cash, net balances with other banks, and bills of very near maturity; here no such distinctions will be made, all "cash" being assumed (1) to provide no earnings and (2) to be completely free of risk of capital value change. The category "securities" will be assumed to include a homogeneous group of securities (1) without default risk, (2) readily salable upon established markets, (3) with maturity date beyond the end of the bank's present planning horizon, and (4) with a fixed coupon per bond per planning period. The distinction between "cash" and "securities" is clearly one of degree and not of kind. The portfolio of an actual bank will invariably consist of a variety of assets in the range from cash to fairly long-term bonds; in this simplified representation, the choice of the bank is narrowed. "Loans" are assumed (1) to be not callable during the planning period, (2) to be not marketable, and (3) to be "shiftable" only to the extent that they are eligible as collateral for borrowing from the Federal Reserve Banks. Thus, the essential difference between "securities" and "loans" is that there is a market for the former so that securities may be readily converted into cash, although at an uncertain price, while loans can be so converted only through the Federal Reserve Bank. Since these are assumed to be the only assets which the bank can hold,[10] it must be true that cash plus securities plus loans equals deposits[11] plus total capital accounts; the bank is assumed to have no liabilities other than deposits, and, of course, no part of the total capital accounts (which will be called simply "net worth") can be withdrawn from the bank.

What has been called the "planning period" is that span of time upon which the bank concentrates all its attention and over which it sets, and does not plan to alter, its asset portfolio. This is obviously unrealistic, for every bank is always planning and re-planning its asset portfolio. Even if the fact of continually maturing securities—which forces the bank to re-plan by automatically replacing securities with cash assets—were removed, as it is in the model, actual banks would make continual changes in their portfolio plans. Nevertheless, it is equally true that portfolios are not planned with the intention of making frequent changes, and it seems more realistic to assume that the basic portfolio decisions with respect to the fundamental components, cash, securities, and loans, are made fairly seldom and with reference to a sizable span of time. Forcing

---

[10] Non-financial assets comprised less than one per cent of the assets of member banks of the Federal Reserve System in 1956.

[11] Deposits are also assumed internally homogeneous, i.e., no distinctions are made between demand and time deposits. The question of the bank's optimal proportion of time to demand deposits is briefly treated in Appendix D.

this flexible procedure into a planning period of fixed length is very simplifying but, it is hoped, not badly distorting.

The choice of this portfolio is assumed to depend *entirely* upon anticipations concerning the circumstances of the ensuing period and in no way upon past events, past portfolio selections, or expectations of events occurring after the end of the ensuing period. To expose the importance of the assumptions of this last sentence some further amplification is required. First, it is assumed that the bank is not influenced by past events except insofar as these affect its estimates of the future. Thus, if the bank has had an unusual proportion of its loans defaulted in the previous period (the third element of uncertainty), this may induce it to re-value its estimates of such risk but it does not reduce its loans solely on the basis of a "once burnt, twice shy" code of behavior. More relevant to the real world is the connection to the "pin-in" effect. Any such effect is assumed away in the model; previous declines in the security price level (as a result of the second element of uncertainty) cannot cause the bank to carry a greater proportion of securities than it otherwise would desire. Second, past portfolio selections do not influence the current choice (except, of course, through their influence on the bank's appraisal of the ensuing period); this requires that there be leeway in the portfolio at the start of any period. Clearly, cash and securities can be converted into other assets at any time[12] so this assumption really applies only to loans—if all the bank's borrowers "required" renewals of their loans (the fourth element of uncertainty) for the ensuing period, the bank would not be able to reduce its loans, whether it wished to or not. Thus, under this assumption the model can only consider those banks for which the proportion of "required" renewals, while perhaps large, is never so large that the bank cannot start the new period with the exact quantity of loans it wishes to make. Third, the bank knows, or estimates with complete confidence, all the parameters of its environment that are relevant to its portfolio choice for the ensuing period. Fourth, the portfolio of the current period is not affected by expectations of change in the parametric climate of the next period. In short, the assumptions about the "period" are those required to keep the model manageable and static—"once burned, *once* shy," unitary elasticity of expectations (in the Hicksian sense[13]), and limits to the degree of the fourth area of uncertainty.

---

[12] The fact that transaction costs of change give the existing portfolio some inertia is assumed to be of little importance at the margin.

[13] J. R. Hicks, *Value and Capital*, 2nd ed. (Oxford: Oxford University Press, 1946), p. 205. This is not strictly correct since expectations are there assumed single-valued. In this chapter, any expectations that are not single-valued are assumed to have a probability distribution which at every moment of time has an arithmetic mean equal to the current market value.

The first area of uncertainty, that of the future course of the level of deposits, implies that the bank must be prepared for the possibility that withdrawals exceed additions to deposits over a particular time-span. A net reduction of deposits will always occur over the moment of time during which one depositor makes a withdrawal. Not infrequently, a bank will find its deposit levels declining over a few days or weeks. It is not impossible that seasonal, cyclical, or secular factors will cause a fall in deposits over longer periods. At the beginning of the planning period, the bank recognizes that its level of deposits during the period may follow a myriad of possible paths, of which continuous rises or continuous falls are but two. In reality, the complete shapes of the possible paths are implicitly considered in the specification of the bank's asset portfolio. But one aspect of the shape of each of these possible paths is of such great importance to the bank that it is here assumed the only aspect considered by the bank—namely, the lowest point to which deposits fall in each of the paths. For it is at this "deposit-low" of the period that the bank is forced to make the most radical adjustment of its asset portfolio in order to meet the demands of its depositors.[14]

This assumption of sole concern with "deposit-lows" is not in itself sufficient to permit complete neglect of the time-shape of deposit changes since the date of occurrence of any "deposit-low" may still be important to the bank. In the interest of simplicity, this problem of the time-path of deposits will be avoided in the following way. At some point toward the end of the period, deposits will reach their low,[15] at which time the bank makes any asset adjustments required; this perhaps necessitates selling some of its securities and/or borrowing on the collateral of some of its securities or loans.

This is not the place for a full discussion of the complex manner (use of Federal Funds, security sales, Federal Reserve Bank discounts, etc.) in which banks in fact can and do meet the problem of insufficient reserves

---

[14] Of course, if deposits rise throughout the period, the "deposit-low" is zero and the bank need make no adjustments as far as meeting withdrawals is concerned. Thus, the "most radical" adjustment may well be no adjustment at all. This "most radical" adjustment may also be slight if the bank has access to short-term borrowings (such as Federal Funds or the discount window) and is not reticent to use them for short periods in hope of improvement in its deposit position. In this case, end-of-period deposits may be a more important variable than the "deposit-low" of the period. The conservative bias that the "deposit-low" assumption gives the portfolio is indicated in Appendix F.

[15] If deposits, on the average, should rise during the period, the "deposit-low" will probably not be much, if at all, below zero and will probably occur toward the beginning of the period. Since little asset readjustment is required in this case and since we neglect the net rise in deposits that follows, the assumption that the "deposit-low" occurs toward the end of the period is innocuous.

(i.e., insufficient cash assets). Basically, the process may be simplified into the following stages:

Stage 1. The bank meets net withdrawals from its cash assets as long as it can without drawing these assets down below their minimum required level.

Stage 2. Should the cash assets prove insufficient, the bank sells from its security portfolio, at the going market price, and continues to do so as long as it has securities to sell.[16]

Stage 3. Should the sale of all its securities also be inadequate to meet the deposit depletions, the bank borrows from the Federal Reserve Bank on the collateral of its outstanding loans.[17] This it continues to do as long as necessary or until its stock of such collateral is exhausted.

To these three stages, a fourth might be added: should all its assets be converted, to the greatest extent possible, into means of payment and still be insufficient to cover deposit withdrawals, Edgeworth's "great disaster" would occur par excellence—the bank would then be in the throes of a liquidity crisis beyond its ability to handle. At the very least, it would have to call for exceptional aid from the Federal Reserve System; it might be forced to close its doors, and it might find itself insolvent as well. However, it will be assumed that such a "Stage 4" is so costly to the bank that no bank's optimum portfolio permits any possibility of this occurrence. Such a result may (and, in fact, does, if seldom) occur, but it could only happen, by the assumptions here, through a misestimation by the bank of the parameters of its operations.[18]

The method of treatment of the four areas of uncertainty may now be more accurately specified.

1. *The size of deposits at any moment of the future.* Although the bank expects (in the probability sense) deposits to stay at their start-of-period level, it recognizes that they may fall or rise. The relevant distribution

---

[16] For simplicity, it is assumed that the banks sell securities, rather than borrow from the Federal Reserve Banks on the collateral of securities. Given bankers' dislike of debt and the fact that interest charges would probably exceed transaction costs of selling and later repurchasing, sales rather than borrowing *would* occur in the world postulated by the model, that is, a world of no "pin-in" effects and unitary elasticity of expectations of bond prices.

[17] Alternatively, one may think of this process as straightforward rediscounting in the traditional, if in fact little used, manner.

[18] It is possible that some bank might be forced to accept the possibility of such a "Stage 4" if its net worth were low and its lowest possible "deposit-low" very near zero. Of course, the bank could meet this situation by holding very large cash assets, but this may be so unprofitable as to induce it to accept the possibility of "Stage 4." Such a bank is not considered in this chapter.

function is that relating each of the various "deposit-lows" during the ensuing period to the probability of its occurrence. If the random variable, u, is defined to be the "deposit-low" as a fraction of initial deposits, the distribution of u may be defined only over the range zero to unity. For simplicity, the frequency distribution of u, $f(u)$, is assumed to be a linearly increasing function of the amount by which u exceeds s, where s is the smallest "deposit-low" (as a fraction of initial deposits) to which the bank assigns a non-zero probability (and clearly $0 < s < 1$).[19] Since the cumulative of $f(u)$ must equal one, specification of s is sufficient to determine:

$$f(u) = \frac{2(u - s)}{(1 - s)^2}$$

2. *The market value of its securities at any moment in the future.* A "unit" of securities is defined as a dollar's worth at the market prices prevailing at the start of the planning period; this "unit" carries a coupon paying g dollars per "unit" per period where it is assumed, without undue restriction, that $0 < g < 1$. The market price at the end of the period may be written as $(1 + w)$ where w, the change in security prices during the period (absolute and percentage), is assumed to be uniformly distributed over the range $-a$ to $a\,(0 < a < 1)$.[20] Since the "deposit-low" occurs toward the end of the period, the price of securities sold at the moment of the "deposit-low" may also be considered to be $(1 + w)$.

3. *The proportion of loans defaulted.* This aspect of bank uncertainty will be most summarily treated, not because it is felt to be unimportant to a complete theory of bank operations but because its basic effects upon the bank's portfolio can be seen in the present model without complex treatment. It is assumed that the bank charges a pure interest rate of e per

---

[19] This "triangular" distribution is assumed because it is believed to be the best *simple* approximation to the actual distribution of banks' "deposit-lows." For a theoretical derivation of the distribution, see Appendix A. Alternatively, a uniform distribution of "deposit-lows" is considered in Appendix E.

[20] Unfortunately, fixing the distribution of w so that its expected value is zero implies that the expected value of the equivalent distribution of interest rates is greater than zero, in contradiction of the assumption of static expectations with respect to interest rates. In the case of consols the expected value of the distribution of changes in the interest rate is:

$$g\left[\frac{a^2}{3} + \frac{a^4}{5} + \frac{a^6}{7} + \cdots\right]$$

which is sufficiently near zero for small value of g and a that this contradiction is not serious. This results from the property of the number system, whereby the average of the reciprocals does not equal the reciprocal of the average.

dollar of its loans; it then adds to this rate some amount according to the default risk which just suffices to insure that the bank will not lose through defaults in the long run. The final "gross" rate is e' (where $0 < e < e' < 1$), but we shall here concern ourselves only with the bank's earnings net of default.[21]

4. *The degree of intra-period "frozen-ness" of the loan portfolio.* The fear on the part of the bank that it may not be able in an emergency to reduce its loans sufficiently, even over several periods, means that any debt incurred to help meet deposit depletions may well be long-term debt, a position which bankers dislike.[22] It is because of this that Stage 2, sales of securities, is assumed to precede Stage 3, borrowing on loan collateral, in the process of meeting deposit depletions. For the same reason, the cost of such borrowing in Stage 3 may be interpreted to include not only the charge of the Federal Reserve Bank but also a subjective "cost" of being in what may prove long-term debt.

While use of the "discount window" is a privilege and not a right, no Federal Reserve Bank would refuse to extend advances to a bank which found itself unable to cover exceptionally large deposit withdrawals without such aid. The only questions before the bank are, then, how much borrowing could they do on the basis of their total loan portfolio and how much would it cost. If the bank gets into Stage 3, it can take a typical dollar's worth of its loans to the Federal Reserve Bank and receive an advance of $(1 - m)$ dollars, where m, which might be labeled the "excess-collateral rate," is, of course, between zero and unity. On this advance, the borrowing bank is charged an interest cost which, it is here assumed, is different from the real "cost" because of bankers' dislike of such debt. There are many ways in which such a "cost" might be handled, but the

---

[21] It must always be remembered, however, that to the extent that the bank is worried about the time-path of defaults or the default rate is positively related to the quantity of loans, the present model will overstate the amount of loans which the bank will desire to make.

[22] Much nebulous writing has appeared on this subject, but the bankers' aversion seems real enough, probably basically deriving from their fear that heavy indebtedness will have adverse effects upon their relations with depositors, borrowers, and correspondent banks. The view is not without its dissenters, however; for example, see A. Murad, "The Ineffectiveness of Monetary Policy," *Southern Economic Journal*, Vol. 22, No. 3 (January 1956), pp. 339–351. Of bankers' supposed aversion to steady borrowing, Murad says (p. 346): "It may be that bankers feel that way or say that they feel that way, but they certainly do not act that way. Whenever they have reserve deficiencies they borrow and if necessary remain for years in debt to the Federal Reserve banks." As a general phenomenon, this last sentence is open to great doubt, for the fact of increasing or large aggregate indebtedness is not proof of a decreasing or small antipathy toward permanent indebtedness.

one to be assumed in this chapter is that the real "cost," q, of such borrowing is to some extent greater than the interest charge, where $0 < q < 1$.[23]

Cash assets are of two types, those required to be held as reserves in the Federal Reserve Bank and those which the bank holds (in various forms) in excess of these requirements. The amount of the former at any moment of time must be a specified fraction of the bank's deposit liabilities. While, in fact, a rise in reserve requirements usually results in the lowering of the amount of other cash assets which the bank feels it requires, it is here assumed that the amount of cash assets other than required reserves is also a specified fraction of its current deposit liabilities. Thus, the "required" amount of cash assets can be written as a fraction, k, of the bank's deposit liabilities, where k is somewhat larger than the reserve requirement ratio. Most banks would meet these requirements almost continually, but as the model is set up, it need only be prepared to meet them at the moment of the "deposit-low" to be sure of having a sufficient amount at every other moment of the period. Assuming a fixed fraction of cash assets in this fashion means that Stage 1 is not possible. But this assumption is not as restrictive as it might seem at first since the excess of cash assets over k would probably be very small unless g were near zero and/or a extremely large.[24]

Each of the balance sheet items will be written as a fraction of start-of-period deposits—the fraction of cash assets being k, of securities, B, of loans, L, and of net worth, N. B and L are variables under the control of the bank, while N is assumed previously determined and unalterable at least over the ensuing period.

It remains only to fix the criterion by which the bank balances its portfolio between possible gains and losses. One often stated by bankers themselves is that they minimize the probability of losses (or, in reverse, maximize the probability of some gain); but this implies that the portfolio be prepared to meet any possible deposit reduction out of cash assets, while in fact banks do incur an unnecessary, if small and profitable, risk of losses. A variant of the above is the minimization of the probability of incurring losses within the constraint of a reasonable expected profit. Such a criterion is rejected on the grounds that setting the definition of

---

[23] If there were no addition of a subjective "cost" and the bank knew that it could repay its debt in exactly one period, q would be equal to the Federal Reserve Bank discount rate (per period). To the extent that there is a subjective element or such last-resort borrowing is felt to be of longer duration, q may be well above the discount rate.

[24] The real-world analog to the parameter g is the difference between long-term security rates and the bill rate. Not infrequently, this difference is very slight, but such times have little relevance here for the assumption of static expectations concerning future interest rates is then almost certainly violated.

"reasonable" is more important than the minimization process that follows. A criterion advanced by recent portfolio theory[25] is that some point is chosen, according to the selector's preferences, on the frontier (or locus) of the maximum expected return for every possible variance of return. This criterion was introduced because it was useful in explaining diversification; in the present model, the variable, variance of return, is not needed to explain diversification and so, for simplicity, will not be included in the text.[26] Here, the bank is assumed to choose its asset portfolio so as to maximize its expected additions to net worth during the period. Thus, it maximizes its expected additions to net worth function with respect to one of the asset variables, B and L, the other being then determined by the accounting identity:

$$1 + N = k + B + L \tag{1}$$

In summary, the symbols to be used in the chapter are:

Variables
1. B, securities as a fraction of initial deposits.
2. L, loans as a fraction of initial deposits.
Random elements
3. u, the "deposit-low" of the period, as a fraction of initial deposits. u is defined over the range $0 < s < u < 1$ by the distribution $f(u) = 2(u - s)/(1 - s)^2$.
4. w, the change between the start of the period and the "deposit-low" (and the end) of the period in the market price of securities. w is defined over the range $-a < w < a \,(0 < a < 1)$ by a uniform distribution $f(w) = 1/2a$.
Parameters
5. N, net worth, unchanging, as a fraction of initial deposits.
6. g, the coupon per dollar's worth of securities (at initial market prices); $0 < g < 1$.
7. e, the earning rate on loans (net of default risk); $0 < e < 1$.
8. k, the amount of cash assets which the bank holds, as a fraction of current deposit liabilities; $0 < k < 1$.

---

[25] *Cf.* H. Markowitz, *Portfolio Selection* (New York: John Wiley and Sons, 1959), Part IV; J. Tobin, "Liquidity Preference as Behavior Towards Risk," *Review of Economic Studies*, Vol. 25, No. 2 (February 1958), pp. 65–86, reprinted in *Risk Aversion and Portfolio Choice*, Cowles Foundation Monograph 19 (New York: John Wiley and Sons, 1967), Chapter 1; and I. O. Scott, "The Availability Doctrine: Theoretical Underpinnings," *Review of Economic Studies*, Vol. 25, No. 1 (October 1957), pp. 41–48.

[26] The implications of a bank preference map which is a function of both expected gain and variance of gain are drawn, for a simplified version of the model, in Appendix B. Also, some inference about the change in results which this would cause is made there.

9. q, the "cost," both actual and subjective, of borrowing a dollar during the period from the Federal Reserve Bank; $0 < q < 1$.

10. m, the "excess-collateral rate." A dollar of loans as collateral enables the bank to borrow $(1 - m)$ dollars from the Federal Reserve Bank (the latter acting in its capacity of "lender of last resort"); $0 < m < 1$.

STRUCTURE OF THE MODEL

The amount of profit which the bank makes during the period will clearly depend upon the "stage" into which the "deposit-low" forces it, and, for Stage 3, upon how far into that stage it goes. The expected addition to net worth (ΔN) for each stage is:

Stage 2. (Securities sales are required to handle the "deposit-low.")

$$\Delta N = gB + wB + eL. \tag{2}$$

The profit is composed of: gB, earnings on securities; wB, capital gains or losses on securities; and eL, earnings (net) on loans.

Stage 3. (Borrowing on loan collateral is required.)

$$\Delta N = gB + wB + eL - q(1 - m)x. \tag{3}$$

where x is the amount of loans put up as collateral [and $(1 - m)x$ the amount borrowed] and

$$(1 - m)x = (1 - k)(1 - u) - (1 + w)B. \tag{4}$$

The profit is composed of: gB, securities earnings; wB, capital gains or losses on the (completely) sold securities; eL, earnings on loans; and $q(1 - m)x$, the cost of the bank's borrowings.

According to the values assumed by the random variables, u and w, the bank finds itself in one of these two stages. The ranges of u and w which bring about each stage are:

Stage 2. This may occur in either of two ways:

$$\text{(i)} \quad s < u < 1; \qquad -1 + \frac{(1 - s)(1 - k)}{B} < w < a.$$

It may be possible that the most extreme (conceivable) deposit depletion can be met through bond sales alone, provided that the price of securities rises sufficiently (or falls sufficiently little) during the period.

$$\text{(ii)} \quad 1 - \frac{(1 + w)B}{1 - k} < u < 1; \qquad -a < w < -1 + \frac{(1 - s)(1 - k)}{B}.$$

If securities prices do not rise enough, only a certain degree of possible deposit withdrawals can be handled by means of bond sales alone.

Stage 3.

$$s < u < 1 - \frac{(1 + w)B}{1 - k} \; ; \quad -a < w < -1 + \frac{(1 - s)(1 - k)}{B}.$$

Any deposit depletion too extreme to be met by securities sales alone *can* be met by bond sales *plus* borrowings on loan collateral.

These three cases are exhaustive since we have already excluded the possibility of a Stage 1, the running down of cash assets to meet withdrawals, and of a Stage 4, where even borrowings on all the bank's loan collateral are insufficient to cope with the deposit losses. But the fact that the three possibilities listed above cover the entirety of the ranges of w and u does not automatically imply that every stage is relevant for every bank—for example, the net worth of a bank may be so high that it is able to cover any conceivable deposit depletion by bond sales alone, even if the price of bonds drops to their lowest conceivable level. In technical terms, for a stage to be possible of occurrence, the lower limits of both u and w (for that stage) must indeed be lower than the upper limits. If all three of these cases cited above—Stage 2(i), Stage 2(ii), and Stage 3—are considered relevant to the bank, then the following assumption about the size of the bank's securities holdings is being made implicitly:

$$\frac{(1 - s)(1 - k)}{1 + a} < B < \frac{(1 - s)(1 - k)}{1 - a} \tag{5}$$

for if the left-hand inequality does not hold, Stage 2(i) does not exist; and if the right-hand inequality does not hold, Stage 2(ii) and Stage 3 do not exist.

The bank for which Stage 3 is not even a remote possibility is not only rare but uninteresting, so there should be few qualms about assuming the right-hand inequality. But the left-hand inequality is not so easily handled; a taxonomic approach would construct the model for both directions of the inequality sign, but here only that one which is felt most closely to describe reality will be extensively treated.[27] In a world where banks do not expect extremely large bond price fluctuations and do make a significant amount of loans relative to their net worth and lowest possible "deposit-lows," most banks are probably *not* able to cover their lowest conceivable

---

[27] Enough has been worked through for the other case to indicate that the results are similar. See Appendix C for a brief treatment of the bank which is able, for some conceivable level of bond prices, to meet the worst conceivable "deposit-low" without recourse to borrowing.

"deposit-lows" by means of securities sales alone, even if bond prices rise to as high a level as is considered possible. Thus, in what follows, it is assumed that Stage 2(i) is not a possibility, or, in other words, that inequalities of equation 5 may be replaced by:

$$0 < B < \frac{(1-s)(1-k)}{1+a} \tag{6}$$

DETERMINATION OF THE OPTIMUM PORTFOLIO

The stage in which the bank finds itself is determined, as follows, by the value assumed by the random variable u:

Stage 2(ii).

$$1 - \frac{(1+w)B}{1-k} < u < 1; \qquad -a < w < a.$$

Stage 3.

$$s < u < 1 - \frac{(1+w)B}{1-k}; \qquad -a < w < a.$$

The expression for the expected addition to net worth, $E[\Delta N]$, is:

$$E[\Delta N] = \int_{w=-a}^{a} \int_{u=s}^{1} [gB + wB + eL] \left[\frac{u-s}{a(1-s)^2} \right] du \, dw$$
$$+ \int_{w=-a}^{a} \int_{u=s}^{1-\frac{(1+w)B}{1-k}} [-q(1-k) + q(1+w)B + q(1-k)u]$$
$$\times \left[\frac{u-s}{a(1-s)^2} \right] du \, dw \tag{7}$$

which becomes, after integration,

$$E[\Delta N] = gB + eL - \frac{q}{3(1-s)^2(1-k)^2} [(1-s)(1-k) - B]^3$$
$$- \frac{a^2qB^2}{3(1-s)^2(1-k)^2} [(1-s)(1-k) - B]. \tag{8}$$

L may be eliminated as a variable by means of the accounting identity of equation 1; then the derivative of $E[\Delta N]$ with respect to B is:

$$\frac{dE[\Delta N]}{dB} = g - e + \frac{q}{(1-s)^2(1-k)^2} [(1-s)(1-k) - B]^2$$
$$- \frac{a^2qB}{3(1-s)^2(1-k)^2} [2(1-s)(1-k) - 3B] \tag{9}$$

and the second derivative:

$$\frac{d^2E[\Delta N]}{dB^2} = \frac{2q}{(1-s)^2(1-k)^2}\left[-(1-s)(1-k)\left(1+\frac{a^2}{3}\right)+(1+a^2)B\right].$$ (10)

If B is at its lowest permissible level (i.e., zero)[28] the first derivative, $dE[\Delta N]/dB$, is positive, and, if B is at its highest value [i.e., $(1-s)(1-k)/(1+a)$], the derivative is negative, provided that the following inequalities hold:[29]

$$\frac{2a^2(2-a)}{3(1+a)^2} < \frac{e-g}{q} < 1.$$ (11)

If inequalities of equation 11 hold, there exists a regular maximum and the optimum fraction of assets in securities can be found by setting the derivative of equation 9 equal to zero. Solving this quadratic equation in B yields:

$$B = \frac{(1-s)(1-k)[1+(a^2/3)]}{1+a^2}\left\{1-\sqrt{1-\frac{(1+a^2)[1-(e-g)/q]}{(1+a^2/3)^2}}\right\}$$ (12)

Much of the complexity (or rather simplicity!) of the form of equation 12 results from the particular functional representation of the distribution of the random variables, u and w; but there are three interesting properties of equation 12 which are not dependent upon the choice of distribution functions:

1. *The fact that* $(1-s)(1-k)$ *enters in linear fashion.* In words, this quantity is the fraction which does not need to be held in cash assets $(1-k)$ of the largest conceivable loss in deposits $(1-s)$. The rest of equation 12, involving the parameters a, e, g, and q, serves to fix the quantity of securities as a fraction of this term $(1-s)(1-k)$. Thus, the determination of the optimum portfolio can be divided into two problems, first, the calculation of the maximum amount of securities which the bank would ever need to sell to meet deposit losses (on the assumption that bond prices do not change), and second, the decision as to what fraction of this amount the bank will actually hold (which will depend upon the various earning and borrowing cost rates as well as the expected fluctuation in security values).

---

[28] See inequalities of equation 6.

[29] See Appendix C. If the left-hand inequality does not hold, the present model is inapplicable and that treated in Appendix C becomes the relevant one. Unless very high values of a are considered, however, the expression on the left will be very close to zero. If the right-hand inequality does not hold, there is a corner maximum, with no securities entering into the portfolio.

2. *The manner in which the earning and borrowing cost rates enter the equation.* By means of the single expression $(e - g)/q$, the bank measures the relative advantage of loans vis-à-vis securities, the advantage being greater the larger is the difference in earning rates and/or the lower is the cost of borrowing on loan collateral. It is interesting to note that, if the bank is to include any securities at all in its optimal portfolio, it is not necessary that the borrowing cost be greater than the loan earning rate (i.e., a "penalty" rate is not essential), but only that it be larger than the difference between the earning rate on loans and that on securities.

3. *The fact that* N, *the net worth of the bank, plays no part in the determination of the optimum quantity of securities.* This independence between optimum B and N implies that any change in N induces a change in the bank's loans of the same amount and direction. This conclusion is not surprising if one recognizes that net worth, from the viewpoint of the bank's liquidity problems, can be treated as a deposit liability with no possibility of withdrawal.

What is really interesting about equation 12 is not the level of B, and hence of L, but rather the way in which the optimum holdings of these assets vary as a result of changes in the different parameters. The first and second partial derivatives of B with respect to the various parameters are given in the table below.

Table 1 $\partial B/\partial x$ $\partial^2 B/\partial x \partial y$ where:

	$\partial B/\partial x$	$y = a$	$y = q$	$y = g$	$y = e$	$y = k$	$y = s$
where $x = s$	$-$	$\pm^1$	$-$	$-$	$+$	$+$	0
$x = k$	$-$	$\pm^1$	$-$	$-$	$+$	0	
$x = e$	$-$	$\pm^2$	$+$	$-$	$+$		
$x = g$	$+$	$\mp^2$	$-$	$+$			
$x = q$	$+$	$\mp^2$	$-$				
$x = a$	$\mp^1$	$\mp^3$					

1. Upper or lower sign holds according as: $(e - g)/q \gtrless 1/9$.
2. Upper or lower sign holds according as: $(e - g)/q \gtrless (3 - 2a^2)/9$.
3. Evaluated at $a = 0$; upper or lower sign holds according as: $(e - g)/q \gtrless 1/9$.

Note: See Appendix E for the signs when a uniform distribution of "deposit-lows" is used.

A similar table of partial derivatives could be constructed for the changes in optimum holdings of loans, but this is not necessary; since, by accounting identity (1), $L = 1 + N - k - B$, the first and second partial of L with respect to any parameter (except k) is simply the negative of the relevant partial of B. It can be shown that an increase in k decreases L as well as B, and that the second derivative $(\partial^2 L/\partial k^2)$ is zero.

One could find quantitative estimates of these derivatives by assuming particular parameter values, but more generally we can plot the value assumed by $B/(1 - s)(1 - k)$ (written hereafter as B') for all possible values of a and of the composite parameter $(e - g)/q$. This is done, for

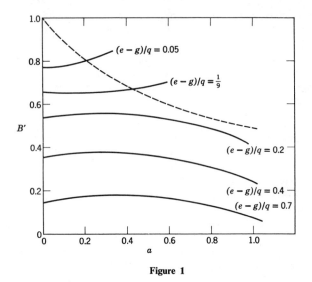

Figure 1

various fixed levels of $(e - g)/q$, in Figure 1. The dotted line is the border above and to the right of which Stage 2(i) becomes a possibility.[30]

The most obvious lesson of Figure 1 is that the effect of changes in the anticipated fluctuation in security prices is uncertain, with respect to both direction and magnitude. When $(e - g)/q$ is in the neighborhood of $\frac{1}{9}$ or of unity (i.e., when B' is in the neighborhood of 0.67 or zero), changes in the parameter a have almost no effect upon the composition of the optimum portfolio. The farther $(e - g)/q$ is from these critical values, the greater will be the effect on the portfolio of a. If $(e - g)/q$ is less than $\frac{1}{9}$, greater certainty about the course of future bond prices will induce the bank

[30] Although that region is neglected in Figure 1, numerical examples based on Appendix C indicate that the curves could be smoothly extrapolated into the Stage 2(i) area without much, if any, error.

to hold *less* securities; while if $(e - g)/q$ is between $\frac{1}{9}$ and unity, greater bond-price certainty will induce larger holdings of securities.

Lest Figure 1 give the impression that the value of a is a critical determinant of the portfolio composition, another diagram, Figure 2, is included which relates B' to $(e - g)/q$ for two very different values of a. The solid line shows the relation at $a = 0$ and the dotted line at $a = \frac{1}{2}$.[31]

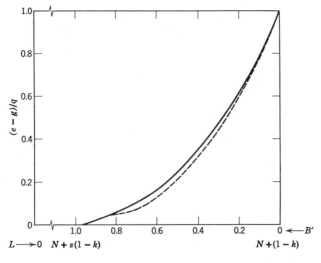

Figure 2

It will be seen from Figure 2 that a has no more than a very marginal effect upon the portfolio,[32] and that the important parameters for the division of the portfolio between loans and securities are, not surprisingly, the difference in earning rate between loans and securities $(e - g)$ and the cost of borrowing, q. It is the influence of these latter parameters (as well, of course, as s and k) with which the rest of this chapter is concerned; considerable simplification will henceforth be achieved by the assumption that a is zero. The first step will be to drop the unrealistic assumption that e is a constant, unaffected by the quantity of loans which the bank makes.

---

[31] The dotted line is not continued to the point where $(e - g)/q$ is zero because, for the very low values, Stage 2(i) becomes possible. For some values of a, as Figure 1 shows, the dotted line will cross the solid one for low values of $(e - g)/q$.

[32] A rise in a from 0 to 0.50 never decreases the optimum security holdings by more than $0.022(1 - s)(1 - k)$ (i.e., by more than $\frac{1}{46}$ of deposits even if both s and k are zero).

IMPERFECT COMPETITION IN THE LOAN MARKET

In order to conceive of the bank as, to some degree, a monopolist in its loan market, the meaning of the loan demand curve must be analyzed. As long as banks are a homogeneous group, each of which have available the same information concerning the credit-worthiness of every potential borrower, the rate of interest charged a customer for a loan is simply the going market rate on riskless lending (the "pure" or "prime" rate, e) plus a certain risk premium.[33] It would be a matter of indifference to both borrowers and banks to which bank a particular borrower went; each bank would get no business if it charged more than the going rate and more business than it could handle if less.

The actual banking mechanism differs, fundamentally, in two ways from this hypothetical competitive system.[34] First, banks do not all have the same knowledge concerning the credit worthiness of a potential borrower, and as a result, different banks do not add onto the pure rate the same risk premium for the same borrower. Other things being equal, the typical businessman is able to borrow at a lower gross rate in his own locale than elsewhere and at a still lower rate at his customary bank than at a new one. The stranger the borrower, the less sure is the bank of his ability and reliability,[35] and hence the higher will be the risk premium that is added to the prime rate. Second, the potential borrower knows all this and therefore tends not to shop around each time he seeks a loan; he will accept the rate quoted by his traditional bank unless he is convinced that it is far out of line with the market situation.

Consequently, the bank is not faced with a horizontal demand curve for loans (in terms of the net rate) but has two degrees of freedom concerning the rate it charges. It can demand a rate higher than the prime rate plus its proper estimate of the risk premium and not lose all its customers because even this gross rate will be lower than many of its borrowers could get elsewhere. Moreover, even those of its borrowers who could do better by taking a higher risk premium but a lower gross rate at another bank are not likely to realize this immediately.[36]

---

[33] This "certain risk premium" is here, it will be recalled, such as to insure the bank against default losses in the long run.

[34] It differs as well in a third way, in that two banks (or the same bank at two different moments of time) may differ in their attitudes toward making risky loans. Certainly the assumption that all banks merely mark up the pure rate, e, so as to avoid default losses in the long run is no better than a very crude first approximation; but it is sufficient for present purposes.

[35] And the more expensive it is to ascertain. If the bank has been dealing with the borrower for a long time, it does not need to incur the costs of careful credit investigation.

[36] And having realized it, many may not wish and/or be able to take advantage of it immediately.

Just as the bank does not lose all its loan business by raising its pure rate above the going market rate, so also does it not gain an infinite amount of new loan demand by undercutting the going rate. For it would need to undervalue its risk premiums and overcome other bank-borrower inertias in order to gain the new business.

All the above assumes that the same pure rate must be charged to all borrowers. To the extent to which the bank can discriminate between borrowers,[37] it improves its situation (at least until its customers find out). At the extreme of perfect discrimination, the demand curve for the bank's loans in terms of the pure rate represents not its average but its marginal earning rate (net of default) per dollar of loans. While the following argument applies, with the requisite adjustments, equally well for this case, it will not be explicitly treated.

The marginal earning rate, or marginal revenue, of loans (net of default), e, should in the general case be written as a function of the amount of loans which the bank makes; however, since the fraction of initial deposits which the bank lends (L) is a linear transformation of the dollar *amount* of loans it makes, e may equally well be considered a function of L. It is far beyond the scope of this chapter to specify the details of this functional relationship; the only property it is safe to assume is that e declines as L increases

One possible procedure from this point would be to hypothesize a specific form for the function; for example, that e is linear in L:

$$e = h - jL \tag{13}$$

where h and j are both positive; the *average* earning rate on loans would then be $(h - \frac{1}{2}jL)$. The technique of the previous section can again be used to derive an explicit expression for the fraction of initial deposits which the bank optimally carries in securities. The monopolistic analog of equation 12, written for simplicity on the assumption that $a = 0$, is:

$$B = \frac{j}{q}(1 - s)^2(1 - k)^2 + (1 - s)(1 - k)$$
$$\times \left\{ 1 - \sqrt{\frac{h - g}{q} + \frac{j}{q}[(1-s)(1-k) - 2(1+N-k)] + \frac{j^2}{q^2}(1-s)^2(1-k)^2} \right\} \tag{14}$$

---

[37] The probability that this occurs is augmented by the fact that the gross rate will differ between borrowers anyway, and differential risk premiums help to disguise the existence of differential pure rates as well. Furthermore, the fraction (if any) of the loan which the bank insists (or strongly suggests) be retained in the borrower's deposit may vary among borrowers, and this practice is essentially nothing more than a rate increase.

which reduces to equation 12 with $a = 0$ whenever $j = 0$ and $e = h$. It is interesting to note three important differences between equations 12 and 14: first, the term $(1 - s)(1 - k)$ no longer enters as a mere proportioning factor in the determination of optimum B; second, j, slope of the marginal revenue from loans function, is an essential element in the determination of B; and third, N now has an effect upon the size of B as well as L.

One could now proceed, as in the previous section, to derive the various properties of the derivatives of equation 14, but this will not be done partly because of the mathematical complication, partly because the results would have validity only for the special case of a linear demand for loans function,[38] but mostly because it is unnecessary. Traditional economic theory suggests that, if we know the marginal revenue from loans function, we can deduce the relevant implications of the market if only we can discover the marginal cost function. And such a function we have already found—implicitly—in the derivation of equation 12.

THE MARGINAL COST OF LOANS

Equation 12 is the expected profit maximizing relation between the optimum quantity of bonds and the parameters of the model. By means of the accounting identity in equation 1, the following equation for the optimum amount of loans may also be found:[39]

$$L = N + s(1 - k) + (1 - s)(1 - k)\sqrt{(e - g)/q}. \qquad (15)$$

So long as all the parameters on the right side of equation 15 are considered unalterable constants, L is simply a function of these parameters, and there is no need to go further. But in a previous section, the possibility was introduced that the marginal earning rate of loans depends upon the quantity of loans made. When this is so, it is better to view equation 15 as a relationship between two variables, the optimum proportion of loans, L, and the marginal loan earning rate, e.[40] Then equation 15 may be put into a form more readily seen as a marginal cost function merely by

---

[38] If e were made a function of powers of L higher than the first, the maximization equation would involve third (or higher) powers of B, and hence B could not be written as a simple explicit function of the parameters. Implicit differentiation would, of course, still be possible.

[39] Throughout this section, too, the parameter a is assumed zero for simplicity.

[40] The e which enters in equations 12 and 15 is the marginal and not the average earning rate on loans. This can be seen by looking at equations 8 and 9; the e appears as a result of the differentiation of the term (eL), and this derivative of the total revenue of loans is the marginal revenue of loans.

algebraic manipulation of e to the left side of the equation:

$$e = q\left[\frac{L - N - s(1 - k)}{(1 - s)(1 - k)}\right]^2 + g. \tag{16}$$

In effect, equation 16 is the bank's "marginal cost of loans" schedule in that it shows what the marginal revenue (or marginal earning rate) of loans must be if the bank is to make any given amount of loans.

The range of L over which equation 16 is relevant is, however, limited. First, L must be less than (or equal to) the total of the non-cash asset portfolio, $(1 + N - k)$, since B has then taken its smallest possible value, zero. Once L has attained this limit, the marginal cost of loans, e, will equal $(g + q)$, and no further increases in e can induce the bank to augment its loan portfolio. Hence, "capacity" limitations imply that the marginal cost of loans curve becomes vertical (i.e., perfectly inelastic with respect to e) at a value of L equal to $(1 + N - k)$. The second limitation is less obvious. Equation 12, and hence equation 16, has been derived on the assumption that there is a possibility of Stage 3 (where borrowing on the collateral of loans is required if the bank is to meet the withdrawals of its worst possible "deposit-low"). But this assumption is violated if L becomes less than $[N + s(1 - k)]$. Thus equation 16 is the relevant marginal cost function only over the range

$$[N + s(1 - k)] < L < (1 + N - k).$$

No elaborate theory is needed to understand the bank's actions in the range $0 < L < [N + s(1 - k)]$, for then the bank faces no potential liquidity problems—sales of securities will always suffice to cover any conceivable amount of withdrawals. The bank's only concern is its earnings, and it will maximize these by making loans as long as the marginal earnings rate on loans exceeds the earning rate on securities; once e equals g, the bank will expand loans no further, holding the remainder of its non-cash asset portfolio in securities. The marginal cost of loans function is, therefore, horizontal (i.e., infinitely elastic with respect to e) at the level of g over the range of L less than $[N + s(1 - k)]$.

This marginal cost of loans curve is shown in Figure 3, where $L_0 = [N + s(1 - k)]$, $L_1 = (1 + N - k)$, and $e^* = g + q$. The function has three principal regions: one of infinite elasticity for low values of L; one of zero elasticity once all possible loans have been made; and one of intermediate values of L where the elasticity declines continuously from infinity to zero as L increases. It is true that the resemblance of this to the traditional manufacturing cost curve is slight—both are equated to marginal revenue to determine the optimum "output"—but this follows from the fact that manufacturing cost curves are only indirectly aligned to opportunity costs. As long as L is less than $[N + s(1 - k)]$, the bank's loan costs are simply the opportunity costs of an alternative "output," i.e., holding securities. If L is large enough to make Stage 3 possible, to these opportunity costs is added an illiquidity-incurring cost of increasingly greater size as L rises.

Throughout this chapter, we have neglected the possibility of a Stage 4 (where sale of *all* securities and borrowing on the collateral of all loans are insufficient to cover the withdrawals of the worst conceivable "deposit-low"). This neglect was justified on the grounds that no bank would ever

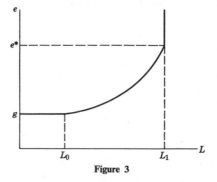

Figure 3

choose a portfolio that permitted any possibility of so fearful an occurrence. But it is possible that Figure 3, as drawn, violates this assumption. Stage 4 emerges as a possibility if L is greater than $[N + s(1 - k)]/m$, where m is the "excess-collateral rate" required by the Federal Reserve Bank for the bank's borrowing on the collateral of its loans. For very small values of m, it is clear that this consideration will be irrelevant,[41] but there are also values of m large enough to induce the Stage-4-avoiding bank to cease its loan expansion, regardless of the marginal earning rate, before loans comprise the entire non-cash asset portfolio. This Stage 4 constraint becomes potentially operative if

$$m > \frac{N + s(1 - k)}{1 + N - k} . \tag{17}$$

That bankers talk of being "loaned-up" while their portfolios still carry some securities is perhaps partial evidence that some such Stage 4 restriction generally does occur.[42] If so, the marginal cost curve becomes vertical

---

[41] In the extreme case, where m equals zero, Stage 4 can never occur, even if N and/or s are zero.

[42] However, as long as m is not one, there are always some (large) values of N and s that make Stage 4 impossible.

not at L_1 but at L_2 (where loans equal $[N + s(1 - k)]/m$);[43] this is shown in Figure 4, where the dotted curve indicates the part of the Figure 3 marginal cost curve which becomes irrelevant as a result of Stage 4 considerations.

Perhaps more important than the shape of the bank's marginal cost of loans function is the way in which this function changes as a result of changes in the different parameters. Given the demand curve for the bank's loans, any factor that causes the marginal cost function to rise (and/or shift to the left) will tend to bring about a reduction in the amount

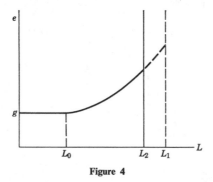

Figure 4

of loans which the bank wishes to make (and vice versa). The changes in the marginal cost function for the five parameters s, k, q, g, and N are illustrated in Figures 5 to 9 respectively; the solid line is the marginal cost for a lower value of the parameter and the dotted one for a higher, and L_0' and L_2' represent the values of L_0 and L_2 pertinent to the higher parameter value.

A fall in s and N and a rise in k, q, and g all have the same general effect of raising the marginal cost function, but the details of these shifts differ. Only s, k, and N are capable of affecting the "loaned-up" limit (imposed by Stage 4 possibilities); and only g can affect the curve in

---

[43] If there is uncertainty about the value of m (i.e., the bank is unsure to what extent the Federal Reserve System will support it in a liquidity crisis), the "loaned-up" limit will probably occur at a value of L less than that calculated by using the expected value of m. How much less we are not equipped to say, on the basis of our too simple assumption that the bank *never* incurs any possibility of Stage 4. Scott suggests the possibility that each bank's "loaned-up" limit of L is based upon other banks', on the grounds that it *is* certain that the Federal Reserve System will not permit a general liquidity crisis to occur under any conditions. See p. 219 (especially footnote 15) of I. O. Scott, "The Changing Significance of Treasury Obligations in Commercial Bank Portfolios," *Journal of Finance*, Vol. XII, No. 2 (May 1957), pp. 213–222.

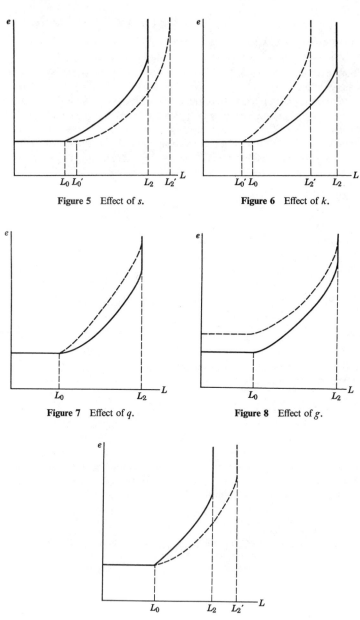

Figure 5 Effect of *s*.

Figure 6 Effect of *k*.

Figure 7 Effect of *q*.

Figure 8 Effect of *g*.

Figure 9 Effect of *N*.

its perfectly elastic range, although changes in s and k can alter the point at which the elasticity becomes finite. Although Figures 5 to 9 are illustrative and not empirically derived, they help to show how Federal Reserve System actions may achieve an impact upon bank portfolios; the traditional central bank policy weapons of reserve requirements, discount rate, and open-market operations are seen to operate primarily, in the world of the model, through the parameters k, q, and g respectively. If these (or any other) central bank measures should alter the bank's uncertainty about its deposit future, then there is an effect through s. A rise in g will generally inflict capital losses on the bank and, to the extent that these reduce N, will further raise the marginal cost of loans schedule of the bank.

The preceding discussion of the bank's supply of loans little resembles the current literature on credit "availability." Although a rise in bond interest rates is effective in shifting the schedule upward and/or to the left (through g, N, and possibly q or s), there is in the model nothing to indicate that small changes in interest rates will have large effects, a basic tenet of the "new theory of credit control."[44] Notice of this incompatibility is worthwhile, for it implies that availability theories rest upon assumptions different from, or supplementary to, those of the model. Some of the more obvious are: (1) explicit consideration of multi-period profit maximization, which might frequently mean a failure to maximize in the short-run; (2) oligopolistic pricing policies (through prime rate conventions, usury laws, or market leadership) which distort the individual bank's effective loan demand schedule; (3) expectations that are not so simple as here assumed (i.e., unitary elasticity); (4) and inter-relationship of loan demand with the level of security interest rates (and possible lags in the adjustments); and (5) greater concern with uncertainty of profits, credit-worthiness of borrowers and the non-price factors of loans than has here been included. This list, certainly not exhaustive, indicates some of the ways that the model would have to be extended if the availability implications were to be more closely approached. It is perhaps at least as important to know what *cannot* be derived from a particular set of assumptions as to know what can.

To derive implications for monetary policy directly from the bank's marginal cost of loans function is a great temptation, but a dangerous one. For the model here presented is no more than a theory of the "firm;" no theoretical structure has been developed about the adjustment mechanism of the banking "industry" nor of the other sectors of the economy, from whence comes the banks' demand for loans. Knowledge about macro-economic behavior requires, ultimately, macro-economic analysis. The

---

[44] This phrase is the title of an excellent summary of the innovations to monetary theory of the 1950s by A. Lindbeck (Stockholm: Almqvist & Wiksell, 1959).

hypotheses about the individual bank's loan behavior here developed are only of value, from the viewpoint of aggregative analysis, if they help to place it upon a more sound micro-economic foundation.

CONCLUSION

Not too long ago, it would have been considered presumptuous to claim that knowledge of the bank's portfolio of earning assets could be useful to analysis of monetary theory or policy. Once economists had become convinced that commercial banks really could "create" money,[45] they became enamored with the fact that the amount of money thus created was limited by the quantity of currency and reserves which the central bank issued. To give precision to the formula relating currency and reserves to the money supply, all that was needed was knowledge of the public's and the banks' propensities to hold currency and the circumstances in which the banks keep excess reserves. Behind such total concern for the money supply always lies the assumption, explicit or implicit, that the velocity of money (or, in more acceptable modern terminology, the relationship of aggregate demand to the money supply) was constant, or at least fairly predictable.

In a world where money was used primarily for transactions purposes, and where only a small and relatively unchanging fraction of the total was used as a way of holding wealth, the quantity theory, at least in its more sophisticated presentations, would be a good approximation of reality. And neglect of bank portfolios, beyond the problem of changes in currency and reserve holdings (either required or desired) would be thoroughly consistent with the theory. What the bank's earning assets were technically labeled—securities, advances, call loans, etc.—might, and obviously would, matter to the banker, but to the monetary theorist they would be just different ways of placing active money balances in the hands of the public.[46] Should the bank decide to alter its portfolio somewhat from securities to loans, the final result would be merely to reduce the spending potential

---

[45] And this was not so long ago as we would like to think. As late as 1921, Professor Cannan wrote: "If cloak-room attendants managed to lend out three-quarters of the bags entrusted to them . . . we should certainly not accuse the cloak-room attendants of having 'created' the number of bags indicated by the excess of bags on deposit over bags in the cloak-rooms." Page 31 of "The Meaning of Bank Deposits," *Economica*, No. 1 (January 1921), pp. 28–36.

[46] Rather curiously, through most of the nineteenth century, a great many bankers and economists did believe that certain classes of bank assets were inherently less inflationary than others. But the "real bills" doctrine was founded not on a belief that the money thereby created was any less "active," but on a mistaken notion concerning aggregate supply.

of those individuals who increased their holdings of securities while increasing, to the same extent, the spending potential of the recipients of the new loans.

Recognition that "idle" balances are neither an insignificant nor an unchanging fraction of the total money supply and the fact that contemporary governments provide a wide range of default-free forms of wealth-holding, from currency to consols (varying each from the other only slightly in liquidity and yield), forces upon monetary theorists an entirely different mode of analysis. While the theory of the determination of the velocity of money was dramatically revised by Keynes' *General Theory*, the relevance of this to monetary policy has only gradually become apparent. It is only during the current decade that monetary authorities have finally become as concerned with the *manner* in which the banking system makes money available to the public as with the total quantity. A movement by banks out of securities into loans cannot be uninteresting to monetary policy; the bond-buying public may be merely transferring a part of its wealth to a less liquid form, while the recipients of new loans are almost certainly increasing their spending.

Thus the division of the bank's earning assets between securities and loans is of relevance not only to the bank itself (concerned as it is with liquidity and profits) but also to analysis of the inflationary impact of different allocations of a given supply of money. Coincidentally—though perhaps providentally so—the bank's choice between greater liquidity and greater earnings is also society's choice between lesser and greater inflationary forces. Most of the weapons of contemporary monetary policy can be understood, and are in fact proposed, as an effort by the central bank to "encourage" (where that word covers a spectrum of meanings from "suggest" to "force") the commercial banks to hold assets which are relatively more liquid (though the means of achieving this often involves making such assets less liquid). It is toward an improved understanding of the ways in which various aspects of monetary policy affect the bank's choice between different earning assets, and hence aggregate demand, that this chapter is aimed.

APPENDIX A: THE "DEPOSIT-LOW"

Most banks have many depositors and the typical deposit transaction involves but a small fraction of the owner's account. For this reason, any attempt to derive theoretically the shape of the distribution of "deposit-lows" for a bank must recognize that any particular "deposit-low" is the result of a long series of individual deposit withdrawals and additions. Avoiding the question of what causes a depositor to alter the size of his account, we will deduce the "deposit-low" distribution on various assumptions about the probability of each deposit account transaction being an addition to or depletion of total deposits.

In line with the static nature of expectations in the text, let us assume that the bank "expects" no change in its total deposits during the ensuing period; this may be interpreted to mean that it believes that every dollar of transactions in its deposit accounts has a fifty-fifty chance of being a withdrawal of a dollar or a deposit of a dollar. It is certainly true, then, that the expected change of deposits, no matter how many transactions occur, will then be zero. But there will still be finite probabilities attached to "deposit-lows" less than zero. In general, if $(2N)$ transactions occur, the probabilities of the "deposit-lows" are given by:

$$\text{Prob } [0] = \frac{(2N)!}{2^{2N} \cdot (N!)^2}$$

$$\text{Prob } [-2x] = \text{Prob } [-2x + 1] = \frac{(2N)!}{2^{2N} \cdot (N - x)! \cdot (N + x)!}$$

where x is a positive integer, Prob $[-2x]$ means the probability of a "deposit-low" of $(2x)$ dollars less than initial deposits, and $1 \leq x \leq N$.[47]

---

[47] *Cf.* J. L. Doob, *Stochastic Processes* (New York: John Wiley & Sons, 1953), pp. 106–108. Let L be the "deposit-low" and A the level of deposits after the completion of all $(2N)$ transactions. Doob proves, with the "reflection principle," that

$$\text{Prob } [L < -2x] = 2 \text{ Prob } [A \leq -2x] - \text{Prob } [A = -2x]$$

Since

$$\text{Prob } [L = -2x] = \text{Prob } [L < -2x + 1] - \text{Prob } [L < -2x],$$

it follows that

$$\text{Prob } [L = -2x] = \text{Prob } [A = -2x + 1] + \text{Prob } [A = -2x].$$

But Prob $[A = -2x + 1] = 0$ (since an even number of $+\$1$ or $-\$1$ transactions can never result in an odd number of dollars withdrawn). Thus,

$$\text{Prob } [L = -2x] = \text{Prob } [A = -2x].$$

It can easily be shown also that

$$\text{Prob } [L = -2x] = \text{Prob } [L = -2x + 1].$$

Thus the distribution of "deposit-lows" is the same (with twice the density) as the distribution of end-of-period deposits over the range of net decreases of deposits. Clearly, as N becomes larger, the "deposit-low" distribution, being binomial, approaches a truncated (at zero) normal distribution.

A smoothed picture of such a discrete probability function is given in Figure A-1,[48] where the solid curve represents the distribution for $(2N)$ transactions and the dotted curve for a larger number of total transactions.[49]

It is unlikely that any bank is in a position, however, to consider each transaction as totally independent of all or any previous transactions in the deposit accounts. At one extreme, if there is only one bank in the economy and there is no change in the public's desire to hold cash (as opposed to deposits), then any withdrawal must appear later as an addition; there is

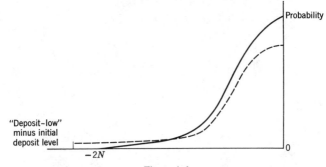

Figure A-1

definitely an inverse relation between the probability that a given transaction will be an addition and the proportion of previous transactions which were additions. The more usual case, however, is that of a bank which experiences or expects, or fears, positive correlation between the probability that a given transaction will be a deposit and the relative number of previous transactions which were deposits.

As an example of this, suppose that, whenever a majority of the previous transactions have been deposits, the probability that the next transaction will also be a deposit is somewhere between 0.5 and unity. In order to maintain the assumption of static expectations, the probability of a withdrawal when a majority of the previous transactions were withdrawals must

---

[48] It should perhaps be noted that this distribution differs from Patinkin's receipts-expenditures distribution for individuals because there is here no assumption that withdrawals *must* equal accretions (i.e., both equal to N). *Cf.* D. Patinkin, *Money, Interest and Prices* (Evanston: Row, Peterson and Company, 1956), Chapter 7 and Appendix to Chapter 7 (by Aryeh Dvoretzky). Note especially the difference between Figure A-1 here and Patinkin's Figure 9, p. 92.

[49] The slope of the frequency distribution is positive over its entire range, from $(-2N)$ to zero. It increases first at an increasing rate, but at a decreasing rate in the area to the immediate left of zero. The inflexion point occurs at $x^2 = \frac{1}{2}(N + 1)$.

be equal to the probability of a deposit when a majority were deposits. The earlier formulae are now seen as the special case where these probabilities are 0.5. A rough picture of the effect of raising them above 0.5 is shown in Figure A-2, where the solid curve represents the same distribution as in Figure A-1, and the dotted curve the distribution when autocorrelation is introduced in the above manner. It is doubtful if the autocorrelation of deposit transactions is sufficiently large, for most banks, to cause a negative slope in the frequency distribution of "deposit-lows," but it may suffice to keep the probability of relatively low "deposit-lows" from being so small as to be negligible.

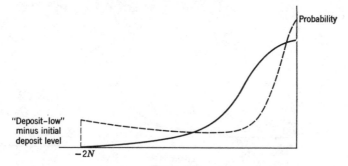

Figure A-2

The "triangular" distribution has been chosen in the text as the closest simple approximation to this distribution. If a straight line were fitted through the distributions of Figure A-2, it could be seen that the "triangular" distribution understates the probability of occurrence of extremely low and zero-neighborhood "deposit-lows" and overstates the probability of the middle range of "deposit-lows."

APPENDIX B: VARIANCE OF PROFITS

Because the consideration of variance of earnings involves great complication of the model, only a very simplified version of it will be discussed here. In addition to the assumptions of the text, it is assumed that the bank has no cash requirements ($k = 0$), it has no net worth ($N = 0$), there is no "excess-collateral rate" ($m = 0$), securities have no earnings ($g = 0$)

and no possibility of price change ($a = 0$), and it is considered possible that all deposits be withdrawn during the period ($s = 0$). Thus the accounting identity (1) of the text becomes:

$$1 = B + L. \tag{B-1}$$

The distribution of "deposit-lows" is $f(u) = 2u$; and the expected additions to net worth function is simply:

$$E[\Delta N] = 2 \int_{u=L}^{1} (eL)u \, du + 2 \int_{u=0}^{L} (eL - qL + qu)u \, du = eL - \frac{qL^3}{3}. \tag{B-2}$$

Maximization of expected profit implies that:

$$L = \sqrt{e/q}. \tag{B-3}$$

A regular maximum will occur, with L between zero and one, as long as $e < q$ (both are positive).

The variance of profit, written $S^2(\Delta N)$, is:

$$S^2(\Delta N) = 2 \int_{u=L}^{1} (eL)^2 u \, du + 2 \int_{u=0}^{L} (eL - qL + qu)^2 u \, du - (E[\Delta N])^2$$
$$= q^2 L^4 \left(\frac{1}{6} - \frac{L^2}{9} \right). \tag{B-4}$$

Minimization of S^2 (in the relevant range, $0 < L < 1$) clearly requires $L = 0$, at which point both E and S^2 are zero. No maximization process is needed to find the frontier of maximum E for each given S since, once one is specified, the other is uniquely determined. Although the equation of this frontier is complex, its slope at any point (determined by the value of L) is:

$$\frac{dE}{dS} = \left(\frac{e}{q} - L^2 \right) \frac{\sqrt{3/2 - L^2}}{L(1 - L^2)} \tag{B-5}$$

which is positive in the range $0 < L < \sqrt{e/q}$, and negative beyond. Thus, the expected gain (E) can be increased only at the expense of increased variance of gain (S^2) up to the point of maximum E. These opportunity loci are plotted in Figure B-1 for three sets of values of e and q.

On the assumption that bankers are "risk-averters" and "diversifiers,"[50]

---

[50] *Cf.* Tobin, *op. cit.*, Sections 3.2 and 3.3, pp. 16–22. The labels "risk-averter" and "diversifier" are applied to those investors whose indifference curves between E and S are concave upward. For opportunity loci such as those of Figure B-1, "plungers" and "risk-lovers" might also diversify (i.e., choose L not equal to zero or one), but "diversifiers" necessarily will diversify.

it can be easily seen from Figure B-1 that they will choose L at least somewhat smaller than that value which maximizes E. However, the change in the portfolio induced by a change in e or q can only be guessed unless the bank's complete preference function between E and S is specified, a task which will not be attempted.

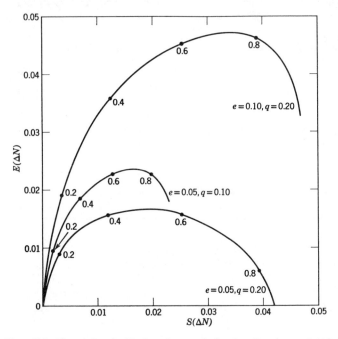

Figure B-1 The numbers beside the points are the fraction of total assets held in loans at that point; the curves end at the point $L = 1.00$ except for the curve $e = 0.05$, $q = 0.20$, which ends at $L = 0.86$, where E becomes negative.

Three conclusions may be drawn from this discussion:

1. The assumption that the bank maximizes E and neglects S entirely is equivalent in the Tobin sense to assuming that the bank is on the border between risk-averting and risk-loving.[51] This is not as serious as the words imply since much of the bank's risk is reflected in the model of the text in the expected profit function itself.

---

[51] *Ibid.*, p. 19. In Tobin's equation 3.7 maximizing expected return implies a marginal utility of return $[U'(R)]$ which is constant with respect to changes in R.

2. The size of the larger earning (and less liquid) portion of the bank's portfolio (i.e., L) would generally be somewhat smaller than the values derived in the text if variance of return were explicitly considered and the bank assumed a "diversifier." While this might be more realistic than to place all the risk elements in the expected return function, the complications of such a procedure can be seen from the simple version of the model presented here.

3. The effects of changes in parameters upon the various assets become less determinate when variance is introduced. Even if the indifference curves between E and S are assumed to be concave upward (i.e., risk-averting), the effect of an increase in e on the bank's willingness to make loans depends upon the relative slopes of successively higher indifference curves. If the slopes are believed to increase rapidly, then it is possible that higher values of e will reduce the amount of loans the bank makes.[52] But inspection of Figure B-1 indicates that the direction of changes is probably not altered for plausible shapes of the indifference loci.

Risk aversion on the part of the bank undoubtedly plays a critical role in the determination of the *composition within* its loan and security portfolios. As between two loans with the same expected earning rate, the one whose returns have lower variance and/or lower correlation with the returns of those loans already in the portfolio will certainly be preferred; similarly, the bank will often accept a low-yield security into its bond portfolio because its potential capital variation is small. While not denying the importance of these considerations in the bank's choice between different loans and between different securities, the model of the text maintains that they are not crucial in the bank's prior choice as to the basic division of the portfolio between loans and securities. The determinancy gained by assuming the bank is an expected profit maximizer is felt to be worth the perhaps slight loss of realism.

APPENDIX C: STAGE 2(i)

If the left-hand inequality of equation 5 of the text is assumed, then Stage 2(i) becomes a possibility, as well as Stage 2(ii) and Stage 3. Then the

---

[52] This possibility has been called an "income" effect by J. Aschheim in "Open-market Operations versus Reserve-requirement Variation," *Economic Journal*, LXIX (December 1959), pp. 697–704, where it is suggested that greater bank profits, *ceteris paribus*, will reduce the quantity of loans.

expected addition to net worth, $E[\Delta N]$, is as follows:

$$E[\Delta N] = \int_{w=-1+\frac{(1-s)(1-k)}{B}}^{a} \int_{u=s}^{1} [gB + wB + eL]\left[\frac{u-s}{a(1-s)^2}\right] du \, dw$$

$$+ \int_{w=-a}^{-1+\frac{(1-s)(1-k)}{B}} \int_{u=1-\frac{(1+w)B}{1-k}}^{1} [gB + wB + eL]\left[\frac{u-s}{a(1-s)^2}\right] du \, dw$$

$$+ \int_{w=-a}^{-1+\frac{(1-s)(-k)}{B}} \int_{u=s}^{1-\frac{(1+w)B}{1-k}} [gB + wB + eL - q(1-k)$$

$$+ q(1+w)B + q(1-k)u]\left[\frac{u-s}{a(1-s)^2}\right] du \, dw. \qquad \text{(C-1)}$$

This becomes, once the integrations are performed:

$$E[\Delta N] = gB + eL - \frac{q(1-a)^4}{24Ba(1-s)^2(1-k)^2}\left[\frac{(1-s)(1-k)}{1-a} - B\right]^4. \qquad \text{(C-2)}$$

After elimination of L by means of the accounting identity (1), the derivative of the expected profit with respect to B is:

$$\frac{dE[\Delta N]}{dB} = -(e-g) + \frac{q(1-a)^4}{24B^2a(1-s)^2(1-k)^2}$$

$$\times \left[\frac{(1-s)(1-k)}{1-a} - B\right]^3\left[\frac{(1-s)(1-k)}{1-a} + 3B\right]. \qquad \text{(C-3)}$$

The second derivative (d^2E/dB^2) is negative throughout the range of B, the first derivative (equation C-3) is negative when B assumes its largest value [i.e., $B = (1-s)(1-k)/(1-a)$], and the first derivative is positive when B assumes its smallest possible value [i.e., $B = (1-s)(1-k)/(1+a)$], provided that the following inequality holds:

$$0 < \frac{e-g}{q} < \frac{2a^2(2-a)}{3(1+a)^2}. \qquad \text{(C-4)}$$

Thus, if equation C-4 holds, there is a value of B in the permissible range for which equation C-3 is equal to zero, and it is that value of B which maximizes expected profits.

If the right-hand inequality of equation C-4 does not hold, expected profits decline continually as B rises from its smallest to its largest permissible value. In that case, the maximizing value of B is smaller than $(1 - s)(1 - k)/(1 + a)$, and the model of the text is the appropriate one [i.e., Stage 2(i) is impossible]. The common sense argument for choosing the assumption of the text that there is no Stage 2(i) is greatly strengthened by a consideration of the parameter values required if the right-hand inequality of equation C-4 is to hold; the table below gives the highest possible values of $(e - g)$, consistent with the existence of a Stage 2(i), for several combinations of values of a and q:

Table C-1

	$q = 0.05$	$q = 0.10$	$q = 0.30$
$a = 0$	0	0	0
$a = 0.1$	0.0005	0.0011	0.0033
$a = 0.25$	0.0023	0.0047	0.0141
$a = 0.50$	0.0055	0.0111	0.0333

Inasmuch as e generally could be expected to exceed g (on any definition of loans and securities) by at least one or two per cent, surprisingly—if not implausibly—large values of a and q are required if the bank is to choose to hold enough securities to be able to meet its worst deposit depletions by securities sales alone—even if bond prices rise to their highest conceivable value.

Nevertheless, the implications for the bank's optimum asset portfolio of changes in various parameters can be determined by taking partial derivatives of equation C-3 while holding that equation equal to zero. The changes in optimum B are as follows:[53]

$$\partial B / \partial e < 0$$

$$\partial B / \partial g > 0$$

$$\partial B / \partial q > 0$$

$$\partial B / \partial s < 0$$

$$\partial B / \partial k < 0$$

---

[53] The arithmetic is sufficiently messy that only the first derivatives have been calculated.

The sign of $\partial B/\partial a$ cannot be determined generally. That these signs are the same as those derived in the text, on the assumption that Stage 2(i) does not exist, is partial evidence that the influence of parameter changes upon optimum portfolios does not depend critically upon this choice of assumption.

APPENDIX D: TIME DEPOSITS

No distinction has been made, anywhere in the text, between different types of deposits, a neglect which will be here repaired by introducing time, as well as demand, deposits. The most obvious difference between the two classes of deposits lies in their cost, for time deposits are still permitted to, and do, earn interest for the depositor. On the other hand, the "earning power" of time deposits may exceed that of demand deposits in either or both of two ways. First, it is an institutional fact in most countries that the cash, or low-yield, reserve requirements on time deposits are lower than those on demand deposits. Second, to the extent that the lowest conceivable "deposit-low" is raised by the addition of less volatile time deposits, the bank may hold a larger portion of its portfolio in less liquid, but higher earning, assets.[54]

Banks attract new time deposits by offering to pay higher interest rates on them. Such increases in time deposits may "come" from several places: by a transfer from (1) the bank's own demand deposits; (2) the public's deposits with other banks; and (3) deposits and shares of the non-bank financial intermediaries.[55] From the point of view of the individual bank, the relevant division is between the first case and the second and third cases.[56] Here it will be assumed that the bank cannot, through its own volition, alter the total quantity of its deposits, but only, by changing its time deposit interest rate, induce some of its depositors to hold time instead of demand deposits. The fraction of total deposits held as time deposits is assumed to grow from zero, as the time deposit

---

[54] Throughout this section, we neglect the possibility that greater time deposits may imply lesser private (or other financial intermediary) lending, and hence higher lending rates for the bank. *Cf.* J. Tobin and William Brainard "Financial Intermediaries and the Effectiveness of Monetary Controls," in this volume, Chapter 3.

[55] It is assumed that the public's currency needs are fixed.

[56] From the point of view of the banking system, the most interesting division is between the first two cases and the third case.

interest rate (i) increases from zero, to some maximum value at which point further increases in i cannot induce further shifts from demand to time deposits. Thus, time deposits as a fraction of total deposits (T) will lie between zero and some maximum level (T^*) depending upon i, where T^* is less than one.

This transfer of funds from demand to time deposits will affect the values of k and s. The over-all cash requirements, as a fraction of total deposits, will be:

$$k = k_d - (k_d - k_t)T \tag{D-1}$$

where requirements on demand deposits (k_d) are assumed to exceed those on time deposits (k_t). The value of s, and the frequency distribution of the possible "deposit-lows," is not so easily calculated. It will depend upon the lowest possible "deposit-low" of time deposits (as a fraction of initial time deposits), s_t, and that of demand deposits (as a fraction of initial demand deposits), s_d; but it will also depend upon the form of the distribution of each of these "deposit-lows" and the covariance of the changes of each of these two types of deposits. If the frequency distribution of each type's "deposit-low" is assumed "triangular" (with a lowest possible "deposit-low" of s_t and s_d for time and demand deposits, respectively) and the two changes are uncorrelated, the resulting distribution of "deposit-lows" for the total of deposits will not be "triangular" but will have a convex (from below) segment over very low "deposit-lows" and a concave segment for "deposit-lows" near unity.[57] Since the assumption

---

[57] If the fraction in time deposits is small enough that

$$T \leq \frac{1 - s_d}{(1 - s_d) + (1 - s_t)}, \tag{D-2}$$

the frequency distribution of "deposit-lows" of total deposits, $f(u)$, will be:

$$f(u) = \frac{2}{3} \frac{[u - Ts_t - (1 - T)s_d]^3}{T^2(1 - T)^2(1 - s_d)^2(1 - s_t)^2} \quad \text{where: } Ts_t + (1 - T)s_d < u < T + (1 - T)s_d$$

$$= \frac{2}{3} \frac{3[u - Ts_t - (1 - T)s_d] - 2T(1 - s_t)}{(1 - T)^2(1 - s_d)^2}$$
$$\text{where: } T + (1 - T)s_d < u < (1 - T) + Ts_t$$

$$= 2[u - Ts_t - (1 - T)s_d]\left[\frac{1}{(1 - T)^2(1 - s_d)^2} + \frac{1}{T^2(1 - s_t)^2}\right]$$

$$- \frac{4(1 - T)(1 - s_d)}{3T^2(1 - s_t)^2} - \frac{4T(1 - s_t)}{3(1 - T)^2(1 - s_d)^2} - \frac{2[u - Ts_t - (1 - T)s_d]^3}{3T^2(1 - T)^2(1 - s_d)^2(1 - s_t)^2} \tag{D-3}$$
$$\text{where: } (1 - T) + Ts_t < u < 1.$$

The distribution, $f(u)$, will be "triangular" only if s_t is one, i.e., time deposits never decline. If the direction of the inequality of equation D-2 is reversed, the exact form of the distribution is altered, but the general shape is the same (and the distribution is "triangular" only if s_d is one).

of zero covariance between "deposit-lows" of time and demand deposits leads to an understatement of frequencies in the low "deposit-low" segment, and an overstatement in the high range, it will be convenient, and probably less unrealistic, to assume that the aggregate "deposit-low" distribution is also "triangular" with the point of zero probability, s, occurring at:[58]

$$s = Ts_t + (1 - T)s_a. \tag{D-4}$$

The costs of time deposits, iT, are subtracted from equation 8 of the text to give the expected addition to net worth when the bank considers a time deposit policy:

$$E[\Delta N] = gB + e(1 + N - k - B) - \frac{q}{3x^2}(x - B)^3 - iT \tag{D-5}$$

where, for simplicity, bond prices are assumed not to fluctuate (i.e., a equal to zero) and, for brevity, x is written for $(1 - s)(1 - k)$. This expression, equation D-5, is maximized by the bank not only with respect to B, which yields equation 12 of the text (with a equal to zero), but also with respect to i, for the interest rate paid on time deposits is now a variable under the control of the bank. Differentiation of equation D-5 with respect to i yields, after substitution for the profit-maximizing value of B by means of equation 12:

$$\frac{\partial E[\Delta N]}{\partial i} = e(k_a - k_t)\frac{dT}{di} - (e - g)[1 - \tfrac{2}{3}\sqrt{(e - g)/q}]$$
$$\times \frac{dx}{dT} \cdot \frac{dT}{di} - \frac{d(iT)}{di}, \tag{D-6}$$

where

$$\frac{dx}{dT} = \frac{d(1 - s)(1 - k)}{dT} = (1 - s_a)(k_a - k_t) - (1 - k_a)(s_t - s_a)$$
$$- 2T(s_t - s_a)(k_a - k_t). \tag{D-7}$$

Clearly, if i becomes so large that dT/di is zero (i.e., time deposits are at their maximum level, T^*), equation D-6 will be negative; for some high values of i, expected profits will be reduced if time deposit rates are raised. At the other extreme, when i, and hence T, is zero, equation D-6 is positive; costs are not increased as much as expected profits when i is increased slightly from zero. Thus, expected profits at first increase and later decrease as i, and hence T, is raised. We can conclude, on the above

---

[58] This value of s is the lowest conceivable "deposit-low" of the distribution (equation D-3).

assumptions, that the optimum proportion of total deposits in time deposit accounts will always be greater than zero.[59] Moreover this conclusion still follows if time deposits are assumed to be reserve-saving though not deposit-stabilizing (i.e., $k_d > k_t$, $s_d = s_t$), or vice versa (i.e., $k_d = k_t$, $s_d < s_t$). Of course, there are many reasons beyond the scope of the model why the optimum amount of time deposits might be zero for a particular bank. Most obvious of these are that administrative considerations place a minimum on the amount of such deposits which the bank will wish to attract and/or that a time deposit rate markedly above zero is required to induce any time deposits at all. On the other hand, there are reasons other than expected profits (as defined here) for desiring such relatively stable deposits even if not profitable—for example, concern by the bank for the variability of its expected profits (see Appendix B).

APPENDIX E: UNIFORM DISTRIBUTION OF "DEPOSIT-LOWS"

In order to indicate that the results of the model of the text do not depend too critically upon the type of distribution assumed for the bank's "deposit-lows," the same model is here worked through briefly on the alternative assumption that the "deposit-lows" are uniformly distributed over the range from s to unity; that is,

$$f(u) = \frac{1}{(1 - s)} . \tag{E-1}$$

The expected addition to net worth is then exactly as given by equation 7 of the text with the appropriate alteration in the distribution of u. The

---

[59] W. L. Smith uses a simplified version of equation D-6, on the assumption that e equals g (i.e., neglecting the liquidity differences between assets), to show that it is profitable for the bank to induce switches from demand to time deposits, by raising time deposit rate, if:

$$e > \frac{i}{k_d - k_t} \left(1 + \frac{1}{\eta} \right)$$

where η is the time deposit interest elasticity of time deposits. Of course, the above conclusions follow in this special case as well. *Cf.* footnote 7, p. 544 of W. L. Smith, "Financial Intermediaries and Monetary Controls," *Quarterly Journal of Economics*, Vol. 73, No. 4 (November 1959), pp. 533–553.

analog to equation 8, expected profit after the integrations have been performed, is:

$$E[\Delta N] = gB + eL - \frac{q}{2(1-s)(1-k)}\left[(1-s)(1-k) - B\right]^2 - \frac{a^2 qB^2}{6(1-s)(1-k)}. \quad \text{(E-2)}$$

The optimum proportion of securities (see equation 12) is:

$$B = \frac{(1-s)(1-k)}{(1+a^2/3)}\left(1 - \frac{e-g}{q}\right). \quad \text{(E-3)}$$

It should be noted that the parameters enter in a less complex, but similar, manner (see equation 12).

The first and second partial derivatives of B have the following signs:

Table E-1 $\partial B/\partial x \quad \partial^2 B/\partial x\, \partial y$ where:

	$y = a$	$y = q$	$y = g$	$y = e$	$y = k$	$y = s$
where $x = s$	−	+	−	−	+	+	0
$x = k$	−	+	−	−	+	0
$x = e$	−	+	+	0	0	
$x = g$	+	−	−	0		
$x = q$	+	−	−			
$x = a$	−	−				

Again, there is no basic difference between this table and Table 1 although here more second partials are zero and there is no possibility of different signs in different regions of the parameters.

APPENDIX F: END-OF-PERIOD DEPOSITS

In the text it is assumed that the "most radical" adjustment of the bank's portfolio is required at the moment when its deposits reach their lowest point of the period. If the bank is able to postpone this adjustment until the end of the period by means of short-term borrowing, then the relevant distribution for its profit calculations is that of end-of-period deposits. It is interesting to compare the implications for the bank's portfolio of this alternative assumption about the relevant deposit distribution.

In Appendix A it is shown, under certain assumptions, that the "deposit-low" distribution is simply a truncated (at the level of initial deposits) duplication (of twice the density) of the end-of-period deposit distribution. Since this "deposit-low" distribution is approximated in the text by a "triangular" distribution,

$$f(u) = \frac{2(u - s)}{(1 - s)^2} \quad \text{for} \quad 0 < s < u < 1,$$

comparison between the two assumptions is facilitated if the distribution of end-of-period deposits, $f^*(v)$, is approximated by an "isosceles" distribution:

$$f^*(v) = \frac{(v - s)}{(1 - s)^2} \quad \text{for} \quad 0 < s < v < 1.$$

$$f^*(v) = \frac{(2 - s - v)}{(1 - s)^2} \quad \text{for} \quad 1 < v < (2 - s).$$

The distribution of v for values greater than unity need not detain us, for the possible earnings obtained from net increases in deposits are quite independent of the start-of-period portfolio decision.

Therefore the expected addition to net worth may be written, analogously to equation 7 of the text, as:

$$E[\Delta N] = \int_{w=-a}^{a} \int_{v=s}^{1} [gB + wB + eL]\left[\frac{v - s}{2a(1 - s)^2}\right] dv\, dw$$

$$+ \int_{w=-a}^{a} \int_{v=s}^{1 - \frac{(1+w)B}{1-k}} [-q(1 - k) + q(1 + w)B + q(1 - k)v]$$

$$\times \left[\frac{v - s}{2a(1 - s)^2}\right] dv\, dw + \frac{1}{2} \int_{w=-a}^{a} [gB + wB + eL]\left(\frac{1}{2a}\right) dw.$$

$$\text{(F-1)}$$

Maximization yields a value for B, the optimum securities holding, analogous to equation 12 of the text:

$$B = \frac{(1 - s)(1 - k)[1 + (a^2/3)]}{1 + a^2}\left\{1 - \sqrt{1 - \frac{(1 + a^2)[1 - 2(e - g)/q]}{(1 + a^2/3)^2}}\right\}.$$

$$\text{(F-2)}$$

The only difference between equation F-2 and equation 12 is that the term $(e - g)/q$ is multiplied by a factor of two in equation F-2. For equal values of all parameters, the present formulation of the deposit distribution therefore implies a smaller amount of securities and a larger amount of loans.[60] The directions of change in the optimum portfolio induced by variations in the parameters are, however, not affected by this concern for end-of-period deposits instead of the "deposit-low." Of course, the results would be different for other specific forms of the distributions, but this exercise indicates that the conclusions of the model are not critically dependent upon the deposit distribution assumption.

---

[60] A corner maximum with no securities held in the optimum portfolio now occurs when $(e - g)/q$ is greater than 0.5, whereas, on the assumption of the text, the corner maximum occurred when $(e - g)/q$ was greater than 1.0.

3

Financial Intermediaries and the Effectiveness of Monetary Controls*

JAMES TOBIN and WILLIAM C. BRAINARD

Does the existence of uncontrolled financial intermediaries vitiate monetary control? What would be the consequences of subjecting these intermediaries to reserve requirements or to interest rate ceilings?

This chapter is addressed to these questions, but it treats them theoretically and at a high level of abstraction. The method is to set up models of general equilibrium in financial and capital markets and to trace in these models the effects of monetary controls and of structural changes. Equilibrium in these models is an equilibrium of stocks and balance sheets—a situation in which both the public and the financial institutions are content with their portfolios of assets and debts, and the demand to hold each asset is just equal to the stock supply. This approach has obvious limitations, among which the most important is probably that it has nothing to say about speeds of adjustment and other dynamic effects of crucial practical importance. On the other hand, monetary economics has long suffered from trying to discuss these effects without solid foundation in any theory of general financial equilibrium. We feel that we can advance the discussion by outlining

---

* SOURCE: Reprinted from *The American Economic Review*, Vol. LIII, No. 2 (May 1963), pp. 383–400.

a systematic scheme for comparative static analysis of some of the questions at issue.[1]

The models discussed in the text are simple ones, designed to bring out the main points with few enough assets and interest rates so that graphical and verbal exposition can be used. The exposition in the text takes advantage of the fact that introducing nonbank financial intermediaries, uncontrolled or controlled, into a system in which banks are under effective monetary control presents essentially the same problems as introducing commercial banks as an intermediary, uncontrolled or controlled, into a system in which the government's essential control is the supply of its own currency. The analysis therefore centers on the more primitive question: the effects of financial intermediation by banks, the consequences of leaving their operation unregulated, and the effects of regulating them in various ways. The conclusions have some interest in themselves, in clarifying the functions of reserve and rate controls on commercial banks. By analogy they also bear on questions concerning the extension of such controls to other financial intermediaries.

The main conclusions can be briefly stated. The presence of banks, even if they are uncontrolled, does not mean that monetary control through the supply of currency has no effect on the economy. Nor does the presence of nonbank intermediaries mean that monetary control through commercial banks is an empty gesture. Even if increases in the assets and liabilities of uncontrolled intermediaries wholly offset enforced reductions in the supplies of controlled monetary assets, even if monetary expansion means equivalent contraction by uncontrolled intermediaries, monetary controls can still be effective. However, substitutions of this kind do diminish the effectiveness of these controls; for example, a billion dollar change in the supply of currency and bank reserves would have more effect on the economy if such substitutions were prevented.

Whether it is important that monetary controls be more effective in this sense is another question, to which this chapter is not addressed. When a given remedial effect can be achieved either by a small dose of strong medicine or a large dose of weak medicine, it is not obvious that the small dose is preferable. Increasing the responsiveness of the system to instruments of control may also increase its sensitivity to random

---

[1] This chapter is based on work by both authors. Some of its topics were treated in a preliminary way in a Cowles Foundation Discussion Paper (No. 63, January 1958, mimeographed) of the same title, by James Tobin. The general approach of that paper was elaborated and extended in a systematic way by William Brainard in "Financial Intermediaries and a Theory of Monetary Control," in this volume, Chapter 4.

exogenous shocks.[2] Furthermore, extension of controls over financial intermediaries and markets involves considerations beyond those of economic stabilization; it raises also questions of equity, allocative efficiency, and the scope of governmental authority.

THE NATURE OF FINANCIAL INTERMEDIARIES

The essential function of banks and other financial intermediaries is to satisfy simultaneously the portfolio preferences of two types of individuals or firms. On one side are borrowers, who wish to expand their holdings of real assets—inventories, residential real estate, productive plant and equipment, etc.—beyond the limits of their own net worth. On the other side are lenders, who wish to hold part or all of their net worth in assets of stable money value with negligible risk of default. The assets of financial intermediaries are obligations of the borrowers— promissory notes, bonds, mortgages. The liabilities of financial intermediaries are the assets of the lenders—bank deposits, savings and loan shares, insurance policies, pension rights.

Financial intermediaries assume liabilities of smaller default risk and greater predictability of value than their assets. The principal kinds of institutions take on liabilities of greater liquidity, too; thus bank depositors can require payment on demand, while bank loans become due only on specified dates. The reasons that the intermediation of financial institutions can accomplish these transformations between the nature of the obligation of the borrower and the nature of the asset of the ultimate lender are these: (1) administrative economy and expertise in negotiating, accounting, appraising, and collecting; (2) reduction of risk per dollar of lending by the pooling of independent risks, with respect both to loan default and to deposit withdrawal; (3) governmental guarantees of the liabilities of the institutions and other provisions (bank examination, investment regulations, supervision of insurance companies, last-resort lending) designed to assure the solvency and liquidity of the institution. For these reasons, intermediation permits borrowers who wish to expand their investments in real assets to be accommodated at lower rates and easier terms than if they had to borrow directly from the lenders. If the creditors of financial intermediaries had to hold instead the kinds of obligations that private borrowers are capable of providing, they would certainly insist on higher rates and stricter terms. Therefore, any autonomous increase in the amount of financial intermediation in the economy

---

[2] The balancing of these considerations and the desirability of finding structural changes which increase the first kind of responsiveness without increasing the second are discussed in the Brainard paper cited above.

(for example, improvements in the efficiency of financial institutions or the creation of new types of intermediaries) can be expected to be, *ceteris paribus*, an expansionary influence. This is true whether the growth occurs in intermediaries with monetary liabilities, i.e., commercial banks, or in other intermediaries.

In the interests of concise terminology, "banks" will refer to commercial banks and "nonbanks" to other financial institutions, including savings banks. Moreover, "intermediary" will refer to an entire species, or industry, of financial institutions. Thus all commercial banks constitute one intermediary, all life insurance companies another, and so on. An "institution" will mean an individual member of the species, an individual firm in the industry—a bank, or a life insurance company, or a retirement program.

Financial institutions fall fairly easily into distinct categories, each industry offering a differentiated product to its customers, both lenders and borrowers. From the point of view of lenders, the obligations of the various intermediaries are more or less close, but not perfect, substitutes. For example, savings deposits share most of the attributes of demand deposits; but they are not means of payment, and the institution has the right, seldom exercised, to require notice of withdrawal. Similarly, there is differentiation in the kinds of credit offered borrowers. Each intermediary has its speciality, e.g., the commercial loan for banks and the real estate mortgage for the savings and loan association. But the borrowers' market is not completely compartmentalized. The same credit instruments are handled by more than one intermediary, and many borrowers have flexibility in the type of debt they incur. Thus there is some substitutability, in the demand for credit by borrowers, among the assets of the various intermediaries.

There is also product differentiation within intermediaries, between institutions, arising from location, advertising, and the other sources of monopolistic competition. But this is of a smaller order of importance than the differentiation between intermediaries. For present purposes, the products offered by the institutions within a given intermediary can be regarded as homogeneous.

The Substitution Assumption

These observations about the nature of financial intermediaries and the imperfect competition among them lead to a basic assumption of the following analysis. The liabilities of each financial intermediary are considered homogeneous, and their appeal to owners of wealth is described by a single market rate of interest. The portfolios of wealth-owners are made up of currency, real capital, and the liabilities of the various intermediaries.

These assets are assumed to be imperfect substitutes for each other in wealth-owners' portfolios. That is, an increase in the rate of return on any one asset will lead to an increase in the fraction of wealth held in that asset, and to a decrease or at most no change in the fraction held in every other asset. Similarly, borrowers are assumed to regard loans from various intermediaries as imperfect substitutes. That is—given the profitability of the real investment for which borrowing is undertaken—an increase in one intermediary lending rate will reduce borrowing from that intermediary and increase, or at least leave unchanged, borrowing from every other source.

THE CRITERION OF EFFECTIVENESS OF MONETARY CONTROL

A monetary control can be considered expansionary if it lowers the rate of return on ownership of real capital that the community requires to induce it to hold a given stock of capital, and deflationary if it raises that rate of return. (The words expansionary and deflationary are used merely to indicate the direction of influence; the manner in which the influence is divided between price change and output change depends on aspects of the economic situation that are not relevant here.) The value of the rate of return referred to is a hypothetical one: the level at which owners of wealth are content to absorb the given stock of capital into their portfolios or balance sheets along with other assets and debts. In full equilibrium, this critical rate of return must equal the expected marginal productivity of the capital stock, which depends technologically on the size of the stock relative to expected levels of output and employment. If a monetary action lowers the rate of return on capital that owners of wealth will accept, it becomes easier for the economy to accumulate capital. If a monetary action increases the rate of return on equity investments demanded by owners of wealth, then it discourages capital accumulation.

This chapter concerns the financial sector alone, and we make no attempt here to describe the repercussions of a discrepancy between the rate of return on capital required for portfolio balance and the marginal productivity of capital. These repercussions occur in the market for goods and services and labor, and through them feed back to the financial sector itself. Let it suffice here to say that they are qualitatively of the same nature as the consequences of a discrepancy between Wicksell's natural and market rates of interest.

We assume the value of the stock of capital to be given by its replacement cost, which depends not on events in the financial sphere but on prices prevailing for newly produced goods. We make this assumption because the strength of new real investment in the economy depends on the terms on which the community will hold capital goods valued at the prices of current production. Any discrepancy between these terms and the actual marginal productivity of capital can be expressed alternatively as a discrepancy between market valuation of old capital and its replacement cost. But the discrepancy has the same implications for new investment whichever way it is expressed.

This required rate of return on capital is the basic criterion of the effectiveness of a monetary action. To alter the terms on which the community will accumulate real capital—that is what monetary policy is all about. The other criteria commonly discussed—this or that interest rate, this or that concept of the money supply, this or that volume of lending—are at best only instrumental and intermediate and at worst misleading goals.

SUMMARY OF REGIMES TO BE DISCUSSED

The argument proceeds by analysis of a sequence of regimes. A regime is characterized by listing the assets, debts, financial intermediaries, and interest rates which play a part in it. In all the regimes to be discussed, net private wealth is the sum of two components: the fixed capital stock, valued at current replacement cost; and the noninterest-bearing debt of the government, taking the form either of currency publicly held or of the reserves of banks and other intermediaries. In the models of this chapter, there is no government interest-bearing debt.[3] Consequently there are no open market operations proper. Instead the standard monetary action analyzed is a change in the supply of noninterest-bearing debt relative to the value of the stock of capital. (Only the proportions between the two components of wealth matter, because it is assumed that all asset and debt demands are, at given interest rates, homogeneous of degree one with respect to the scale of wealth.)

The public is divided, somewhat artificially, into two parts: wealth-owners and borrowers. Wealth-owners command the total private wealth of the economy and dispose it among the available assets, ranging from currency to direct ownership of capital. Borrowers use the loans they obtain from financial intermediaries to hold capital. This split

---

[3] This complication has been discussed in other works of the authors; in Brainard, *op. cit.*, and in Tobin, "An Essay on Principles of Debt Management," *Fiscal and Debt Management Policies*, prepared for the Commission on Money and Credit (Englewood Cliffs, N.J.: Prentice-Hall, Inc., 1963), pp. 143–218.

should not be taken literally. A borrower may be, and usually is, a wealth-owner—one who desires to hold more capital than his net worth permits.

A final simplification is to ignore the capital and nonfinancial accounts of intermediaries, on the ground that these are inessential to the purposes of the chapter. Table 1 provides a summary of the regimes to be discussed.

Table 1 Summary of Financial Regimes Discussed in Text

Regime	Structure of Assets and Debts		Yields to Be Determined on
	Holder	Assets (+), Debts (−)	
I	Private wealth-owners	+ Currency + Capital	Capital
II	Private wealth-owners	+ Currency, + capital, + Intermediary liabilities	Capital, intermediary liabilities and loans
	Private borrowers	− Loans, + capital	
	Intermediary	− Liabilities, + loans, (+ reserves)	
III	Private wealth-owners	+ Currency, + capital + deposits	(A) Capital, loans, deposits
	Private borrowers	− Loans, + capital	(B) Capital, loans (deposit rate fixed)
	Intermediary (Banks)	− Deposits, + loans, + reserves (currency)	

REGIME I: A CURRENCY-CAPITAL WORLD

It is instructive to begin with a rudimentary financial world in which the only stores of value available are currency and real capital. There are no intermediaries, not even banks, and no credit markets. Private wealth is the sum of the stock of currency and the value of the stock of capital. The stock of currency is, in effect, the government debt, all in noninterest-bearing form. The required rate of return on capital R_0 is simply the rate at which wealth-owners are content to hold the existing currency supply, neither more nor less, along with the existing capital stock, valued at replacement cost. The determination of R_0 is shown in Figure 1. In Figure 1, the return on capital R_0 is measured vertically. Total private wealth is measured by the horizontal length of the box OW, divided between the supply of currency OC and the replacement value of capital CW. Curve DD' is a portfolio choice curve, showing how wealth-owners wish to divide their wealth between currency and capital at various rates R_0. It is a kind of "liquidity preference" curve. The rate which equates currency supply and demand—or, what amounts to the same thing, capital supply and demand—is $\bar{R}_0$.

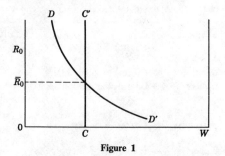

Figure 1

In this rudimentary world, the sole monetary instrument is a change in the supply of currency relative to the supply of capital. An increase in currency supply relative to the capital stock can be shown in Figure 1 simply by moving the vertical line CC' to the right. Clearly this will lower the required rate of return $\bar{R}_0$. Similarly, the monetary effect of a contraction of the currency supply can be represented by a leftward shift of the same vertical line.

REGIME II: AN UNCONTROLLED INTERMEDIARY

Now imagine that a financial intermediary arrives on the scene. The liabilities of the intermediary are a close but imperfect substitute for currency. Its assets are loans which enable private borrowers to hold capital in excess of their own net worth. How does the existence of this intermediary alter the effectiveness of monetary policy? That is, how does the intermediary affect the degree to which the government can change $\bar{R}_0$ by a given change in the supply of currency?

We will assume first that the intermediary is not required to hold reserves and does not hold any. Its sole assets are loans. To any institution the value of acquiring an additional dollar liability to the public is the interest at which it can be re-lent after allowance for administrative costs, default risk, and the like. Consequently, in unrestricted competition this rate will be paid to the intermediary's creditors. In equilibrium, the borrowers' demand for loans at the prevailing interest rate on loans will be the same as the public's supply of credits to the intermediary at the corresponding rate.

This regime is depicted in Figure 2. The axes represent the same variables as in Figure 1, and the supplies of currency and capital are shown in the same manner. But the demand for capital is now shown

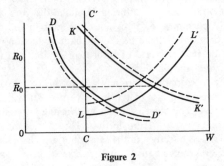

Figure 2

in two parts. The first, measured leftward from the right vertical axis to curve KK', is the direct demand of wealth-owners. The second part, measured rightward from line CC' to curve LL', is the demand for capital by borrowers. This distance also measures the demand of borrowers for loan accommodation by the intermediary. Curve DD' represents, as in Figure 1, the demand of wealth-owners for currency. The horizontal difference between DD' and KK' is their demand for the liabilities of the intermediary.

In this regime there is a second interest rate to be determined, the rate R_2 on intermediary liabilities. The rate on intermediary loans, r_2, is uniquely determined by R_2; competition among institutions keeps the margin between these rates equal to the cost of intermediation. The position of the three curves in Figure 2 and the demands which they depict depend on this rate as well as on R_0. The three dashed curves represent a higher intermediary rate R_2 than the solid curves. However, only the solid curves represent an equilibrium combination of the two rates, at which (1) the demands for capital absorb the entire capital stock, (2) the loan assets of the intermediary equal its liabilities, and (3) the demand for currency is equal to the supply.

We may presume, of course, that the introduction of the intermediary lowers the required rate of return on capital $\bar{R}_0$. For wealth-owners, the intermediary's liabilities satisfy some of the same needs which would be met in Regime I by an increase in the supply of currency. At the same time, some of the capital which wealth-owners formerly held can now be lodged with borrowers, at a lower rate of return. These borrowers were unable to obtain finance to hold capital in Regime I.

An autonomous growth of the intermediary can be formally represented by a reduction in the margin between the intermediary's lending and borrowing rates. As the intermediary becomes more efficient in administration, risk pooling, and in tailoring its liabilities and assets to the preferences of its customers on both sides, this margin will decline under the force of competition. It can be shown that a reduction in the margin always lowers the required rate of return on capital and increases the intermediary's assets and liabilities.

A reduction in the supply of currency will, in this regime, as in the first regime, raise the required rate of return on capital. It will also raise the intermediary's rates. The existence of the intermediary does not, therefore, mean that monetary control is ineffective. However, it normally means that the control is less effective, in the sense that a dollar reduction in the supply of currency brings about a smaller increase in $\bar{R}_0$ when it can be counteracted by expansion of the intermediary. The possibility of substituting the intermediary's liabilities for currency offers a partial escape from the monetary restriction. But as long as the intermediary's liabilities are an imperfect substitute for currency, the escape is only partial.

REGIME II: A CONTROLLED INTERMEDIARY

The proposition that the intermediary weakens monetary control can be demonstrated by imagining that we can impose some quantitative restriction on the expansion of the intermediary. We can then compare the strength of monetary restriction in Regime II, with and without this quantitative control.

Assume, therefore, that the government's noninterest-bearing debt is divided into two segregated parts: currency held by the public and reserves held by the intermediary pursuant to a legal fractional reserve requirement. Assume further that this requirement is effective, i.e., that the aggregate size of intermediary liabilities permitted by the reserve requirement is smaller than the size which would result from unrestricted competition. When the reserve requirement is effective, the margin between the intermediary's lending and borrowing rates is greater than is needed to compensate for risk and administrative costs. Let the supply of currency to the public be reduced. In an uncontrolled Regime II, this will in certain circumstances lead to an expansion of intermediary assets and liabilities. In those circumstances, preventing such expansion by a reserve requirement will increase the effectiveness of monetary control. That is, a dollar reduction in the currency supply will raise $\bar{R}_0$ more if an expansionary response by the intermediary is prevented. There are also circumstances—probably less plausible—where monetary restriction would, in an uncontrolled regime, result in a contraction of the intermediary. In these cases, of course, control of the intermediary does not strengthen monetary control.

The example just discussed is a simple and artificial one. But the point it makes is of quite general applicability. In the more complex real world, currency and commercial bank liabilities are together subject to control via monetary policy, while the scales of operations of other financial intermediaries are not. The freedom of these intermediaries offers an escape from monetary controls over commercial banks, but only a partial escape. Likewise, the effectiveness of monetary controls would be enhanced if each nonbank intermediary was subject to a specific reserve requirement which would keep it from expanding counter to policies which contract commercial banks.

REGIME III: COMMERCIAL BANKING

The reserve requirement introduced in Regime II was expressed in terms of a specific government debt instrument, available only for this purpose and only in amounts determined by the government. The more familiar situation is that the reserve asset is, for all practical purposes, currency itself. Currency, that is, can serve either as a means of payment in the hands of the public, or as reserves for the intermediary. The government determines the total size of its noninterest-bearing debt, but its allocation between currency and reserves is a matter of public choice. It is, of course, this kind of reserve and reserve requirement that we associate with commercial banks—the most prominent intermediary. Indeed, the traditional business of banks is to accept deposit liabilities payable in currency on demand, and this obligation is the historical reason for banks' holding reserves in currency or its equivalent in "high-powered" money.

Let us consider, therefore, a third regime in which the one intermediary is a commercial banking system required to hold as reserves in currency a certain fraction of its deposit liabilities. Total private wealth is, as in the first two regimes, the sum of currency supply and the capital stock. Wealth-owners divide their holdings among currency, bank deposits, and direct ownership of capital. Banks dispose their deposits between reserves in currency and loans to borrowers, in proportions dictated by the legal reserve requirement. Borrowers hold that part of the capital stock not directly held by wealth-owners. So far as interest rates are concerned, there are two important variants:

A. Interest on bank deposits is competitively determined, and stands in competitive relation to the interest rate on bank loans. This relationship will depend on, among other things, the reserve requirement, which compels a bank to place a fraction of any additional deposit in noninterest-bearing reserves.

B. Interest on deposits is subject to an effective legal ceiling, and at the same time the reserve requirement normally restricts the banking industry to a scale at which the loan rate exceeds this fixed deposit interest rate by more than the competitive margin.

In this regime, there are two sources of demand for currency. One is the direct demand of the public. The other is the banks' reserve requirement; in effect, the public demand for deposits creates a fractional indirect demand for currency. This creates an interesting complication, as follows: The basic assumption about the portfolio behavior of wealth-owners is that assets are all substitutes for each other. Essentially the same assumption is applied to the behavior of borrowers, that is, a rise in the interest rate on any asset (A) induces, *ceteris paribus*, an increase in desired holdings of (A) and a decrease, or at most no change, in the desired holdings of every other asset. It is this assumption which enabled us to state unambiguously the direction of the effects of monetary actions in the regimes previously discussed. In the present regime the same substitution assumption still applies to the portfolio behavior of wealth-owners and borrowers. This means, among other things, that the public's direct demand for currency is assumed to decline, or at most not to rise, in response to an increase in the rate offered on bank deposits. But, of course, an increase in this rate also increases the demand for bank deposits. Thus it indirectly increases the demand for currency to serve as bank reserves.

It is certainly conceivable, especially if the required reserve ratio is high, that the indirect effect of an increase in the deposit rate outweighs the direct effect. In that event, currency and deposits are, taking account of public and banks together, complements rather than substitutes. This possibility is the simplest example of a very general phenomenon. Even though the substitution assumption applies to the portfolio choices of the public, and of every intermediary, taken separately, it is possible that assets will be complements in the system as a whole. This can happen whenever the public and intermediaries hold the same assets (currency, or government bonds, or other securities) or whenever one intermediary holds as assets the liabilities of another intermediary. Some of the implications of complementarity for both the stability of the system and its responses to various changes in parameters and in structure can be illustrated in the present regime.

Equilibrium in Regime III may be depicted by considering separately the conditions of equilibrium in the market for currency and in the

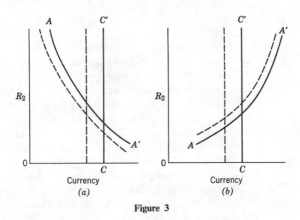

Figure 3

market for loans. In Figure 3 the supply of currency is shown as the vertical line CC'. The demand for currency, in relation to the deposit rate R_2, is the curve AA'. This includes both the direct and the indirect demand for currency. As noted above, this relationship may be either downward-sloping, as in Figure 3*a* or upward-sloping, as in Figure 3*b*. The upward-sloping case is that of complementarity. In each case the position of the demand curve depends on the level of R_0; the dashed curve represents a higher R_0, which tends to reduce the demand for currency. From the relationships involved in Figure 3 can be derived a locus of pairs of rates R_0 and R_2 which equate demand and supply for currency. Such a relationship is shown in Figure 5 by the curve E_c. In the "substitutes case," corresponding to Figure 3*a*, it is downward-sloping, as shown in Figure 5*a*. In the "complements case," corresponding to Figure 3*b*, it is upward-sloping, as shown in Figures 5*b* and 5*c*.

In Figure 4 the loan market is shown, the volume of loans on the horizontal axis and the deposit rate on the vertical axis. The supply of loans, BB', is essentially the public demand for deposits, after allowance

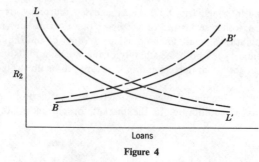

Figure 4

for the fractional reserve requirement. The demand for loans, LL', is the amount of loan accommodation borrowers wish at various deposit rates, taking account of the fact that the loan rate systematically exceeds the deposit rate for the reasons already mentioned. The positions of the loan supply and demand curves depend on R_0, the rate of return on capital. A higher R_0 shifts both curves upward, as indicated by the dashed curves. From these relationships a second locus of the two rates R_0 and R_2 can be derived, the pairs of rates which equilibrate the loan market. This is the upward-sloping relationship E_l, also shown in Figure 5.

Three possible cases for the system as a whole are shown in the three parts of Figure 5: the first, or substitutes case, in Figure 5a, a moderate complements case in Figure 5b, and an extreme complements case in Figure 5c. Now if there is a reduction in the supply of currency, equilibrium in the currency market can be maintained only by an increase in the rate on capital R_0 associated with any given deposit rate R_2. This can be seen by a shift left in the currency supply in Figure 3. Consequently the effect of a reduction in the currency supply can be shown in Figure 5 by a rightward shift in the curve E_c. In the first two cases, Figures 5a and 5b, this means an increase in both rates, as would be expected. However, in the extreme complements case, Figure 5c, it indicates a decrease in both rates!

This implausible result arouses the suspicion that the solution indicated in Figure 5c is an unstable equilibrium. We have examined the question of stability under the assumption that excess demand for capital leads to a fall in the rate of return on capital R_0, while excess borrowers' demand for loans, relative to the supply permitted by reserve requirements and depositor preferences, leads to a rise in loan-deposit rate R_2. The case exhibited in Figure 5c is indeed unstable, while the other two cases are stable.

Consider now alternative (B), in which the interest rate on deposits is subject to an effective legal ceiling. The competitive link between the

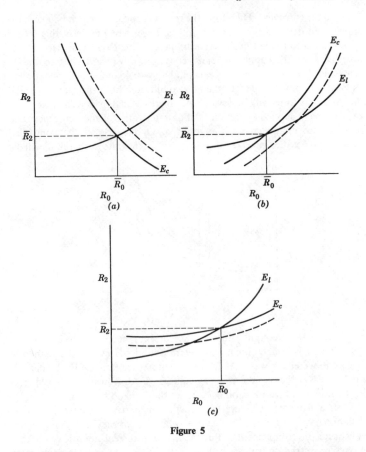

Figure 5

deposit and loan rates is broken by this regulation. In Figure 3, in other words, there is only one applicable level of the deposit rate. Consequently, there is only one rate on capital which is consistent with equilibrium in the "market" for currency. Figure 6 exhibits this situation. The currency equilibrium curve of Figure 6 is simply a vertical line; although the loan rate r_2 measured on the vertical axis of Figure 6 can vary, its variation does not affect either the deposit rate or equilibrium in the currency market.

The effect of an increase in the controlled deposit rate depends on whether currency and deposits are, when both indirect and direct demands are taken into account, substitutes or complements. If they are substitutes, an increase in the controlled deposit rate will reduce the net demand for currency. Therefore, the rate on capital R_0 which balances the supply and demand for currency will be lower. In Figure 6, this means a movement to the left in the vertical line. An increase in the deposit rate also increases the supply of loans, causing a downward shift in the E_l schedule. For any given rate on capital a lower loan rate will be required to clear the loan market. In the new equilibrium both the rate on capital and the loan rate will be lower. An increase in the deposit rate is an expansionary monetary action.[4] If, on the other hand, currency and deposits are complements, the result of an increase in the controlled deposit rate is the reverse. An increase in the rate on capital will be

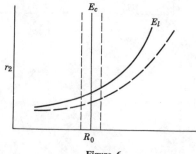

Figure 6

required to restore equilibrium in the currency market; the increase in deposit rate is a deflationary monetary action. However the loan rate r_2 may move either way. As in the substitutes case, a rise in the deposit rate increases the supply of loans, shifting E_l downward. But the rise in the rate of return on capital R_0 raises the demand for loans.

With a fixed deposit rate, a reduction in currency supply is always deflationary. This is true, of course, whether currency and deposits are substitutes or complements. But the question of real interest is whether monetary restriction is more deflationary—i.e., produces a bigger increase in the return on capital—when the deposit rate is flexible or when it is fixed. Monetary restriction will, in the flexible case, increase the deposit rate; in the other case the legal ceiling prevents this reaction. Now if currency and deposits are substitutes, an increase in the deposit rate is

---

[4] It is perhaps not too fanciful to refer, as an example of this kind of effect, to the consequences of the increases in Regulation Q ceiling rates on time and savings deposits in commercial banks permitted in 1961. Contrary to many predictions, these increases led to lower, rather than higher, mortgage lending rates; they were expansionary. Given the low reserve requirement against these deposits, especially when compared to demand deposits, it is to be expected that time and savings deposits are strong substitutes for currency and reserves.

expansionary; it opposes and weakens the monetary contraction. But if they are complements, the reverse is true; flexibility in the deposit rate reinforces and strengthens quantitative monetary control.

Once there is a reserve requirement, variation in the required ratio is another instrument of monetary control. There are two questions to ask about such variation. The first concerns its effect upon the required rate of return on capital. The second concerns its effect on the strength of quantitative monetary control.

With a fixed deposit rate, an increase in the reserve requirement is always deflationary. With a given currency supply, the higher reserve requirement necessarily means that the public must curtail its holdings of currency or deposits or both. The only way they can be induced to do so is by an increase in R_0.

With a flexible deposit rate the same conclusion applies when currency and deposits are substitutes. However, it is conceivable, when they are complements, that an increase in the reserve requirement will be expansionary.[5]

We may now ask what is the effect of introducing or in general of increasing the reserve requirement on the strength of quantitative monetary control. The answer may depend on whether the deposit rate is fixed or flexible. With a fixed deposit rate an increase in the reserve requirement will decrease the response to changes in currency supply. This can be seen by imagining that uncontrolled Regime II is modified, first, by fixing the deposit rate and, second, by imposing a reserve requirement. With a fixed deposit rate and no reserve requirement, any reduction in the supply of currency is at the expense of the public's direct holdings of currency. The increase in the rate of return on capital necessary to reconcile the public to these reduced holdings of currency will also diminish their demand for bank deposits. But when banks hold no reserves, this cannot release any currency.

On the other hand, once banks are required to hold reserves, a contraction of bank deposits releases currency. Therefore, direct holdings of currency do not have to absorb the full reduction in the currency

---

[5] This may be seen in the following way: The initial effect of an increase in the reserve requirement may be divided into two parts: (*a*) the increase in the demand for currency and decrease in the supply of loans which result from banks' attempts to meet the higher reserve requirement; and (*b*) the increased margin banks will require between their deposit and loan rates when they have to place a higher proportion of deposits in non-interest-bearing reserves. The first of these effects is always contractionary. The second effect will also be contractionary in the substitutes case. In the complements case, however, the effect of increasing the margin between the rates is expansionary, and may even outweigh the first effect. At the same loan rate the deposit rate will be lower; as we have already noticed, lowering the deposit rate is expansionary in the complements case.

supply. Consequently, the necessary increase in the rate of return on capital is smaller.

When the deposit rate is free to rise, we would expect an increase in the rate in the wake of currency contraction to increase the volume of bank deposits. This expansion tends to offset the reduction in the public's currency holdings. Substitution of deposits for currency moderates the increase in R_0 necessary to reconcile the public to smaller holdings of currency. When banks hold no reserves, this substitution can proceed without any brake. But when banks are subject to a reserve requirement, it can proceed only to the extent that the public is induced to give up additional currency to serve as bank reserves. Therefore, a reserve requirement means that a larger increase in R_0, the rate of return on capital, is needed to make the public content with a larger reduction in its direct holdings of currency.

This is the essential reason why regulations preventing or limiting expansion of the intermediary strengthen monetary control. It may be observed that such regulations are of two kinds: either a rate ceiling which prevents the intermediary from bidding for funds, or a reserve requirement, or both. Once there is an effective rate ceiling, however, increasing the required reserve ratio—though itself an effective instrument of control—reduces the effectiveness of a given change in the supply of currency. It is possible, even when the deposit rate is flexible, that bank deposits decline in response to a contraction of the currency supply. Then, just as in the case of a fixed deposit rate, increasing the reserve requirement diminishes the response of the system to such contraction. A reserve requirement is not necessary to prevent expansion of the intermediary from offering an escape from monetary control, because the intermediary would not expand anyway.[6]

The principal results for Regime III are summarized in Table 2.

Table 2   Summary of Results for Regime III

Currency and Deposits Are:	Substitutes	Complements	Extreme Complements
System is	Stable	Stable	Unstable
Increase in deposit rate is	Expansionary	Deflationary	
Variation of currency supply more effective when deposit rate is	Fixed	Flexible	

[6] This statement needs to be somewhat qualified to allow for the fact that a higher reserve ratio enlarges the competitively required margin between deposit and loan rates. This strengthens the contribution of a higher reserve requirement to the effectiveness of a reduction in the currency supply, and makes it possible for this contribution to be positive even when deposits do not expand.

These conclusions have been reached by adding one intermediary, banks, to a currency-capital model and then imposing rate and reserve regulations on banks. But they are illustrative of more general conclusions. In a many-intermediary world, similar propositions apply to the extension to nonbank intermediaries of the rate and reserve regulations to which banks are subject.

APPENDIX

Part I: Notation and Assumptions

Suppose there are n types of financial assets that owners of wealth can hold; the first currency, the remaining $(n - 1)$ the liabilities of $(n - 1)$ financial intermediaries. An $(n + 1)$ asset, direct equity in capital, is designated by subscript 0. Let $D_i \geq 0$ be the proportion of the value of total wealth the public desires to hold in the ith asset $(i = 0, 1, 2, \ldots, n)$. Let R_i be the rate of return offered owners of the ith asset. Since the first financial asset is currency, R_1 is taken to be fixed at zero. Each D_i may be taken to be a function of all the R_i. We shall further assume that the demand for the various assets is homogeneous in wealth, i.e., the D_i do not depend on the level of wealth. There are n independent functions to distribute total wealth into $n + 1$ categories. Thus we may represent wealthowners' desired allocation by:

$$D_i = D_i(R_0, R_2, \ldots, R_n) \qquad (i = 1, 2, \ldots, n) \qquad \text{(A-1)}$$

The assets are assumed to be imperfect substitutes, so that the effect of a reduction in the jth interest rate, other rates remaining constant, is to diminish D_j and to increase or at least to leave unchanged the demand for each of the other assets, including D_0. Similarly, it is assumed that the effect of a reduction in R_0 is to increase or leave unchanged every financial asset holding. Using the notation D_{ij} to represent the partial derivative of the function D_i with respect to the jth rate, these assumptions are as follows:

$$
\begin{aligned}
&D_{ij} > 0 \, (i = j) \\
&D_{ij} \leq 0 \, (i \neq j) \qquad (i, = 1, 2, \ldots, n) \\
&\sum_{i=1}^{n} D_{ij} > 0 \qquad\quad (j = 2, \ldots, n) \\
&D_{i0} \leq 0
\end{aligned}
\qquad \text{(A-2)}
$$

Each of the financial intermediaries offers its own variety of loan to individuals who would like to hold capital beyond their net worth. The demands of borrowers for loans of each type depend jointly on the rate of return on capital, R_0, and on the $(n-1)$ different borrowers' interest rates r_i:

$$L_i = L_i(R_0, r_2, \ldots, r_n) \qquad (i = 2, 3, \ldots, n) \qquad \text{(A-3)}$$

Debts of different types are assumed to be gross substitutes, so that the effect of a reduction in the jth borrower's rate, other rates remaining constant, is to increase both total borrowing $\sum_{i=2}^{n} L_i$ and L_j specifically and to diminish or leave unchanged all other debts. The effect of a reduction in R_0 is to diminish or leave unchanged borrowers' demands for each type of loan. These assumptions are as follows:

$$L_{ij} < 0 \, (i = j)$$
$$L_{ij} \geq 0 \, (i \neq j)$$
$$\sum_{i=1}^{n} L_{ij} < 0 \qquad (i, j = 2, \ldots, n) \qquad \text{(A-4)}$$
$$L_{i0} \geq 0$$

In addition to loans, an intermediary may hold other assets. The regimes considered in Part II (and their n-intermediary counterparts in Part III) make different assumptions about intermediaries' portfolios of loans, currency and other assets. The portfolio choices of intermediaries are constrained by the requirement that their assets equal their liabilities. (For the present purposes no harm is done by assuming shareholders' equity in intermediaries to be zero.) To simplify presentation, the balance sheet identity for each financial intermediary will be used to translate wealth-owners demand for each intermediary's liability into indirect demand for loans, currency, etc. Equilibrium in the various asset markets may then be represented by a system of equations of the following form:

Capital $A_0(R_0, R_2, \ldots, R_n, r_2, \ldots, r_n) = S_0$

Currency $A_1(R_0, R_2, \ldots, R_n, r_2, \ldots, r_n) = S_1$

Loans $\underline{A_i(R_0, R_2, \ldots, R_n, r_2, \ldots, r_n) = 0} \qquad (i = 2, \ldots, n) \qquad \text{(A-5)}$

$$\sum_{0}^{n} A_i \qquad \qquad = \sum S_i = 1$$

The functions A_0, A_1, and A_i are derived from the demand functions D_i and L_i already discussed. A_0 and A_1 represent the total private demand for capital and currency respectively. The supply of these assets, which comprise private wealth, are S_0 and S_1. The A_i in the remaining $(n - 1)$ equations represent the excess demand functions for the various types of intermediary loans. When there are additional forms of government debt, this system is correspondingly augmented with equations like that relating to currency. The last equation indicates that the demands for the various assets always sum up to private wealth; hence one of the preceding demand equations is redundant. We follow the convention of omitting the first equation.

The n independent equations of A-5 contain $(2n - 1)$ rates: R_0 the yield of capital, $(n - 1)$ intermediary lending rates, and $(n - 1)$ intermediary borrowing rates. Consequently, $(n - 1)$ additional equations are needed. For example, lending and borrowing rates may be assumed equal for all intermediaries in a competitive regime where intermediaries hold no assets but loans. Then

$$R_i = r_i \qquad (i = 2, \ldots, n) \tag{A-6}$$

This need not be literally interpreted to mean that competition among financial institutions within a given intermediary brings the rates into equality. The assumption could be relaxed to permit a premium to compensate for administrative costs and risks of default and illiquidity, without essential difference so long as the premium is a constant or increasing function of the total volume of assets and liabilities of the intermediary.

When the deposit rates are regulated, or competition is ineffective, a different set of $(n - 1)$ conditions will apply to the rates.

Use of equations A-6 or their counterpart will enable us to eliminate all but n variables from the system of equations A-5. The effects of changes in parameters on the rates, and in particular on R_0, may then be found by differentiating this system. The results depend crucially upon the partial derivatives of the demand equations A_i, which differ from regime to regime.

Part II: Analysis of Regimes Discussed in Text

Regime I

$$D_1(R_0) = S_1 \qquad \text{Currency}$$

$$\frac{\partial R_0}{\partial S_1} = \frac{1}{D_{10}} < 0 \tag{A-7}$$

Regime II

A. Uncontrolled Intermediary

$$D_1(R_0, R_2) = S_1 \qquad \text{Currency}$$

$$D_2(R_0, R_2) - L_2(R_0, r_2) = 0 \qquad \text{Intermediary} \tag{A-8}$$

$$r_2 - R_2 = a \qquad \text{Relation between rates}$$

(i) Effect of reduction in margin between rates.

$$\begin{bmatrix} D_{10} & D_{12} \\ \\ D_{20} - L_{20} & D_{22} - L_{22} \end{bmatrix} \begin{bmatrix} \dfrac{\partial R_0}{\partial a} \\ \\ \dfrac{\partial R_2}{\partial a} \end{bmatrix} = \begin{bmatrix} 0 \\ \\ L_{22} \end{bmatrix} \qquad (A-9)$$

The restrictions on D_i and L_i assumed in Part I assure that the Jacobian is negative, that $\partial R_0/\partial a \geq 0$, that $\partial R_2/\partial a \leq 0$, and that $\partial D_2/\partial a = D_{20}(\partial R_0/\partial a) + D_{22}(\partial R_2/\partial a) \leq 0$. That is, an increase in the efficiency of intermediation lowers the required return on capital, raises the deposit rate, and expands the liabilities and assets of the intermediary.

(ii) Effect of change in currency supply.

$$J' \begin{bmatrix} \dfrac{\partial R_0}{\partial S_1} \\ \\ \dfrac{\partial R_2}{\partial S_1} \end{bmatrix} = \begin{bmatrix} 1 \\ \\ 0 \end{bmatrix} \qquad (A-10)$$

where J' is the Jacobian of equation A-9. It follows that $\partial R_0/\partial S_1$, $\partial R_2/\partial S_1$, $\partial r_2/\partial S_1 \leq 0$. However $\partial D_2/\partial S_1 = D_{20}(\partial R_0/\partial S_1) + D_{22}(\partial R_2/\partial S_1)$ may have either sign.

B. *Controlled Intermediary*

$$\begin{aligned} D_1(R_0, R_2) &= S_1 & \text{Currency} \\ e D_2(R_0, R_2) &= S_2 & \text{Specific reserve} \quad (A-11) \\ (1 - e)D_2(R_0, R_2) - L_2(R_0, r_2) &= 0 & \text{Intermediary} \end{aligned}$$

Here S_2 is the supply of government debt in the form of the reserve asset, expressed as a proportion of total wealth. The required ratio is $0 \leq e \leq 1$. There are three equations in the three rates R_0, R_2, r_2; the third equation of A-8 drops out. (However, the inequality $r_2 - R_2 \geq a$ must hold; otherwise equations A-11 are supplanted by equations A-8.)

(i) Effect of change in currency supply.

$$\begin{bmatrix} D_{10} & D_{12} & 0 \\ \\ D_{20} & D_{22} & 0 \\ \\ (1-e)D_{20} - L_{20} & (1-e)D_{22} & -L_{22} \end{bmatrix} \begin{bmatrix} \dfrac{\partial R_0}{\partial S_1} \\ \\ \dfrac{\partial R_2}{\partial S_1} \\ \\ \dfrac{\partial r_2}{\partial S_1} \end{bmatrix} = \begin{bmatrix} 1 \\ \\ 0 \\ \\ 0 \end{bmatrix} \qquad (A-12)$$

The first two equations can be solved separately, and it is easily seen that $\partial R_0/\partial S_1$, $\partial R_2/\partial S_1 \leq 0$. Since $D_{20}(\partial R_0/\partial S_1) = -D_{22}(\partial R_2/\partial S_1)$ from the second equation the third equation reduces to

$$-L_{20}\frac{\partial R_0}{\partial S_1} = L_{22}\frac{\partial r_2}{\partial S_1}.$$

Therefore $\partial r_2/\partial S_1$ is also nonpositive.

(ii) Comparison with uncontrolled regime.

The effect of restraining the expansion of the intermediary can be found by substracting equation system A-10 from the first two equations of A-12.

$$\begin{bmatrix} D_{10} & D_{12} \\ D_{20} & D_{22} \end{bmatrix}\begin{bmatrix} \dfrac{\partial R_0}{\partial S_1} \\ \dfrac{\partial R_2}{\partial S_1} \end{bmatrix}_{\text{A-12}} - \begin{bmatrix} D_{10} & D_{12} \\ D_{20}-L_{20} & D_{22}-L_{22} \end{bmatrix}\begin{bmatrix} \dfrac{\partial R_0}{\partial S_1} \\ \dfrac{\partial R_2}{\partial S_1} \end{bmatrix}_{\text{A-10}} = \begin{bmatrix} 0 \\ 0 \end{bmatrix}$$

$$\begin{bmatrix} D_{10} & D_{12} \\ D_{20} & D_{22} \end{bmatrix}\left[\begin{pmatrix} \dfrac{\partial R_0}{\partial S_1} \\ \dfrac{\partial R_2}{\partial S_1} \end{pmatrix}_{\text{A-12}} - \begin{pmatrix} \dfrac{\partial R_0}{\partial S_1} \\ \dfrac{\partial R_2}{\partial S_1} \end{pmatrix}_{\text{A-10}} \right] = \begin{bmatrix} 0 & 0 \\ -L_{20} & -L_{22} \end{bmatrix}\begin{bmatrix} \dfrac{\partial R_0}{\partial S_1} \\ \dfrac{\partial R_2}{\partial S_1} \end{bmatrix}_{\text{A-10}} \quad \text{(A-13)}$$

$$= \begin{bmatrix} 0 \\ -\left(\dfrac{\partial D_2}{\partial S_1}\right)_{\text{A-10}} \end{bmatrix}$$

It follows that

$$\text{sign}\left(\frac{\partial R_o}{\partial S_1}\right)_{\text{A-12}} - \left(\frac{\partial R_o}{\partial S_1}\right)_{\text{A-10}} = \text{sign}\left(\frac{\partial D_2}{\partial S_1}\right)_{\text{A-10}}$$

$$\text{sign}\left(\frac{\partial R_2}{\partial S_1}\right)_{\text{A-12}} - \left(\frac{\partial R_2}{\partial S_1}\right)_{\text{A-10}} = \text{sign} -\left(\frac{\partial D_2}{\partial S_1}\right)_{\text{A-10}}$$

If reduction of currency supply would lead to an expansion of the intermediary when it is uncontrolled, then preventing this expansion will enhance the effectiveness of the currency restriction.

Regime III

A. Deposit Rate Flexible

$$D_1(R_0, R_2) + cD_2(R_0, R_2) = S_1 \quad \text{Currency}$$
$$(1 - c)D_2(R_0, R_2) - L_2(R_0, r_2) = 0 \quad \text{Intermediary (banks)} \quad \text{(A-14)}$$
$$\frac{R_2}{1 - c} - r_2 = 0 \quad \text{Relation between rates}$$

Here the required reserve is in currency, and the required ratio is $0 \leq c \leq 1$. The three equations determine R_0, R_2, r_2.

B. Deposit Rate Fixed

$$D_1(R_0, \bar{R}_2) + cD_2(R_0, \bar{R}_2) = S_1 \qquad \text{Currency} \qquad \text{(A-15)}$$

$$(1 - c)D_2(R_0, \bar{R}_2) - L_2(R_0, r_2) = 0 \qquad \text{Intermediary (banks)}$$

Here the deposit rate is fixed at $\bar{R}_2$, and the two equations determine R_0, r_2. In order for this regime to apply, the following inequality must hold:

$$\frac{\bar{R}_2}{1 - c} \leq r_2$$

(i) Change in fixed deposit rate in B.

$$\begin{bmatrix} D_{10} + cD_{20} & 0 \\ \\ (1 - c)D_{20} - L_{20} & -L_{22} \end{bmatrix} \begin{bmatrix} \dfrac{\partial R_0}{\partial \bar{R}_2} \\ \\ \dfrac{\partial r_2}{\partial \bar{R}_2} \end{bmatrix} = - \begin{bmatrix} D_{12} + cD_{22} \\ \\ (1 - c)D_{22} \end{bmatrix} \qquad \text{(A-16)}$$

The Jacobian is negative. Therefore

$$\text{sign } \frac{\partial R_0}{\partial \bar{R}_2} = \text{sign}\,(D_{12} + cD_{22}) \qquad \text{(A-17)}$$

Currency and deposits are defined to be *substitutes* if $(D_{12} + cD_{22}) < 0$, and *complements* if $(D_{12} + cD_{22}) > 0$. Thus equation A-17 says that raising the fixed deposit rate is *expansionary* if currency and deposits are substitutes and *deflationary* if they are complements.
The sign of $\partial r_2 / \partial R_2$ is also ambiguous:

$$\text{sign } \frac{\partial r_2}{\partial R_2} = \text{sign} \begin{vmatrix} D_{10} + cD_{20} & D_{12} + cD_{22} \\ (1 - c)D_{20} - L_{20} & (1 - c)D_{22} \end{vmatrix}$$

In the substitutes case $\partial r_2 / \partial \bar{R}_2 < 0$.

(ii) Complementarity and stability.

The sign of $D_{12} + cD_{22}$ is also important in determining the stability of the equilibrium represented by the solution of equations A-14. Let the Jacobian of equations A-14 be:

$$J' = \begin{bmatrix} D_{10} + cD_{20} & D_{12} + cD_{22} \\ \\ (1 - c)D_{20} - L_{20} & (1 - c)D_{22} - L_{22} \cdot \dfrac{1}{1 - c} \end{bmatrix}$$

The solution is stable if $|J'| < 0$ and unstable if $|J'| > 0$. If $D_{12} + cD_{22} < 0$, $|J'| < 0$. That is, a sufficient condition for stability is that currency and deposits be substitutes. This is not a necessary condition. But "extreme" complementarity is associated with instability. The proof that stability depends on the sign of $|J'|$ is as follows.

Assume that excess demand for capital leads to a fall in the rate of return on capital and that an excess of borrowers' demand for loans over banks' supply of loans leads to a rise in the deposit rate R_2 and accordingly in the loan rate r_2.[1]

$$\dot{R}_0 = -K_0 A_0(R_0, R_2)$$
$$\dot{R}_2 = -K_2 A_2(R_0, R_2) \quad \text{(A-18)}$$

where K_0, $K_2 > 0$ are speeds of adjustment, which by choice of units may be taken as unity.

Here,

$$A_0 = 1 - D_1 - D_2 + L_2 - S_0$$
$$= S_1 - D_1 - D_2 + L_2$$

and

$$A_2 = (1 - c)D_2 - L_2$$

By Taylor's theorem we can approximate A_i in the neighborhood of equilibrium by the linear expression:

$$A_i = \sum_j a_{ij}(R_j - \bar{R}_j) \qquad i = 0, 2 \quad \text{(A-19)}$$

where a_{ij} is the partial derivative of excess demand for the ith asset with respect to the jth rate and $\bar{R}_j$ is the equilibrium R_j.

Substituting equation A-19 in equation A-18 and using the relationships given in equation A-14 we obtain:

$$\begin{bmatrix} \dot{R}_0 \\ \dot{R}_2 \end{bmatrix} = \begin{bmatrix} D_{10} + D_{20} - L_{20} & D_{12} + D_{22} - \dfrac{L_{22}}{1-c} \\ -(1-c)D_{20} + L_{20} & -(1-c)D_{22} + \dfrac{L_{22}}{1-c} \end{bmatrix} \begin{bmatrix} R_0 - \bar{R}_0 \\ R_2 - \bar{R}_2 \end{bmatrix}$$

$$= A[R_i - \bar{R}_i] \quad \text{(A-20)}$$

This system is stable if and only if the real parts of the characteristic roots of the Jacobian A are all negative. A 2 by 2 matrix with negative diagonal elements (always the case in our system) has the real parts of

[1] We assume that the relation $R_2/(1 - c) - r_2 = 0$ always holds. Our results would not be altered if we allowed a "profit" margin in disequilibrium and assumed that it tends toward zero.

its characteristic roots negative if and only if the determinant of the matrix is positive. That is, stability under our assumptions requires $|A| > 0$.

By adding the last row of the determinant of A to the first row it can be seen that:

$$|J'| = -|A|$$

hence $|J'| < 0$ is a necessary and sufficient condition for stability under our assumptions.

In the text we defined "extreme" complementarity as the case where the currency equilibrium curve E_c cuts the loan equilibrium curve E_l above from the left as in Figure 5c. Let $E_l(R_0)$ be the value of R_2 which clears the loan market, and $E_c(R_0)$ the value of R_2 which clears the currency "market."

Then for the "extreme" complements case

$$\frac{\partial E_l}{\partial R_0} > \frac{\partial E_c}{\partial R_0} > 0 \qquad \text{for} \quad (D_{12} + cD_{22}) > 0$$

since

$$\frac{\partial E_l}{\partial R_0} = \frac{-[(1-c)D_{20} - L_{20}]}{[(1-c)D_{22} - L_{22}/(1-c)]}$$

and

$$\frac{\partial E_c}{\partial R_0} = \frac{-(D_{10} + cD_{20})}{(D_{12} + cD_{22})}$$

and

$$|J'| = (D_{10} + cD_{20})\left[(1-c)D_{22} - \frac{L_{22}}{1-c}\right] - [(1-c)D_{10} - L_{20}](D_{12} + cD_{22})$$

it is clear that in the complements case:

$$\frac{\partial E_l}{\partial R_0} \gtrless \frac{\partial E_c}{\partial R_0} \qquad \text{implies } |J'| \gtrless 0$$

The "extreme" complements case is unstable; the "moderate" complements case is stable.

(iii) Effect of change in currency supply.

(a) Deposit rate flexible.

Differentiating equations A-14 gives:

$$\left[J' \right]\begin{bmatrix} \dfrac{\partial R_0}{\partial S_1} \\[2mm] \dfrac{\partial R_2}{\partial S_1} \end{bmatrix} = \begin{bmatrix} 1 \\[2mm] 0 \end{bmatrix} \tag{A-21}$$

Assuming stability, $|J'| < 0$, and $\partial R_0/\partial S_1$, $\partial R_2/\partial S_1 \leq 0$.

(b) Deposit rate fixed:

Differentiating equations A-15 and letting J^2 be the Jacobian of this system, written out in A-16, we have:

$$
\begin{bmatrix} \\ J^2 \\ \\ \end{bmatrix} \begin{bmatrix} \dfrac{\partial R_0}{\partial S_1} \\[2ex] \dfrac{\partial r_2}{\partial S_1} \end{bmatrix} = \begin{bmatrix} 1 \\[2ex] 0 \end{bmatrix} \tag{A-22}
$$

Again,

$$
\frac{\partial R_0}{\partial S_1}, \frac{\partial r_2}{\partial S_1} \leq 0.
$$

We can compare the responses in the two cases by assuming a restriction of currency supply beginning at the same equilibrium. In one case, (b), the deposit rate is prevented from rising, but the loan rate may rise. In the other case, (a), the two rates remain in the equilibrium relationship given by the third equation of A-14. However, in order to make the comparison, we must use that equation to eliminate R_2, rather than r_2, from the first two equations of A-14. Denoting the solutions to A-14 and A-15 by 1 and 2 respectively we find:

$$
\begin{bmatrix} D_{10} + cD_{20} & (D_{12} + cD_{22})(1-c) \\[2ex] (1-c)D_{20} - L_{20} & (1-c)^2 D_{22} - L_{22} \end{bmatrix} \begin{bmatrix} \dfrac{\partial R_0}{\partial S_1} \\[2ex] \dfrac{\partial r_2}{\partial S_1} \end{bmatrix}_1
$$

$$
- \begin{bmatrix} D_{10} + cD_{20} & 0 \\[2ex] (1-c)D_{20} - L_{20} & -L_{22} \end{bmatrix} \begin{bmatrix} \dfrac{\partial R_0}{\partial S_1} \\[2ex] \dfrac{\partial r_2}{\partial S_1} \end{bmatrix}_2 = \begin{bmatrix} 0 \\[2ex] 0 \end{bmatrix} \tag{A-23}
$$

Therefore

$$
\begin{bmatrix} D_{10} + cD_{20} & (D_{12} + cD_{22})(1-c) \\[2ex] (1-c)D_{20} - L_{20} & (1-c)^2 D_{22} - L_{22} \end{bmatrix} \begin{bmatrix} \left(\dfrac{\partial R_0}{\partial S_1}\right)_1 - \left(\dfrac{\partial R_0}{\partial S_1}\right)_2 \\[2ex] \left(\dfrac{\partial r_2}{\partial S_1}\right)_1 - \left(\dfrac{\partial r_2}{\partial S_1}\right)_2 \end{bmatrix}
$$

$$
= - \left(\frac{\partial r_2}{\partial S_1}\right)_2 \begin{bmatrix} (D_{12} + cD_{22})(1-c) \\[2ex] (1-c)^2 D_{22} \end{bmatrix} \tag{A-24}
$$

The determinant of the Jacobian in equation A-24 is $(1 - c)|J^2|$, and is therefore negative whenever the system is stable. We know also that $(\partial r_2/\partial S_1)_2$ is negative. Therefore:

$$\left(\frac{\partial R_0}{\partial S_1}\right)_1 - \left(\frac{\partial R_0}{\partial S_1}\right)_2 = \frac{-(\partial r_2/\partial S_1)_2}{|J^2|} \cdot \begin{vmatrix} D_{12} + cD_{22} & 0 \\ (1 - c)^2 D_{22} & -L_{22} \end{vmatrix}$$

Therefore

$$\text{sign}\left[\left(\frac{\partial R_0}{\partial S_1}\right)_1 - \left(\frac{\partial R_0}{\partial S_1}\right)_2\right] = \text{sign} - (D_{12} + cD_{22}),$$

or

$$\text{sign}\left[\left|\left(\frac{\partial R_0}{\partial S_1}\right)_1\right| - \left|\left(\frac{\partial R_0}{\partial S_1}\right)_2\right|\right] = \text{sign}\,(D_{12} + cD_{22})$$

That is, changes in currency supply are more (less) effective with a *fixed* deposit rate if currency and deposits are substitutes (complements).

(iv) Effect of change in reserve requirement.

(a) Deposit rate flexible.

Differentiating equation A-14 gives:

$$[J']\begin{bmatrix} \dfrac{\partial R_0}{\partial c} \\[2mm] \dfrac{\partial R_2}{\partial c} \end{bmatrix} = \begin{bmatrix} -D_2 \\[2mm] D_2 + \dfrac{L_{22}R_2}{(1 - c)^2} \end{bmatrix} \qquad (A-25)$$

Since $|J'|$ is negative for stable solutions,

$$\text{sign}\,\frac{\partial R_0}{\partial c} = \text{sign}\begin{vmatrix} D_2 & D_{12} + cD_{22} \\[2mm] -D_2 - \dfrac{L_{22}R_2}{(1 - c)^2} & (1 - c)D_{22} - \dfrac{L_{22}}{1 - c} \end{vmatrix}$$

$$= \text{sign}\begin{vmatrix} D_2 & D_{12} + cD_{22} \\[2mm] -\dfrac{L_{22}R_2}{(1 - c)^2} & D_{12} + D_{22} - \dfrac{L_{22}}{1 - c} \end{vmatrix}$$

Therefore, if $D_{12} + cD_{22} < 0$, then $\partial R_0/\partial c > 0$ (substitutes case). But if $D_{12} + cD_{22} > 0$ (complements case), $\partial R_0/\partial c$ may be negative. For example, let $D_2 = 0$.

(b) Deposit rate fixed.

Differentiating equation A-15 gives

$$[J^2]\begin{bmatrix} \dfrac{\partial R_0}{\partial c} \\[2mm] \dfrac{\partial r_2}{\partial c} \end{bmatrix} = \begin{bmatrix} -D_2 \\[4mm] D_2 \end{bmatrix} \tag{A-26}$$

Therefore,

$$\frac{\partial R_0}{\partial c} = \frac{D_2 L_{22}}{|J^2|} > 0.$$

(v) Effect of change in reserve requirement on response of system to change in currency supply.

(*a*) Deposit rate flexible.

Differentiating equation A-21 with respect to c gives:

$$[J']\begin{bmatrix} \dfrac{\partial}{\partial c}\left(\dfrac{\partial R_0}{\partial S_1}\right) \\[3mm] \dfrac{\partial}{\partial c}\left(\dfrac{\partial R_2}{\partial S_1}\right) \end{bmatrix} = -\begin{bmatrix} D_{20} & D_{22} \\[3mm] -D_{20} & -D_{22} - \dfrac{L_{22}}{(1-c)^2} \end{bmatrix}\begin{bmatrix} \dfrac{\partial R_0}{\partial S_1} \\[3mm] \dfrac{\partial R_2}{\partial S_1} \end{bmatrix}$$

$$= -\begin{bmatrix} \dfrac{\partial D_2}{\partial S_1} \\[3mm] -\dfrac{\partial D_2}{\partial S_1} - \dfrac{L_{22}}{(1-c)^2}\dfrac{\partial R_2}{\partial S_1} \end{bmatrix}$$

$$\text{sign}\,\frac{\partial}{\partial c}\left(\frac{\partial R_0}{\partial S_1}\right) = \text{sign}\begin{vmatrix} \dfrac{\partial D_2}{\partial S_1} & D_{12} + cD_{22} \\[4mm] -\dfrac{\partial D_2}{\partial S_1} - \dfrac{L_{22}}{(1-c)^2}\dfrac{\partial R_2}{\partial S_1} & (1-c)D_{22} - \dfrac{L_{22}}{1-c} \end{vmatrix}$$

$$= \text{sign}\begin{vmatrix} \dfrac{\partial D_2}{\partial S_1} & D_{12} + cD_{22} \\[4mm] -\dfrac{L_{22}}{(1-c)^2}\dfrac{\partial R_2}{\partial S_1} & D_{12} + D_{22} - \dfrac{L_{22}}{1-c} \end{vmatrix}$$

If $D_{12} + cD_{22} < 0$ (substitutes case) and $\partial D_2/\partial S_1 < 0$, then $\partial(\partial R_0/\partial S_1)/\partial c < 0$, i.e., an increase in c increases the response. In particular $D_{12} + cD_{22} < 0$ when $c = 0$. If $D_{12} + cD_{22} > 0$ (complements case) and $\partial D_2/\partial S_1 > 0$, then $\partial(\partial R_0/\partial S_1)/\partial c > 0$.

(*b*) Deposit rate fixed.

Differentiating equation A-22 with respect to c gives:

$$[J^2] \begin{bmatrix} \dfrac{\partial}{\partial c}\left(\dfrac{\partial R_0}{\partial S_1}\right) \\[2ex] \dfrac{\partial}{\partial c}\left(\dfrac{\partial r_2}{\partial S_1}\right) \end{bmatrix} = \begin{bmatrix} -D_{20} & \dfrac{\partial R_0}{\partial S_1} \\[2ex] D_{20} & \dfrac{\partial R_0}{\partial S_1} \end{bmatrix}$$

Therefore

$$\frac{\partial}{\partial c}\left(\frac{\partial R_0}{\partial S_1}\right) = \frac{D_{20}L_{22}(\partial R_0/\partial S_1)}{|J^2|} > 0.$$

That is, increasing the required reserve ratio always diminishes the response.

Part III: Extension to Many Intermediaries

The discussion of regimes below parallels Part II.

Regime II

A. Uncontrolled Intermediaries.

$$\begin{aligned} D_1(R_0, R_2, \ldots, R_n) &= S_1 & &\text{Currency} \\ D_i(R_0, R_2, \ldots, R_n) - L_i(R_0, r_2, \ldots, r_n) &= 0 & &\text{Intermediaries} \quad\text{(A-27)} \\ r_i - R_i &= a_i & &\text{Relation between} \\ i &= 2, \ldots, n & &\text{the rates} \end{aligned}$$

(i) Effect of change in currency supply.

Using the $(n-1)$ rate relations to eliminate the r_i and differentiating with respect to S_1:

$$\begin{bmatrix} D_{10} & D_{12} & \cdots & D_{1n} \\ D_{20} - L_{20} & D_{22} - L_{22} & \cdots & D_{2n} - L_{2n} \\ \cdot & \cdot & \cdots & \cdot \\ \cdot & \cdot & \cdots & \cdot \\ \cdot & \cdot & \cdots & \cdot \\ D_{n0} - L_{n0} & D_{n2} - L_{n2} & \cdots & D_{nn} - L_{nn} \end{bmatrix} \begin{bmatrix} \dfrac{\partial R_0}{\partial S_1} \\[2ex] \dfrac{\partial R_2}{\partial S_1} \\[1ex] \cdot \\ \cdot \\ \cdot \\ \dfrac{\partial R_n}{\partial S_1} \end{bmatrix} = \begin{bmatrix} 1 \\[1ex] 0 \\[1ex] \cdot \\ \cdot \\ \cdot \\ 0 \end{bmatrix} \quad \text{(A-28)}$$

By the assumptions of A-2 and A-4 in Part I the first column of the n by n matrix in equation A-28 is composed entirely of non-positive elements. In the remaining columns, the diagonal elements are positive and the rest non-positive. Moreover, the sum of the elements in every column but the first is positive. It is shown in Part IV that the determinant of such a matrix is negative and that all the cofactors of the first row are positive. Hence all the derivatives that solve equation A-28 are negative. An increase in the supply of currency will lower rates at all intermediaries and will lower the acceptable return on direct equity in capital.

The change in the volume of each intermediary $\partial D_i/\partial S_1 = \sum_j D_{ij}(\partial R_j/\partial S_1)$, $(i = 2, \ldots, n)$, and the corresponding derivative for aggregate intermediary liabilities $\sum_{i=2}^{n}(\partial D_i/\partial S_1) = \sum_i \sum_j D_{ij}(\partial R_j/\partial S_1)$ may have either sign.

B. Controlled Intermediaries.

$$D_1(R_0, R_2, \ldots, R_n) = S_1 \qquad \text{Currency}$$

$$e_i D_i(R_0, R_2, \ldots, R_n) = S_i \qquad \text{Specific Reserves}$$

$$(1 - e_i)D_i(R_0, R_2, \ldots, R_n) - L_i(R_0, r_2, \ldots, r_n) = 0 \qquad \text{Intermediaries}$$

$$i = 2, \ldots, n \qquad \text{(A-29)}$$

Here S_i is the supply of the reserve asset specific to the ith intermediary expressed as a proportion of total wealth. The required ratio for the ith intermediary is $0 \leq e_i \leq 1$. There are $(2n - 1)$ equations in the $(2n - 1)$ rates R_0, R_i, r_i; the last $(n - 1)$ equations in equations A-27 drop out. (However, the inequalities $r_i - R_i \geq a_i$ must hold.)

(i) Effect of change in currency supply.

$$
\begin{bmatrix}
D_{10} & \cdots & D_{1n} & 0 & \cdots & 0 \\
e_2 D_{20} & \cdots & e_2 D_{2n} & & & \\
\cdot & & \cdot & \cdot & & \cdot \\
\cdot & & \cdot & \cdot & & \cdot \\
e_n D_{n0} & \cdots & e_n D_{nn} & 0 & \cdots & 0 \\
\hline
(1-e_2)D_{20}-L_{20} & (1-e_2)D_{22}\cdots(1-e_2)D_{2n} & -L_{22}\cdots-L_{2n} \\
\cdot & \cdot & \cdot \\
\cdot & \cdot & \cdot \\
(1-e_n)D_{n0}-L_{n0} & (1-e_n)D_{n2}\cdots(1-e_n)D_{nn} & -L_{n2}\cdots-L_{nn}
\end{bmatrix}
\begin{bmatrix}
\dfrac{\partial R_0}{\partial S_1} \\[4pt]
\dfrac{\partial R_2}{\partial S_1} \\
\cdot \\
\cdot \\
\dfrac{\partial R_n}{\partial S_1} \\
\hline
\dfrac{\partial r_2}{\partial S_1} \\
\cdot \\
\cdot \\
\dfrac{\partial r_n}{\partial S_1}
\end{bmatrix}
=
\begin{bmatrix}
1 \\
0 \\
\cdot \\
\cdot \\
\cdot \\
\cdot \\
\cdot \\
\cdot \\
0
\end{bmatrix}
$$

$$\text{(A-30)}$$

The first n equations can be solved separately from the last $(n-1)$ equations for the n derivatives $\partial R_0/\partial S_1$, $\partial R_i/\partial S_1$. Since this subsystem has the same features as system A-28 it is easily seen that $\partial R_0/\partial S_1$, $\partial R_i/\partial S_1 \leq 0$ $(i = 2, \ldots, n)$.

The remaining $(n-1)$ equations may be solved for the $\partial r_i/\partial S_1$. Since the first n equations are satisfied, $\sum_j e_i D_{ij}(\partial R_j/\partial S_1) = 0$, this system reduces to:

$$
\begin{bmatrix}
-L_{22} & \cdots & -L_{2n} \\
\cdot & & \\
\cdot & & \\
\cdot & & \\
-L_{n2} & \cdots & -L_{nn}
\end{bmatrix}
\begin{bmatrix}
\dfrac{\partial r_2}{\partial S_1} \\
\cdot \\
\cdot \\
\cdot \\
\dfrac{\partial r_n}{\partial S_1}
\end{bmatrix}
=
\begin{bmatrix}
L_{20} \\
\cdot \\
\cdot \\
\cdot \\
L_{n0}
\end{bmatrix}
\dfrac{\partial R_0}{\partial S_1}
\qquad \text{(A-31)}
$$

The diagonal elements of the matrix in equation A-31 are all positive, the off diagonal elements non-positive, and the column sums positive. In Part IV it is shown that the determinant of such a matrix is positive and that the cofactors of each element are positive. Hence

$$
\frac{\partial r_i}{\partial S_1} \leq 0, \qquad i = 2, \ldots, n.
$$

(ii) Comparison with uncontrolled regime.

The effect of restraining the expansion of each intermediary can be found by subtracting equation system A-28 from the first n equations of A-31.

$$
J_4
\begin{bmatrix}
\dfrac{\partial R_0}{\partial S_1} \\
\cdot \\
\cdot \\
\cdot \\
\dfrac{\partial R_n}{\partial S_1}
\end{bmatrix}_4
-
J_2
\begin{bmatrix}
\dfrac{\partial R_0}{\partial S_1} \\
\cdot \\
\cdot \\
\cdot \\
\dfrac{\partial R_n}{\partial S_1}
\end{bmatrix}_2
= 0
\qquad \text{(A-32)}
$$

where J_4 is the sub-Jacobian in equation A-30 and J_2 the Jacobian in equation A-28.

Given

$$J_2 = J_4 + \begin{bmatrix} 0 & \cdots & 0 \\ -L_{20} & \cdots & -L_{2n} \\ \cdot & & \\ \cdot & & \\ \cdot & & \\ -L_{n0} & \cdots & -L_{nn} \end{bmatrix} = J_4 + \Delta$$

$$J_4\left[\left[\frac{\partial R_i}{\partial S_1}\right]_4 - \left[\frac{\partial R_i}{\partial S_1}\right]_2\right] = \Delta\left[\frac{\partial R_i}{\partial S_1}\right]_2 = -\begin{bmatrix} 0 \\ \dfrac{\partial D_2}{\partial S_1} \\ \cdot \\ \cdot \\ \cdot \\ \dfrac{\partial D_n}{\partial S_1} \end{bmatrix}_2 \qquad \text{(A-33)}$$

Given $J_4 < 0$ it follows that

$$\text{sign}\left[\left(\frac{\partial R_0}{\partial S_1}\right)_4 - \left(\frac{\partial R_0}{\partial S_1}\right)_2\right] = \text{sign}\begin{vmatrix} 0 & D_{12} & \cdots & D_{12} \\ \left(\dfrac{\partial D_2}{\partial S_1}\right)_2 & D_{22} & \cdots & D_{2n} \\ \cdot & \cdot & & \cdot \\ \cdot & \cdot & & \cdot \\ \cdot & \cdot & & \cdot \\ \left(\dfrac{\partial D_n}{\partial S_1}\right)_2 & D_{n2} & \cdots & D_{nn} \end{vmatrix} \qquad \text{(A-34)}$$

If all the $(\partial D_2/\partial S_1)_2$ are negative the determinant at the right will be negative; this is a sufficient, not a necessary, condition.

If reduction of the currency supply would lead to an expansion of all the intermediaries when they are uncontrolled, then preventing this expansion will enhance the effectiveness of currency restriction.

Regime III

A. Deposit Rates Flexible.

$$D_1(R_0, R_2, \ldots, R_n) + c\sum_2^n D_i(R_0, R_2, \ldots, R_n) = S_1 \qquad \text{Currency}$$

$$(1 - c)D_i(R_0, R_2, \ldots, R_n) - L_i(R_0, r_2, \ldots, r_n) = 0 \qquad \text{Intermediaries}$$

$$\frac{R_i}{(1 - c)} - r_i = 0 \qquad \begin{array}{l}\text{Relation} \\ \text{between} \\ \text{rates}\end{array}$$

$$i = 2, \ldots, n \qquad \text{(A-35)}$$

Here the required reserve for each intermediary is in currency, and the required ratio is $0 \leq c \leq 1$. For convenience we assume the required ratio for all intermediaries is equal. The $(2n - 1)$ equations determine the $(2n - 1)$ variables $R_0, R_i, r_i; (i = 2, \ldots, n)$.

B. *Deposit Rates Fixed.*

$$D_1(R_0, \bar{R}_2, \ldots, \bar{R}_n) + c \sum_2^n D_i(R_0, \bar{R}_j) = S_1 \qquad \text{Currency}$$

$$(1 - c)D_i(R_0, \bar{R}_2, \ldots, \bar{R}_n) - L_i(R_0, r_2, \ldots, r_n) = 0 \qquad \text{Intermediaries}$$

$$i = 2, \ldots, n \qquad (A-36)$$

Here the deposit rate at the ith intermediary is fixed at $\bar{R}_i$, and the n equations determine the n variables $R_0, r_i (i = 2, \ldots, n)$. In order for the regime to apply, the following inequality must hold:

$$\frac{\bar{R}_i}{(1 - c)} \leq r_i$$

(i) Effect of change in currency supply.

   (a) Deposit rates flexible.

Differentiating equation A-35 gives:

$$
\begin{bmatrix}
D_{10} + c \sum D_{i0} & D_{12} + c \sum D_{i2} & \cdots & D_{1n} + c \sum D_{in} \\
(1-c)D_{20} - L_{20} & (1-c)D_{22} - \dfrac{L_{22}}{(1-c)} & \cdots & (1-c)D_{2n} - \dfrac{L_{2n}}{(1-c)} \\
\vdots & \vdots & \ddots & \vdots \\
(1-c)D_{n0} - L_{n0} & (1-c)D_{n2} - \dfrac{L_{n2}}{(1-c)} & \cdots & (1-c)D_{nn} - \dfrac{L_{nn}}{(1-c)}
\end{bmatrix}
\begin{bmatrix}
\dfrac{\partial R_0}{\partial S_1} \\
\dfrac{\partial R_2}{\partial S_1} \\
\vdots \\
\dfrac{\partial R_n}{\partial S_1}
\end{bmatrix}
=
\begin{bmatrix}
1 \\
0 \\
\vdots \\
0
\end{bmatrix}
$$

$$(A-37)$$

Since the cofactors of the first row are all positive, the derivatives that solve equation A-37 are all of the same sign:

$$\text{sign}
\begin{bmatrix}
\dfrac{\partial R_0}{\partial S_1} \\
\dfrac{\partial R_2}{\partial S_1} \\
\vdots \\
\dfrac{\partial R_n}{\partial S_1}
\end{bmatrix}
= \text{sign } |J^3|$$

where J^3 is the Jacobian in equation A-37.

A sufficient, but not necessary condition that $|J^3| < 0$ is that all the deposits be "substitutes" with currency:

$$\left(D_{1j} + c\sum_{i=2}^{n} D_{ij}\right) \leq 0, \qquad j = 2, \ldots, n$$

This condition is analogous to the substitutes case discussed in the text and Part II of the Appendix. In this case however an increase in the ith rate causes a decrease in the demand for currency reserves by the other intermediaries as well as an increase in the demand for reserves by the ith intermediary.

(*b*) Deposit rate fixed.

Differentiating equation A-36 gives:

$$
\begin{bmatrix}
D_{10} + c\sum D_{i0} & 0 & \cdots & 0 \\
(1-c)D_{20} - L_{20} & -L_{22} & \cdots & -L_{2n} \\
\cdot & \cdot & & \cdot \\
\cdot & \cdot & & \cdot \\
\cdot & \cdot & & \cdot \\
(1-c)D_{n0} - L_{n0} & -L_{n2} & \cdots & -L_{nn}
\end{bmatrix}
\begin{bmatrix}
\dfrac{\partial R_0}{\partial S_1} \\
\dfrac{\partial r_2}{\partial S_1} \\
\cdot \\
\cdot \\
\cdot \\
\dfrac{\partial r_n}{\partial S_1}
\end{bmatrix}
=
\begin{bmatrix}
1 \\
0 \\
\cdot \\
\cdot \\
\cdot \\
0
\end{bmatrix}
\qquad \text{(A-38)}
$$

The Jacobian in this system of equations meets the same sign conditions as the Jacobian in system A-28, hence $\partial R_0/\partial S_1$, $\partial r_i/\partial S_1 \leq 0$; $(i = 2, \ldots, n)$.

Following the procedure discussed in Part II, Regime III (iii) we may compare the responses in the two cases by subtracting system A-37 (but using the rate relations to eliminate the deposit rather than loan rates) from system A-38:

$$
J^4
\begin{bmatrix}
\dfrac{\partial R_0}{\partial S_1} \\
\dfrac{\partial r_2}{\partial S_1} \\
\cdot \\
\cdot \\
\cdot \\
\dfrac{\partial r_n}{\partial S_1}
\end{bmatrix}_4
-
J^{3'}
\begin{bmatrix}
\dfrac{\partial R_0}{\partial S_1} \\
\dfrac{\partial r_2}{\partial S_1} \\
\cdot \\
\cdot \\
\cdot \\
\dfrac{\partial r_n}{\partial S_1}
\end{bmatrix}_{3'}
=
\begin{bmatrix}
0 \\
0 \\
\cdot \\
\cdot \\
\cdot \\
0
\end{bmatrix}
\qquad \text{(A-39)}
$$

where J^4 is the Jacobian in equation A-38 and $J^{3'}$ is the Jacobian of the system A-37 when the deposit rates rather than the loan rates are eliminated.

$$J^4 \left[\begin{array}{c} \dfrac{\partial R_0}{\partial S_1} \\[8pt] \dfrac{\partial r_2}{\partial S_1} \\[6pt] \cdot \\ \cdot \\ \cdot \\[6pt] \dfrac{\partial r_n}{\partial S_1} \end{array} \right]_4 - \left[\begin{array}{c} \dfrac{\partial R_0}{\partial S_1} \\[8pt] \dfrac{\partial r_2}{\partial S_1} \\[6pt] \cdot \\ \cdot \\ \cdot \\[6pt] \dfrac{\partial r_n}{\partial S_1} \end{array} \right]_{3'} = -[J^4 - J^{3'}] \left[\begin{array}{c} \dfrac{\partial R_0}{\partial S_1} \\[8pt] \cdot \\ \cdot \\ \cdot \\[8pt] \dfrac{\partial r_n}{\partial S_1} \end{array} \right]_{3'} \tag{A-40}$$

$$= (1 - c) \left[\begin{array}{cccc} 0 & \left(D_{12} + c \sum_{2}^{n} D_{i2} \right) & \cdots & \left(D_{1n} + c \sum_{2}^{n} D_{in} \right) \\[10pt] & (1 - c)D_{22} & \cdots & (1 - c)D_{22} \\ \cdot & \cdot & & \cdot \\ \cdot & \cdot & & \cdot \\ \cdot & \cdot & & \cdot \\ 0 & (1 - c)D_{n2} & \cdots & (1 - c)D_{n2} \end{array} \right] \left[\begin{array}{c} \dfrac{\partial R_0}{\partial S_1} \\[8pt] \dfrac{\partial r_2}{\partial S_1} \\[6pt] \cdot \\ \cdot \\ \cdot \\[6pt] \dfrac{\partial r_n}{\partial S_1} \end{array} \right]_{3'}$$

Since $|J^4| < 0$ and the cofactor of the first element in the first row of J^4 is positive:

$$\text{sign} \left[\left(\frac{\partial R_0}{\partial S_1} \right)_4 - \left(\frac{\partial R_0}{\partial S_1} \right)_{3'} \right] = \text{sign} - \sum_{j=2}^{n} \left(D_{1j} + c \sum_{i=2}^{n} D_{ij} \right) \left(\frac{\partial r_j}{\partial S_1} \right)_{3'}$$

when $|J^3| < 0$, $(\partial r_j/\partial S_1)_{3'} \leq 0$ for all j.

Changes in currency supply are more (less) effective with *fixed* deposit rates if currency and each variety of "deposits" are substitutes (complements).

(ii) Effect of change in reserve requirement on response of system to change in currency supply.

(*a*) Deposit rate flexible.

Differentiating equation A-37 with respect to c gives:

$$J^3 \left[\frac{\partial \left(\frac{\partial R_i}{\partial S_1} \right)}{\partial c} \right]$$

$$= - \begin{bmatrix} \sum_2^n D_{i0} & \sum_2^n D_{i2} & \cdots & \sum_2^n D_{in} \\ -D_{20} & -D_{22} - \frac{L_{22}}{(1-c)^2} & \cdots & -D_{2n} - \frac{L_{22}}{(1-c)^2} \\ \cdot & \cdot & \cdots & \cdot \\ \cdot & \cdot & & \cdot \\ \cdot & \cdot & & \cdot \\ -D_{n0} & -D_{n2} - \frac{L_{n2}}{(1-c)^2} & \cdots & -D_{nn} - \frac{L_{nn}}{(1-c)^2} \end{bmatrix} \left[\frac{\partial R_i}{\partial S_1} \right]$$

$$(A\text{-}41)$$

where J^3 is the Jacobian in equation A-37.

This reduces to:

$$J^3 \left[\frac{\partial \left(\frac{\partial R_i}{\partial S_1} \right)}{\partial c} \right] = - \begin{bmatrix} \frac{\partial \sum D_i}{\partial S_1} \\ -\frac{\partial D_2}{\partial S_1} - \sum_2^n \frac{L_{2i}}{(1-c)^2} \frac{\partial R_i}{\partial S_1} \\ \cdot \\ \cdot \\ -\frac{\partial D_n}{\partial S_1} - \sum_2^n \frac{L_{ni}}{(1-c)^2} \frac{\partial R_i}{\partial S_1} \end{bmatrix} \quad (A\text{-}42)$$

Assuming $|J^3| < 0$: if $\partial D_i/\partial S_1 < 0 \, (i = 2, \ldots, n)$, $(D_{ij} + c \sum_{i=2}^n D_{ij}) < 0 \, (j = 2, \ldots, n)$ (all substitutes case), and $\sum_{i=2}^n [L_{ji}/(1-c)^2](\partial R_i/\partial S_1) > 0$ then $\partial(\partial R_0/\partial S_1)/\partial c < 0$, i.e., an increase in c increases the response of the rate on capital.

(*b*) Deposit rates fixed.

Differentiating equation A-38 with respect to c gives:

$$J^4 \left[\frac{\partial \left(\frac{\partial R_i}{\partial S_1} \right)}{\partial c} \right] = - \begin{bmatrix} \sum_{i=2}^n D_{i0} \\ -D_{20} \\ \cdot \\ \cdot \\ -D_{n0} \end{bmatrix} \frac{\partial R_0}{\partial S_1}$$

Therefore,

$$\frac{\partial(\partial R_0/\partial S_1)}{\partial c} = \frac{-(\partial R_0/\partial S_1)}{|J^4|} \begin{vmatrix} \sum_{i=2}^{n} D_{i0} & 0 & \cdots & 0 \\ -D_{20} & -L_{22} & & -L_{2n} \\ \cdot & \cdot & & \cdot \\ \cdot & \cdot & & \cdot \\ \cdot & \cdot & & \cdot \\ -D_{n0} & -L_{n2} & \cdots & -L_{nn} \end{vmatrix} > 0$$

That is, increasing the required reserve ratio always diminishes the response of the rate on capital to changes in the supply of currency.

Part IV: Some Basic Propositions about Matrices

Let A be a non-singular square matrix with non-positive off-diagonal elements, positive diagonal elements, column sums $\sum_i a_{ij}$ positive. To prove that det (A) is positive.

Consider the matrix B where $b_{ij} = -a_{ij}/a_{jj}$ for $i \neq j$ and $b_{jj} = 0$. Then B is a matrix of non-negative elements with column sums $\sum_i b_{ij} < 1$. Det (A) will be positive if det $(I - B)$ is positive, for det $(I - B) = (1/\prod_j a_{jj})$ det (A).

Proof that det $(I - B) > 0$:[2]

Suppose det $(I - B) \leq 0$. Since for sufficiently large λ, det $(\lambda I - B) > 0$, there must exist a root $\lambda_0 \geq 1$ with det $(\lambda_0 I - B) = 0$. The equation system $[\lambda_0 I - B]'x = 0$ has a solution vector $x \neq 0$. Let x_j be the element of largest absolute value $|x_j| > 0$. $|x_j| \leq |\lambda_0 x_j|$. By the jth equation of the system, $|\lambda_0 x_j| = |\sum_i b_{ij}x_i|$. $|\sum_i b_{ij}x_i| \leq \sum_i b_{ij}|x_i| \leq \sum_i b_{ij}|x_j| < |x_j|$. This contradicts $\lambda_0 \geq 1$. Hence det $(I - B) > 0$.

Consider a non-singular matrix A_1 formed by substituting for the first column of A a vector of non-positive elements. The proposition is that det (A_1) is negative. Proof by induction:

If the proposition is true for n by n square matrices, then it is true for $(n + 1)$ by $(n + 1)$ square matrices. Add to $A(n)$ a new first row and first column so that the resulting matrix is $A_1(n + 1)$. Expand A_1 by the first row. The first cofactor is det $[A(n)]$, which is positive according to the first note above. The cofactors of the remaining elements of the first row all involve n by n minors of which the first column consists entirely of non-positive elements, while the remaining columns come from

---

[2] For this proof, we are much indebted to Martin Beckmann.

$A(n)$. The minor of the second element is $A_1(n)$ and by assumption negative; thus the second cofactor is positive. The minor of the third element can be made into an $A_1(n)$ by placing the third row at the top of the minor. This interchange alters the sign; hence the minor and cofactor are both positive. In general, the minor of the ith element can be made into an $A_1(n)$ by the $(i - 2)$ interchanges necessary to place the ith row at the top of the minor. The minors will be positive for i odd and negative for i even; therefore all the cofactors are positive. Since all the elements of the first row are non-positive, $A_1(n + 1)$ is negative.

The proposition is true for $n = 2$. $A_1(2) = \begin{vmatrix} - & - \\ - & + \end{vmatrix}$.

If the first and last rows of the matrix of coefficients in equation A-28 are interchanged, the resulting matrix is $A_1(n + 1)$. Hence the matrix in equation A-28 has a positive determinant, with negative cofactors for the last row.

4

Financial Intermediaries and a Theory of Monetary Control*

WILLIAM C. BRAINARD

1 INTRODUCTION

The inadequacies of contemporary monetary theory are perhaps most obvious when economists get together to discuss some policy proposal. In recent years the growth and wide distribution of public debt and the rapid growth of non-bank financial intermediaries have created concern over the effectiveness of existing methods of monetary control. Opinions have differed widely over the significance of these two developments. While there has been little agreement on the diagnosis, there has been no shortage of prescriptions for our monetary ills. Monetary economists have come forth with a bewildering variety of proposals to improve the monetary system. Some writers propose the complete removal of reserve requirements on time deposits at commercial banks, while others suggest their equalization with the reserve requirement on demand deposits.[1] Some authors have suggested secondary reserve requirements on commercial

* SOURCE: Reprinted from *Yale Economic Essays*, Vol. 4, No. 1 (Fall 1964), pp. 431–482. I am grateful to Arthur Okun, Michael Lovell, and James Tobin for their encouragement and many useful suggestions. I am also indebted to Alan Heston and Menahem Yaari for their continued encouragement and assistance.
[1] For the first proposal see *The Report of the Commission on Money and Credit* (Englewood Cliffs, N.J.: Prentice-Hall, 1961), pp. 168–169, and Joseph Aschheim, *Techniques of Monetary Control* (Baltimore: Johns Hopkins Press, 1961), pp. 135–154. Among the proponents of the second are Milton Friedman, *A Program for Monetary Stability* (New York: Fordham University Press, 1960), and James Henderson, "Monetary Reserves and Credit Control," *American Economic Review*, L (June 1960), pp. 348–369.

banks, possibly in the form of non-negotiable government securities.[2] Others have proposed extension of bank-type regulations to non-bank financial intermediaries.[3] Still others have urged the removal of the regulation of the rates of interest paid on time and savings deposits at commercial banks and some would also repeal the prohibition of the payment of interest on demand deposits.[4] Along with removal of the regulation of the rates of interest paid on deposits, it has been recommended that interest be paid on bank reserves or on the excess of reserves over legal requirements.[5]

In the discussions surrounding these proposals it is difficult to find reference to formal monetary theory. It is not surprising that the niceties of general equilibrium analysis are of little help when policy makers seek answers to questions like: Should the deposit rate at banks be fixed by regulation, or allowed to fluctuate in response to market forces? What would be the consequences of subjecting non-bank intermediaries to reserve requirements or to interest ceilings? These questions are difficult to ask, let alone answer, within the framework of the traditional theoretical models, classical or Keynesian. When confronted with questions of this type, monetary economists tend to rely on a set of *ad hoc*, partial equilibrium observations and assertions, which, while lacking a solid foundation in a theory of general financial equilibrium, do have direct relevance to the questions at issue. One of the major reasons that both classical and Keynesian monetary theory have difficulty in dealing with this type of "practical" problem is that they lack sufficient detail in their description of financial assets and financial markets. It is difficult to analyze the effect of allowing the deposit rates at commercial banks to adjust to market forces in a model which does not give explicit recognition to either banks or their deposit liabilities.

This inadequacy reflects the common tendency of classical and

---

[2] See, for example, A. G. Hart, "Monetary Policy for Income Stabilization," in *Income Stabilization for a Developing Democracy* (New Haven: Yale University Press, 1953) and E. A. Goldenweiser, *American Monetary Policy* (New York: McGraw-Hill, 1951).
[3] J. G. Gurley and E. S. Shaw, in their celebrated "Financial Aspects of Economic Development," *American Economic Review*, XLV (September 1955), pp. 515–538, were among the first to stress the need for control over non-bank financial activity. James Henderson, *op. cit.*, proposed reserve requirements on all savings deposits.
[4] See, for example, Milton Friedman, *op. cit.*, C. Kreps and D. Lapkin, "Public Regulation and Operating Conventions Affecting Sources of Funds of Commercial Banks and Thrift Institutions," *Journal of Finance*, XVII (May 1962), pp. 289–301, and James Tobin, "Towards Improving the Efficiency of the Monetary Mechanism," *Review of Economics and Statistics*, XLII (August 1960), pp. 276–279.
[5] The first recommendation has been made by Milton Friedman, *op. cit.*, and George Tolley, "Providing for Growth of the Money Supply," *Journal of Political Economy*, LXV (December 1957), pp. 465–485; the second by James Tobin, *op. cit.*

Keynesian economics to treat the financial structure as being of secondary importance, netting out the assets and liabilities of the private sector. The lack of financial structure in traditional models, of course, has been subjected to severe criticism in the work of J. Gurley and E. Shaw and other proponents of the "new view."[6] However, their objection to the traditional analysis is different from the one discussed here. According to Gurley and Shaw, essential features of the relationships between the financial system and the real economy are obscured or lost in these models. The view associated with Gurley and Shaw tends to "focus on demands for and supplies of the whole spectrum of assets rather than the quantity and velocity of money; and to regard the structure of interest rates, asset yields and credit availabilities rather than the quantity of money as the linkage between monetary and financial institutions and policies, on the one hand, and the real economy on the other.[7] Even if this view of the linkage were incorrect, and the demand for money were the only link between financial and real activity, it would be important to give formal recognition to non-monetary institutions and assets. Most of the proposals for monetary reform, and some instruments of monetary control, have to be interpreted in the traditional models as shifts in the demand schedule for money. Yet the way in which they would affect the demand for money is neither obvious nor capable of analysis within these models. This is, of course, an old story; in order to understand the way in which changes in "structure" affect equilibrium in a model, one needs to know the structural equations, not just the reduced form. This is a compelling reason for looking at the structure of financial markets quite independently of whether one accepts or rejects the view that the linkage between financial and real markets is through the demand for money.

The discussion of the impact of non-bank financial intermediaries on the effectiveness of monetary control provides an illustration of the type of partial equilibrium analysis used by monetary economists. In this discussion a number of writers have utilized an extension of the deposit creation model used for studying the commercial banking system.[8] This

---

[6] The most complete statement of the view associated with Gurley and Shaw is their *Money in a Theory of Finance* (Washington: Brookings Institution, 1960). Harry Johnson has provided a review of this development in his survey article "Monetary Theory and Policy," *American Economic Review*, LII (June 1962), pp. 335–384.

[7] James Tobin, "Commercial Banks as Creators of 'Money'," *Banking and Monetary Studies*, Deane Carson, ed. (Homewood, Ill.: Richard D. Irwin, Inc., 1963), reprinted in this volume, Chap. 1. Tobin goes on to discuss the implications of the "new view" for the theory of deposit creation.

[8] See, for example, Donald Shelby, "Some Implications of the Growth of Financial Intermediaries," *Journal of Finance*, XIII (December 1958), pp. 527–541, or Warren Smith, "Financial Intermediaries and Monetary Controls," *Quarterly Journal of Economics*, LXXIII (November 1959), pp. 533–553.

analysis emphasizes the indirect use of reserves by intermediaries through holdings of deposits in commercial banks. Typically the "absorption ratios" for various types of liabilities or "credit-creation" multipliers are calculated. These quantities are then used to evaluate the effects of movements of deposits from one type of intermediary to another, and to evaluate the credit-creating power of a specified change in reserves. While this elaboration of the simple deposit creation multiplier model is a step in the right direction, and is perhaps adequate as an expositional device, as a tool of analysis it is subject to a number of reservations.

First, the implications of changes in bank assets and liabilities for the volumes of other assets and liabilities in the system are obscured and easily forgotten in this partial equilibrium model. An increase in the reserve base which results in a four- or five-fold expansion of bank assets and liabilities requires a major reshuffling in the portfolios of wealth owners and borrowers. In this model it is easy to forget that such portfolio adjustments imply changes in the direct demand for capital. It is easy to imagine situations in which the volume of bank loans or "indirect finance" increases, and in which the total demand for capital decreases.

A related inadequacy of this partial equilibrium model is that it ignores the interdependence of the various markets and intermediaries. In a general equilibrium model it would be natural to include the rates of return on all assets in the equations of demand and supply for each asset, in order to make explicit this interdependence. An additional advantage of including the rate of return in the demand equations is that it enables one to consider various proposals dealing with the regulation of rates which are beyond the scope of a simpler model.

Finally, this partial analysis usually ignores the implications of rational behavior for the portfolio choices of individuals and financial institutions. The commercial banks described in this model (and in textbook discussions of multiple deposit creation) mechanically place a constant fraction of their assets in reserves, bonds, and loans. Changes in the relative rates of return on these assets cannot induce banks to change their behavior. Similarly, it is frequently assumed that individuals place a fixed proportion of increases in net worth in each asset. Thus, the multiple expansion of deposits which follows an increase in reserve base proceeds without reference to the preferences of borrowers or lenders.

These comments suggest the possible advantage of formulating a general equilibrium model of financial and capital markets utilizing some specific assumptions about the way in which the demands of individuals and institutions for the various assets depend on the rates of return. The purpose of this essay is to develop such a model and to use it to trace the effects of monetary controls and structural changes. Equilibrium in this model is an equilibrium of stocks and balance sheets—a situation in which both the public and financial institutions are content with their portfolios of assets and debts, and the demand to hold each asset is just equal to the stock supply.

This approach has a number of limitations. One of the most important ones is that it has nothing to say about speeds of adjustment and other dynamic effects. We feel, nevertheless, that by examining the comparative statics of such a general equilibrium system we shall gain important insights on some of the questions at issue.

The usefulness of our analysis is limited in another respect. The model we will construct is designed to illuminate questions which relate to the role of the financial system as the link through which the monetary authority attempts to regulate overall economic activity. That is, we will view the efficiency of the financial system exclusively from the point of view of stabilization. The shortcoming of this emphasis is that it neglects certain other criteria relevant to an evaluation of structural change.

First, we will not consider the impact of existing or proposed legislation on the allocative efficiency of the financial system. One of the persuasive arguments against regulation of the rates paid on the liabilities of commercial banks (and for the payment of interest on reserves) is that such regulation leads to non-productive efforts to economize on money holdings during periods of high interest rates. Second, we shall have nothing to say about the importance of equitable treatment of banks and other intermediaries. Neither shall we discuss the costs and dangers of the extension of government regulation. Both of these considerations involve controversial value judgments.

An undesirable consequence of including greater institutional detail than appears in the existing literature is the necessity of restricting our discussion to financial markets, and abstracting from markets for goods and services. Although this procedure is partially dictated by the necessity of reducing the problem to manageable proportions, it is not entirely without justification.

> In a world of financial assets and well-developed capital markets, Keynes was right in perceiving the tactical advantage to the theorist of treating separately decisions determining total wealth and its rate of growth and decisions regarding the composition of wealth.[9]

It does, however, leave us with the question of the relationship between adjustments on the capital account and the flow variables in the income account. Recently, several authors, in discussing the way in which monetary actions affect economic activity, have emphasized the effects of monetary actions on the terms at which the community will hold the

---

[9] James Tobin, "Money, Capital and Other Stores of Value," *American Economic Review*, LI (May 1961), pp. 26–37.

existing stock of capital.[10]   We shall refer to the rate of return at which the public will hold the existing stock of capital as the *required rate of return* on capital.   The required rate of return should not be confused with the Keynesian interest rate, which is the long-term bond rate.   Numerous examples can be constructed in which the supply price of capital falls as a consequence of an event which causes the bond rate to rise.[11]   Reductions in the required rate of return on capital encourage the production of new capital and increases in it discourage such production.

The mechanism by which changes in the required rate of return on capital originating in the asset markets are translated into changes in the level of economic activity can be of several varieties.   While it is not the purpose of this essay to improve our understanding of that mechanism, it may be useful to briefly discuss the way our results could be integrated into a more complete model.   Perhaps the simplest mechanism is the one described in Hicks' "LM-IS" analysis.   In this analysis an increase, for example, in "the rate of interest" required for portfolio balance at a given level of income (an upward shift in the "LM" curve) leads to a reduction in investment as firms find it more expensive to finance new capital purchases.   In our model we distinguish between the rate of interest on bonds (and other financial assets) and the required rate of return on capital.   Hence it is appropriate to regard the level of investment activity as directly related to the required rate of return on capital, rather than the bond rate.   Increases in the required rate on capital reflect reductions in the demand for capital, whether from firms who find it more expensive to make new security issues, from wealth owners who are attracted out of the equities market by higher yields on substitute assets, or from borrowers who find it more expensive to finance equity holdings.   The consequence of an increase in the required rate of return on capital (a reduction in the demand for capital at the initial rate) is a decrease in production of new capital.   Subsequent changes in the level of economic activity, of course, in turn influence the demand for assets, as transactions needs and savings are altered.   In a complete model of income determination, full equilibrium is reached at a lower level of income and a higher rate of return on capital.   In this chapter we shall only consider the first stage of this process, the adjustments in the rates of return necessary to restore equilibrium in the asset markets.   In the case of the rate of return on capital, this is analogous to exploring the vertical displacements of the "LM" curve which result from monetary actions.

The remainder of this chapter will illustrate the way in which a general

[10] Harry Johnson, *op. cit.*, attributes this view to M. Friedman, K. Brunner and J.Tobin.
[11] Tobin, "Money, Capital and Other Stores of Value," *op. cit.*, gives several examples. We shall encounter several additional cases later in our analysis.

equilibrium model of the capital account may be utilized to clarify some policy issues. In Section 2 we will make explicit the model and the assumptions about the ways the demand of individuals and institutions depend on the rates of return. The assumptions about the demand functions, of course, are important as they are what enable us to obtain specific results. Section 3 demonstrates the continued effectiveness of open market operations in a world with many intermediaries and financial assets. Section 4 explores the question of how structural change alters the effectiveness of monetary control. In that section it is argued that "effectiveness" involves the response of the system to "disturbances" as well as actions of the monetary authority. For illustrative purposes we consider three different types of disturbances as well as open market operations, and investigate the way a particularly simple structural change, a permanent increase in the reserve requirement on banks, affects the system's response to them. In Section 5 we discuss the consequences of removing rate regulations on banks. One consequence of a variable deposit rate which arises is the possibility of complementarity in the system. Following the view taken in Section 4, we discuss the consequences of increasing deposit rate competition on the response of the system to disturbances as well as open market operations. This discussion also provides an illustration of the way results are altered by inclusion of non-bank intermediaries and financial assets other than money.

2   THE MODEL

Notation

Assets.   The structure of asset holdings for the general model is shown in Table 1. Owners of wealth may hold $(n + 1)$ assets; capital, currency, and the deposit liabilities of the various intermediaries.[12] Wealth-owners' demand for these assets is denoted by:[13]

$$
\begin{aligned}
&D_0 &&\text{Wealth-owners' direct demand for capital}\\
&D_1 &&\text{Wealth-owners' direct demand for currency}\\
&D_2 &&\text{Wealth-owners' direct demand for bonds}\\
&D_3 &&\text{Wealth-owners' demand for the deposit liabilities}\\
&&&\text{of banks}\\
&D_i;\ i = 4, \ldots, n &&\text{Wealth-owners' demand for the deposit liabilities}\\
&&&\text{of the ith intermediary}
\end{aligned}
$$

---

[12] We will refer to a class of institutions, for example, savings and loan associations, as an intermediary. All commercial banks constitute the intermediary "banks." Capital, bonds, and the liabilities of any intermediary are each assumed homogeneous. Bonds are issued only by the government.

[13] All demands are in physical, not in value, units. For example, a "physical" unit of a bond is one note, which has certain characteristics, e.g., par value, maturity, and coupon.

Table 1   The Structure of Asset Holdings

Sector	Assets	Liabilities
Government (including central bank)		Currency Bonds
Public (non-intermediary)	Currency Bonds Deposits in intermediaries Capital	Loans from intermediaries
Intermediaries Banks	Reserves (currency or deposit liabilities of central bank) Bonds Loans to public	Deposits
Other	Loans to public	Deposits

Individuals may borrow from banks or the other intermediaries for the purpose of holding capital beyond their net worth:

L_i; $i = 3, \ldots, n$ Borrowers' demand for loans from the ith intermediary

Banks place their disposable assets in currency, bonds, and loans.[14]

b The proportion of banks' asset portfolio held in bonds

c The proportion of banks' asset portfolio held in currency

Rates.   The yields on the $(n + 1)$ assets available to wealth owners are denoted by R_i, $i = 0, \ldots, n$. R_1, the rate on currency, is fixed at zero and omitted from the demand functions. A bar over any other rate indicates that it is institutionally fixed. Hence, $R_3 = \bar{R}_3$ indicates that the bank deposit rate is fixed.

The loan rates at the intermediaries are denoted by r_i; $i = 3, \ldots, n$.

---

[14] Banks (and other intermediaries) do not hold capital in their portfolios.

Parameters.   Various variables, including the supplies of currency, bonds, and capital, and a reserve requirement, are determined exogenously:

S_0 The supply of capital
S_1 The supply of currency
S_2 The supply of bonds
k A legal reserve requirement, in currency, on banks

In addition a number of parameters affecting behavior are used in the analysis:

γ A general shift parameter which is an argument of the demand for every asset
γ_1 A specific shift parameter affecting the demand for bonds and capital
γ_2 A specific shift parameter affecting the demand for loans by borrowers and the indirect demand for capital
γ_3 A specific shift parameter affecting banks' demand for bonds and loans
λ A parameter indicating the degree of rate competition among banks

The significance of these parameters will be discussed later.

Behavioral Assumptions

In order to infer anything about the way events alter the equilibrium in financial markets some assumptions must be made about the demand functions for the various assets. Ideally, these restrictions on the demand functions would be derived from a theory of portfolio choice or would be the result of empirical estimation. Unfortunately, the theory of portfolio choice provides little guidance and empirical studies of individual portfolio behavior are virtually nonexistent. Our procedure, then, will be to investigate the implications of the strong, but plausible, assumption that the demand functions of wealth owners and intermediaries have the property that all assets are gross substitutes, and that demands for loans have a similar property.[15] That is, a rise in the interest rate on any asset results,

---

[15] Recent contributions to the general theory of portfolio selection include James Tobin, "Liquidity Preference as Behavior Towards Risk," *Review of Economic Studies*, XXV (February 1958), reprinted in Cowles Foundation Monograph 19, *Risk Aversion and Portfolio Choice* (New York: John Wiley and Sons, 1967), Chap. 1, and Harry Markowitz, *Portfolio Selection* (New York: John Wiley and Sons, 1959). Tobin shows the plausibility of the gross substitutability assumption in the case of a quadratic utility function. Richard Porter, in "A Model of Bank Portfolio Selection," *Yale Economic Essays*, I (Fall 1961), reprinted in this volume, Chap. 2, has presented a model of bank portfolio selection based on the assumption of expected profit maximization for which banks' demand functions have this property.

ceteris paribus, in an increase in wealth-owners' (or an intermediary's) desired holdings of that asset and a decrease, or at most no change, in desired holdings of every other asset. Although the demand functions undoubtedly depend upon wealth, income, and other variables, assumptions about the form of the dependency are unnecessary for our analysis since these variables are fixed.

The Public. The demand of wealth owners for the various assets is assumed to depend upon the rates of return of all assets and on a shift parameter γ:

$$D_i = D_i(R_0, R_2, \ldots, R_n; \gamma) \qquad i = 0, \ldots, n \qquad (1)$$

These assets are assumed to be gross substitutes in the portfolios of wealth owners, i.e., an increase in the jth rate will increase the demand for the jth asset and decrease or leave unaffected the demand for all other assets:

$$\frac{\delta D_i}{\delta R_i} > 0; \qquad \frac{\delta D_i}{\delta R_j} \leq 0, i \neq j; \qquad \frac{\delta D_0}{\delta R_j} < 0, \quad \text{for at least one } j. \quad (2)$$

To simplify matters, it is assumed that borrowers borrow in order to hold capital, so that the demand for loans at the ith intermediary depends only on the rate on capital, on the $(n - 2)$ intermediary loan rates, and on a shift parameter.

$$L_i = L_i(R_0, r_3, \ldots, r_n; \gamma); \qquad i = 3, \ldots, n \qquad (3)$$

Increases in the rate on capital or decreases in the rate on loans at the ith intermediary increase the demand for loans from that intermediary, and decreases in the loan rate at the other intermediaries decrease it:

$$\frac{\delta L_i}{\delta R_0} \geq 0, \qquad \frac{\delta L_i}{\delta r_i} \leq 0, \qquad \frac{\delta L_i}{\delta r_j} \geq 0 \quad \text{for } i \neq j \text{ and } i, j = 3, \ldots, n \quad (4)$$

Intermediaries. The proportion of their portfolios which banks desire to place in currency, in bonds, and in loans is assumed to depend upon the bond rate, the bank loan rate, the legal reserve requirement (which may be zero), and a shift parameter.[16] Because of transactions needs, and the possibility of deposit withdrawals, banks may demand currency in excess of the legal requirement. Likewise we know that it is possible for banks to hold reserves which fall short of the legal requirement. Thus it seems more reasonable to insert k as an argument of the demand function rather than merely as a constraint on c.

$$\left. \begin{array}{ll} c = c(R_2, r_3, k, \gamma), & 0 \leq c < 1 \\ b = b(R_2, r_3, k, \gamma), & 0 \leq b < 1 \end{array} \right\} \ 0 \leq b + c < 1 \qquad (5)$$

---

[16] Assuming that these proportions depend upon the volume of deposits would not greatly complicate the analysis.

An increase in the bond rate is assumed to increase (or leave unaffected) the proportion of banks' portfolio in bonds and to decrease (or leave unaffected) the proportion in currency and loans:

$$\frac{\delta b}{\delta R_2} \geq 0, \qquad \frac{\delta c}{\delta R_2} \leq 0, \qquad \frac{\delta(b+c)}{\delta R_2} \geq 0 \qquad (6)$$

An increase in the banks' loan rate is assumed to decrease (or leave unaffected) the proportion held in currency and bonds:

$$\frac{\delta b}{\delta r_3} \leq 0, \qquad \frac{\delta c}{\delta r_3} \leq 0 \qquad (7)$$

An increase in the legal reserve requirement is assumed to increase banks' demand for currency, and decrease (or leave unaffected) its demand for bonds and loans:

$$\frac{\delta c}{\delta k} > 0, \qquad \frac{\delta b}{\delta k} \leq 0, \qquad \frac{\delta(b+c)}{\delta k} \geq 0 \qquad (8)$$

Non-bank intermediaries hold all of their assets in the form of loans.

Each intermediary has two rates associated with it, a deposit rate and a loan rate. In the case of non-bank financial intermediaries we will assume that competition among institutions within an intermediary forces institutions in the intermediary to pay a deposit rate equal to the loan rate minus some fixed cost of intermediation:[17]

$$R_i = r_i - m_i; \qquad i = 4, \ldots, n \qquad (9)$$

where m_i represents the cost of intermediation of the ith intermediary. In the case of banks, there are two basic variations. In Sections 3 and 4 we will assume the deposit rate at banks is fixed by regulation and does not respond to changes in the rates of return on banks' portfolios.

$$R_3 = \bar{R}_3 \qquad (10)$$

In Section 5 we will assume that the banks' deposit rate depends on the rate of return on their portfolio and the degree of rate competition, λ.

$$R_3 = f(R_2, r_3, \lambda) \qquad (11)$$

The justification for this assumption is discussed in Section 5.

Equations Representing Equilibrium

Equilibrium in this model requires the demand for every asset, including the deposit liabilities and the loans of intermediaries, to be equal to its supply. Since the portfolio choices of intermediaries are constrained

---

[17] The cost of intermediation could be made an increasing function of the volume of deposits without complicating the analysis.

by the requirement that their assets equal their liabilities, we may simplify presentation by translating the demand of wealth owners for the liability of each intermediary into a direct demand for loans, currency, and bonds.[18] Equilibrium in the various asset markets may then be represented by a system of equations of the following form:

Capital $\qquad D_0(\ ) + \sum_{i=3}^{n} \frac{p_i}{P_0} L_i = S_0$

Currency $\qquad D_1(\ ) + c(\ )P_3 D_3(\ ) = S_1$

Bonds $\qquad D_2(\ ) + b(\ )\frac{P_3}{P_2} D_3(\ ) = S_2 \qquad\qquad (12)$

Bank loans $\qquad (1 - (b + c))\frac{P_3}{p_3} D_3(\ ) - L_3(\ ) = 0$

Non-bank loans $\qquad \frac{P_i}{p_i} D_i(\ ) - L_i(\ ) = 0, \qquad i = 4, \ldots, n$

where the P_i represents the price of a unit of the ith asset held by wealth-owners and p_i represents the price of the ith loan asset.

The total of wealth-owners' demand for assets is constrained to be equal to private net worth:

$$\sum_{i=0}^{n} P_i D_i(\ ) = \sum_{i=0}^{2} P_i S_i \qquad\qquad (13)$$

When each equation in equation 12 is multiplied through by the price of the asset to which it corresponds and the equations are summed, we get equation 13. Hence, one of the equations in equation 12 is redundant. In all subsequent sections we shall omit the first equation.

We have assumed that the demand for the various assets depends on the rates of return, and that equilibrium of this sytem is maintained by adjustment of these rates. For some assets, for example the deposit liabilities of intermediaries, it is natural to assume that these rate adjustments are essentially recontracts of the terms on which individuals hold the asset. For such assets the units can be defined once and for all so that the price of a unit is 1. In the case of other assets, notably bonds and capital, it would seem more appropriate to regard changes in rates as the reflection of changes in the valuation of a given expected stream of return associated with a unit of the asset. For these assets, an increase in the rate of return is the consequence of the reduction in the price of the asset and vice versa. For convenience, we will assume that all assets are of the first

[18] For our purposes no harm is done by assuming the equity of shareholders in the intermediaries to be zero.

type. Our results would not be altered by relaxation of this assumption. The system of equations 12 may now be rewritten as:

$$D_0(\ ) + \sum_{i=3}^{n} L_i(\ ) = S_0$$
$$D_1(\ ) + c(\ )D_3(\ ) = S_1$$
$$D_2(\ ) + b(\ )D_3(\ ) = S_2 \tag{14}$$
$$(1 - (b + c))D_3(\ ) - L_3(\ ) = 0$$
$$D_i(\ ) - L_i(\ ) = 0 \qquad i = 4, \ldots, n$$

Equilibrium requires, in addition to satisfaction of equations 14, that the rates of return on the assets and liabilities of intermediaries be related as indicated in equations 9 to 11. With the exception of banks, we shall use these relationships to eliminate the intermediaries' loan rates. In the case of banks, we shall either fix the deposit rate or replace it with an appropriate function of the rate of return on the assets which comprise banks'

Table 2 Summary of Regimes

	Markets	Restriction	Variables Investigated
Section 3 With banks	Capital Currency Bonds Bank Loans	Bank deposit rate fixed	$\dfrac{dR_i}{dS_2}, \dfrac{dD_3}{dS_2}, \dfrac{dL_3}{dS_2}$
With many intermediaries	Capital Currency Bonds $(n-2)$ Loans	Bank deposit rate fixed	$\dfrac{dR_i}{dS_2}$
Section 4	Capital Currency Bonds Bank loans	Bank deposit rate fixed	$\dfrac{dR_i}{d\gamma_1}, \dfrac{dR_i}{d\gamma_2}, \dfrac{dR_i}{d\gamma_3}$
			$\dfrac{dR_i}{dk}$
			$\dfrac{d\left(\dfrac{dR_i}{dS_2}\right)}{dk} \quad \dfrac{d\left(\dfrac{dR_i}{d\gamma_i}\right)}{dk}$
Section 5	Capital Currency Bonds $(n-2)$ loans		$\dfrac{d\left(\dfrac{dR_i}{dS_2}\right)}{d\lambda} \quad \dfrac{d\left(\dfrac{dR_i}{d\gamma}\right)}{d\lambda}$

portfolios. We are then left with n rates of return; $R_0, R_2, r_3, R_4, \ldots, R_n$ to be determined by the n independent equations in equation 14.

In the remainder of this chapter, we will frequently simplify this system somewhat by eliminating some of the intermediaries, or by placing restrictions on banks' portfolios in order to focus on a particular issue. A summary of the regimes to be considered is provided in Table 2. Once a regime has been specified the effects of changes in parameters on the rates of return may be found by differentiating the system. The resulting system of equations can be differentiated again to show the effect of structural changes on the magnitude of the response of the rates. Although the derivatives give only the consequence of the infinitesimal changes in parameters, many of our results do not depend on the initial values of the dependent variables, and consequently are valid for larger changes.

3 THE EFFECTIVENESS OF OPEN MARKET OPERATIONS

With Banks

In order to illustrate the workings of the model let us first consider a regime with only one intermediary, banks, with a legally fixed deposit rate. Equation system 14 (dropping the equation for capital) then reduces to three equations in the three rates, R_0, R_2, r_3.

$$D_1(\ ) + c(\ )D_3(\ ) = S_1$$
$$D_2(\ ) + b(\ )D_3(\ ) = S_2 \quad (15)$$
$$(1 - (b + c))D_3(\ ) - L_3(\ ) = 0$$

An open market sale of bonds by the Federal Reserve increases the supply of bonds and decreases by an equal amount the supply of currency or bank reserves. The bond and currency markets are out of equilibrium until the rates of return on the various assets adjust so that the public and banks together are satisfied to hold in their portfolios the reduced stock of currency and the increased stock of bonds.

We may find the effect of an open market sale of bonds on the equilibrium rates of return by differentiating equations 15 with respect to S_2.

$$\left(\frac{\delta D_1}{\delta R_0} + c\frac{\delta D_3}{\delta R_0}\right)\frac{dR_0}{dS_2} + \left(\frac{\delta D_1}{\delta R_2} + c\frac{\delta D_3}{\delta R_2} + \frac{\delta c}{\delta R_2}D_3\right)\frac{dR_2}{dS_2} + \frac{\delta c}{\delta r_3}D_3\frac{dr_3}{dS_2} = -1$$

$$\left(\frac{\delta D_2}{\delta R_0} + b\frac{\delta D_3}{\delta R_0}\right)\frac{dR_0}{dS_2} + \left(\frac{\delta D_2}{\delta R_2} + b\frac{\delta D_3}{\delta R_2} + \frac{\delta b}{\delta R_2}D_3\right)\frac{dR_2}{dS_2} + \frac{\delta b}{\delta r_3}D_3\frac{dr_3}{dS_2} = 1$$

$$\left[(1 - (b + c))\frac{\delta D_3}{dR_0} - \frac{\delta L_3}{\delta R_0}\right]\frac{dR_0}{dS_2} + \left[(1 - (b + c))\frac{\delta D_3}{\delta R_2} - \frac{\delta(b + c)}{\delta R_2}D_3\right]\frac{dR_2}{dS_2}$$

$$+ \left[-\frac{\delta(b + c)}{dr_3}D_3 - \frac{\delta L_3}{\delta r_3}\right]\frac{dr_3}{dS_2} = 0 \quad (16)$$

The first equation indicates that the changes in the rates R_0, R_2, and r_3 must together bring about a reduction in the demand for currency by one unit; the second equation says that these changes must increase the demand for bonds by one unit; the third says that they must leave the loan market in equilibrium. The coefficients of the total derivatives dR_0/dS_2, dR_2/dS_2, dr_3/dS_2 are the partial derivatives of the excess demands for the various assets. For example, the coefficient of dR_2/dS_2 in the first equation $(\delta D_1/\delta R_2 + c(\delta D_3/\delta R_2) + (\delta c/\delta R_2)D_3)$ indicates that a unit increase in the rate on bonds would decrease the demand for currency in three ways. First, it would decrease the public's direct demand for currency by $\delta D_1/\delta R_2$. Second, it would decrease the volume of bank liabilities by $\delta D_3/\delta R_2$ and hence, indirectly, decrease banks' demand for currency by $c(\delta D_3/\delta R_2)$. Lastly, it would decrease by $\delta c/\delta R_2$ the proportion of their portfolios banks desire to hold in currency, and hence decrease their demand for currency by $(\delta c/\delta R_2)D_3$. Similarly it can be seen from the first term of the third equation that a unit increase in the rate of return on capital would increase the excess demand for loans; it would decrease the volume of bank deposits by $\delta D_3/\delta R_0$ and hence reduce their supply of loans by $(1 - (b + c))\delta D_3/\delta R_0$ while simultaneously increasing by $\delta L_3/\delta R_0$ the volume of loans borrowers desire at the given loan rate.

For convenience, henceforth systems of equations like equations 16 will be written in the form

$$J_1 \begin{bmatrix} \dfrac{dR_0}{dS_2} \\[2mm] \dfrac{dR_2}{dS_2} \\[2mm] \dfrac{dr_3}{dS_2} \end{bmatrix} = \begin{bmatrix} -1 \\[2mm] 1 \\[2mm] 0 \end{bmatrix} \tag{17}$$

where J_1 (a Jacobian) represents the matrix of partial derivatives of market equations 15. Using the assumption that assets are gross substitutes it can easily be shown (Appendix of this chapter) that the rates on capital, bonds, and loans must all rise if equilibrium is to be restored.

$$\begin{bmatrix} \dfrac{dR_0}{dS_2} \\[2mm] \dfrac{dR_2}{dS_2} \\[2mm] \dfrac{dr_3}{dS_2} \end{bmatrix} > 0 \tag{18}$$

This result is, of course, not surprising to someone accustomed to computing deposit creation multipliers. Although in this model the equilibrium volume of bank deposits is not rigidly tied to the volume of bank reserves, it is easy to show that it must decrease as a consequence of an open market sale of bonds. Since all of the rates (except the fixed rate on bank deposits) increase, and since the public's demand for deposits is negatively related to these rates, the volume of deposits in equilibrium must be smaller:

$$\frac{dD_3}{dS_2} = \frac{\delta D_3}{\delta R_0}\frac{dR_0}{dS_2} + \frac{\delta D_3}{\delta R_2}\frac{dR_2}{dS_2} < 0.$$

$$(-)(+) \quad (-)(+)$$

(19)

Someone accustomed to the more conventional analysis may, however, find it interesting that under our assumptions the sign of the effect of an open market sale of bonds on the volume of loans is not determined.

$$\frac{dL_3}{dS_2} = \frac{\delta L_3}{\delta R_0}\frac{dR_0}{dS_2} + \frac{\delta L_3}{\delta r_3}\frac{dr_3}{dS_2}.$$

$$(+)(+) \quad (-)(+)$$

(20)

Increases in the rate on capital, as wealth-owners move into bonds, increase borrowers' demand for loans. At the same time, because of decreases in the volume of their deposits (and the increased attractiveness of bonds) banks are less willing to lend at any given rate on loans. The shifts in the supply and demand curves work together in raising r_3, but work in opposite directions in affecting L_3. If borrowers are not discouraged by increases in the loan rate and banks can be induced to increase the proportion of their portfolios placed in loans, the volume of loans will increase. The precise condition on the sign of dL_3/dS_2 is given by:

$$\text{sign}\frac{dL_3}{dS_2} = \text{sign} \begin{vmatrix} \frac{\delta D_0}{\delta R_0} & \frac{\delta D_0}{\delta R_2} & 0 \\ (1-(b+c))\frac{\delta D_3}{\delta R_0} & (1-(b+c))\frac{\delta D_3}{\delta R_2} - \left(\frac{\delta(b+c)}{\delta R_2}\right)D_3 & -\left(\frac{\delta(b+c)}{\delta r_3}\right)D_3 \\ -\frac{\delta L_3}{\delta R_0} & 0 & -\frac{\delta L_3}{\delta r_3} \end{vmatrix}$$

(21)

An increase in the volume of loans, should it occur, does not indicate that the open market sale of bonds has been expansionary. Even under the conditions which give rise to an increase in the volume of loans, the rate of return on capital (as well as on other assets) increases; this is the sole and sufficient criterion that the action is contractionary. This is perhaps the simplest instance where reliance on a variable other than the rate of return on capital may give a misleading indication of expansion (or contraction).

With Many Intermediaries

Open market sales of bonds were effective in raising the required rate of return on capital in a world of one intermediary, subject to a reserve requirement and with a legally fixed deposit rate. Would monetary control remain effective in a world where there were many intermediaries and where credit markets were not subject to these restraints?[19] The results of the preceding section are easily extended to answer this question.

Consider the regime represented by equation system 14, continuing to assume the banks' deposit rate is fixed:

$$
\begin{aligned}
D_1(\ ) + c(\ )D_3(\ ) &= S_1 \\
D_2(\ ) + b(\ )D_3(\ ) &= S_2 \\
(1 - (b + c))D_3(\ ) - L_3(\ ) &= 0 \\
\left.
\begin{aligned}
D_i(\ ) - L_i(\ ) &= 0 \\
R_i = r_i - m_i
\end{aligned}
\right\} \ & i = 4, \ldots, n
\end{aligned}
\tag{22}
$$

This is the same regime as the one considered in the previous section except for the addition of $(n - 3)$ "intermediary" loan markets. These markets may equally well be regarded as markets for various types of private debt issue used to finance holdings of real capital (e.g. corporate bonds). With this interpretation, of course, the "deposit" rate is identical to the "loan" rate.

Differentiating this system with respect to the supply of bonds we find:

$$
J_2
\begin{bmatrix}
\dfrac{dR_0}{dS_2} \\[2ex]
\dfrac{dR_2}{dS_2} \\[2ex]
\dfrac{dr_3}{dS_2} \\[2ex]
\dfrac{dR_4}{dS_2} \\[1ex]
\cdot \\
\cdot \\
\cdot \\
\dfrac{dR_n}{dS_2}
\end{bmatrix}
=
\begin{bmatrix}
-1 \\[2ex]
1 \\[2ex]
0 \\[2ex]
\cdot \\[1ex]
\cdot \\
\cdot \\
0
\end{bmatrix}
\tag{23}
$$

---

[19] This discussion parallels Tobin and Brainard, "Financial Intermediaries and The Effectiveness of Monetary Controls," *American Economic Review*, LII (May 1963), reproduced in this volume as Chapter 3.

where

$$
J_2 \equiv \left[
\begin{array}{c|cccc}
& \dfrac{\delta_1 D}{\delta R_4} + c\,\dfrac{\delta D_3}{\delta R_4} & \cdots & \dfrac{\delta D_1}{\delta R_n} + c\,\dfrac{\delta D_3}{\delta R_n} \\[2ex]
J_1 & \dfrac{\delta D_2}{\delta R_4} + b\,\dfrac{\delta D_3}{\delta R_4} & \cdots & \\[2ex]
& (1-(b+c))\dfrac{\delta D_3}{\delta R_4} - \dfrac{\delta L_3}{\delta R_4} & \cdots & \vdots \\[2ex]
\hline
\dfrac{\delta D_4}{\delta R_0} - \dfrac{\delta L_4}{\delta R_0}\,\dfrac{\delta D_4}{\delta R_2}\,\dfrac{\delta L_4}{\delta r_3} & \dfrac{\delta D_4}{\delta R_4} - \dfrac{\delta L_4}{\delta R_4} & \cdots & \dfrac{\delta D_4}{\delta R_n} - \dfrac{\delta L_4}{\delta R_n} \\[2ex]
\vdots \qquad \vdots & \vdots & & \vdots \\[2ex]
\dfrac{\delta D_n}{\delta R_0} - \dfrac{\delta L_n}{\delta R_0}\,\dfrac{\delta D_n}{\delta R_2}\,\dfrac{\delta L_n}{\delta r_3} & \dfrac{\delta D_n}{\delta R_4} - \dfrac{\delta L_n}{\delta R_4} & \cdots & \dfrac{\delta D_n}{\delta R_n} - \dfrac{\delta L_n}{\delta R_n}
\end{array}
\right]
$$

With the use of the assumptions we have made about asset substitution it is easily shown (Appendix of this chapter) that:

$$
\begin{bmatrix}
\dfrac{dR_0}{dS_2} \\[2ex]
\dfrac{dR_2}{dS_2} \\[2ex]
\dfrac{dr_3}{dS_2} \\[2ex]
\dfrac{dR_4}{dS_2} \\[1ex]
\vdots \\[1ex]
\dfrac{dR_n}{dS_2}
\end{bmatrix} > 0
\tag{24}
$$

Even though the deposit liabilities of non-bank intermediaries may expand to wholly offset enforced reductions in the supplies of controlled monetary assets and even if monetary expansion means equivalent contraction by uncontrolled intermediaries, monetary controls can still be effective. However, it has been shown elsewhere that substitutions of this kind *diminish* the effectiveness of these controls; for example, a billion dollar change in the supply of currency and bank reserves would have more effect on the economy if asset substitutions were prevented.[20]

----

[20] *Ibid.*

It is not obvious, of course, that the volume of deposits (and loans) at non-bank intermediaries will in fact increase in the wake of an open market sale of bonds. It is possible, however, that the increase in the deposit rate at a particular intermediary will attract deposits in spite of increases in the rates on competing assets; deposits, bonds, and capital. Of course, if the deposit rate at any intermediary is fixed, then an open market sale of bonds leads to a reduction in the volume of its deposits.

4   RESERVE REQUIREMENTS AND THE EFFECTIVENESS OF MONETARY CONTROL

Introduction: The Problem of Evaluation

The structure of the financial system is constantly changing. New conventions, new assets, and new institutions emerge and old ones disappear. Monetary economists devote a good deal of time to studying and debating the way in which these structural changes alter the effectiveness of monetary control. Despite the great interest in the way structural changes alter the effectiveness of monetary control, there has been relatively little discussion of what "effectiveness" is, what determines it and what changes it. For example, most of those who oppose the extension of controls to non-bank financial intermediaries do so on the grounds that the diminution in effectiveness of monetary control, caused by these intermediaries, is slight, rather than challenging the appropriateness of the conventional notion of effectiveness. In most discussions effectiveness is measured by the magnitude of the response of some crucial variable, e.g., the rate of interest on bonds, the money supply, or the volume of loans, to an open market operation of a given size. Yet it is far from obvious that a structural change which leads to a reduction of effectiveness in this sense is necessarily undesirable.

Few economists express alarm over the automatic stabilization of the tax structure; yet this stabilizer decreases the response of the economy to discretionary fiscal actions. Structural changes which reduce the response of interest rates to open market operations may also reduce their response to "disturbances" which the Federal Reserve is trying to offset. Even if the monetary authority makes no allowance for changes in the potency of its medicine, it seems plausible that structural changes which proportionately decrease the response to controls and disturbances leave the system no worse off. In fact, in an uncertain world, where the regulatory authority is not able to make perfect predictions of either the disturbances or of the response of the system to its own actions, such a reduction is desirable.[21] In such a world, the authority can only partially offset disturbances. Structural changes which reduce the importance of the "residual" disturbances improve the performance of the system. If the monetary authority is free to adjust its dosage the argument is stronger. In that case, structural changes are desirable even if they act more strongly to decrease the response to policy variables than they do to immunize the system against disturbances.

There are, of course, reasons why it may be undesirable to have to increase the dosage of a diluted medicine. It seems reasonable to suppose, for example, that fluctuations in government expenditures per se are undesirable. Similarly it has been argued that large doses of monetary medicine are dangerous. If financial markets are "thin," large monetary actions may be discontinuous rather than continuous in their effect. Hence, a large open market sale of bonds might cause erratic price adjustments rather than a smooth movement of prices to a new equilibrium. Such price movements would in turn further "thin" the market.

In any case, the above arguments suggest that an important part of the evaluation of a given structural change is assessing the way in which it alters the response of the system to "disturbances." How does a given structural change affect the response of interest rates to shifts in the demand for bonds or capital? Are shifts in demand from bank deposits to deposits in savings and loan associations more or less disruptive if the deposit rate at banks is fixed or free to respond to competitive pressures? In this section, and also in Section 5, we will explore the usefulness of our analytic framework in answering this type of question. Although the structural changes we consider are quite simple, and they relate to proposals for changes in government regulation, the same theoretical considerations are relevant to structural changes beyond the control of the monetary authority. Not surprisingly, we frequently find that theoretical arguments alone will not resolve the question of whether a particular change is desirable or not. For some disturbances it is not possible to tell whether a structural change increases or decreases the response of the system without quantitative information about demand elasticities. Perhaps more significantly, a structural change which increases the response of the system to one disturbance may decrease its response to another. In these cases, an empirical judgment has to be made about the relative frequency and the relative magnitude of the two disturbances.

---

[21] This statement, and the ones that follow, are based on a simple model presented in Brainard, "Financial Intermediaries and a Theory of Monetary Control," unpublished Yale dissertation, 1962. The model assumed that "disutility" is associated with the squared difference between actual income and some target value.

We shall now proceed to consider the effects of three disturbances: a shift in the demands of wealth owners for bonds and for capital, a shift in the demand for loans by borrowers, and a shift in the desired portfolio composition of banks. Following this discussion, we will investigate the effect of permanent increases in reserve requirements on the response of the system to open market operations and these disturbances. These items comprise the remainder of this section.

The Effect of Disturbances: Three Types of Shifts in Demand

Shifts in demand schedules reflect changes in tastes, in expectations, or in variables other than the rates of return, which enter into the demand equations. Shifts in demand in this sense should not be confused with portfolio adjustments by the public or by banks which result from rate changes, e.g., the "shift" of banks out of bonds and into loans during an expansionary period, which is usually regarded as a response to changes in the relative profitability of these assets and not to a change in banks' preferences at a given set of rates. In our discussion, a change in tastes or in expectations, which results in a shift in the demand schedule for an asset, is represented by a change in the shift parameter which was introduced for this purpose in the demand equations for the various assets.

A Decrease in the Demand for Bonds and an Increase in the Demand for Capital. A change in preferences which results in an increase in the direct demand for capital at the expense of the direct demand for bonds is represented in our system by an increase in the shift parameter γ_1,

$$D_0 = D_0(R_0, R_2, \bar{R}_3; \gamma_1),$$
$$D_2 = D_2(R_0, R_2, \bar{R}_3; \gamma_1),$$

where by assumption,

$$\frac{\delta D_0}{\delta \gamma_1} = -\frac{\delta D_2}{\delta \gamma_1} > 0.$$

Differentiating the system of equations 15 with respect to γ_1 gives:

$$J_1 \begin{bmatrix} \dfrac{dR_0}{d\gamma_1} \\ \cdot \\ \cdot \\ \cdot \\ \dfrac{dr_3}{d\gamma_1} \end{bmatrix} = - \begin{bmatrix} 0 \\ \dfrac{\delta D_2}{\delta \gamma_1} \\ 0 \end{bmatrix} \tag{25}$$

where J_1 is the Jacobian in equation 16. As one would expect, it is easily shown that a decrease in the public's demand for bonds and an equal increase in its demand for capital results in a decrease in the rate on capital and an increase in the rate on bonds.

$$\frac{dR_0}{d\gamma_1} < 0, \qquad \frac{dR_2}{d\gamma_1} > 0. \tag{26}$$

The loan rate, on the other hand, may either increase or decrease. This is most easily seen by supposing that the demand for cash is unaffected by changes in the rate on bonds and capital. That is, the increase in the public's and banks' demand for cash resulting from the lower rate on capital is exactly offset by the decrease in the public's and banks' demand for cash resulting from increases in the rate on bonds. We may then ask whether at the initial loan rate there is an excess supply or an excess demand for loans.[22] Banks will tend to lend less at a given loan rate for two reasons: (1) the higher bond rate tends to increase the proportion of their portfolio in bonds, and therefore decrease the proportion held in loans; (2) the higher bond rate tends to reduce the volume of their deposit liabilities, and, hence, the size of their earning portfolio. This will be offset to the extent that the lower rate on capital tends to increase the volume of their deposits. Borrowers will desire fewer loans at a given loan rate because the rate on capital has fallen. If, at the initial loan rate, the decrease in the supply of loans by banks is greater than the decrease in the demand for loans by borrowers, then the loan rate will have to increase to clear the loan market. If the decrease in the supply of loans by banks is less than the decrease in the demand for loans by borrowers (or if the supply of loans by banks should increase), then the loan rate will have to decrease to clear the market. The precise condition indicating whether the rate on loans increases or decreases is shown in Table 3.

An Increase in the Demand for Loans. The effect of an increase in the demand for loans for the purpose of capital purchases may be analyzed in the same way. The demand for loans includes a shift parameter γ_2:

$$L_3 = L_3(R_0, r_3; \gamma_2)$$

where $\delta L_3/\delta \gamma_2 > 0$. Differentiating equation 15 with respect to γ_2 we

---

[22] This explanation is, of course, not a proof. Which one of the very great number of possible paths of adjustment is actually followed by the system will depend on the relative speeds of adjustment of the various markets. This example assumes that the markets for capital and bonds adjust rapidly as compared to the market for loans.

Table 3 The Effect of Shifts in Demand on the Various Rates

Case	$\dfrac{dR_0}{d\gamma_i}$	$\dfrac{dR_2}{d\gamma_i}$	$\dfrac{dr_3}{d\gamma_i}$
$i = 1$ Demand for bonds down $(D_2\downarrow)$	$-$	$+$	$\dfrac{\left(\dfrac{\delta D_1}{\delta R_0} + c\dfrac{\delta D_3}{\delta R_0}\right)\dfrac{\delta L_3}{\delta R_0}}{[1-(b+c)]\dfrac{\delta D_3}{\delta R_0}} \gtreqless 0$
Demand for capital up $(D_0\uparrow)$			$\dfrac{\left(\dfrac{\delta D_1}{\delta R_2} + c\dfrac{\delta D_3}{\delta R_2} + \dfrac{\delta c}{\delta r_2}D_3\right)}{[1-(b+c)]\dfrac{\delta D_3}{\delta R_2} - \left(\dfrac{\delta b}{\delta R_2} + \dfrac{\delta c}{\delta R_2}D_3\right)D_3}$
$i = 2$ Demand for loans up $(L_3\uparrow)$ Indirect demand for capital up	$-$	$\dfrac{\left(\dfrac{\delta D_2}{\delta R_0} + b\dfrac{\delta D_3}{\delta R_0}\right)D_3}{\dfrac{\delta b}{\delta r_3}D_3} \gtreqless 0$	$\dfrac{\left(\dfrac{\delta D_1}{\delta R_0} + c\dfrac{\delta D_3}{\delta R_0}\right)D_3}{\dfrac{\delta c}{\delta r_3}D_3} \gtrless$
$i = 3$ Bank demand for bonds down $(b_3\downarrow)$ Bank demand for loans up	$\dfrac{\dfrac{\delta D_0}{\delta R_2}}{\dfrac{\delta L_3}{\delta r_3}} \gtreqless 0$	$+$	$\dfrac{\left(\dfrac{\delta D_1}{\delta R_2} + c\dfrac{\delta D_3}{\delta R_2} + \dfrac{\delta c}{\delta R_2}D_3\right)}{\dfrac{\delta c}{\delta r_3}D_3}$
			$-$

find:

$$J_1 \begin{bmatrix} \dfrac{dR_0}{d\gamma_2} \\ \cdot \\ \cdot \\ \cdot \\ \dfrac{dr_3}{d\gamma_2} \end{bmatrix} = \begin{bmatrix} 0 \\ 0 \\ \dfrac{\delta L_3}{\delta \gamma_2} \end{bmatrix} \tag{27}$$

Not surprisingly, it is easily shown that an increase in the demand for loans results in a decrease in the rate on capital, and an increase in the rate on loans.

$$\frac{dR_0}{d\gamma_2} < 0, \qquad \frac{dr_3}{d\gamma_2} > 0.$$

In this case, however, the rate on bonds may either increase or decrease. Assume, for example, that the changes in the rates on capital and on loans offset each other and leave the demand for cash unaffected. At the initial rate on bonds, the increased loan rate induces intermediaries to sell bonds in order to make more loans. At the same time, the lowered rate on capital increases the demand for bonds for two reasons: (1) it increases the public's direct demand for bonds, and (2) it increases the public's demand for deposits, which results in banks increasing their demand for bonds for their enlarged earning portfolio. If, at the initial bond rate, the decrease in demand for bonds by banks (because of the increased attractiveness of loans) is more than offset by the increase in the public's and banks' demand for bonds (because of the decreased rate on capital) the rate on bonds will decrease, and vice versa. The precise condition for the rate on bonds to increase or decrease when changes in the rate on capital and loans affect the demand for cash is shown in Table 3.

Changes in the Bond and Loan Proportions in Bank Portfolios. A change in the portfolio demand of banks for bonds (as against loans) is represented in our system by a change in the shift parameter γ_3:

$$b = b(R_2, r_3; \ \gamma_3)$$

where $\delta b / \delta \gamma_3 < 0$. In this case we find that

$$J_1 \begin{bmatrix} \dfrac{dR_0}{d\gamma_3} \\ \dfrac{dR_2}{d\gamma_3} \\ \dfrac{dr_3}{d\gamma_3} \end{bmatrix} = -D_3 \begin{bmatrix} 0 \\ \dfrac{\delta b}{\delta \gamma_3} \\ \dfrac{-\delta b}{\delta \gamma_3} \end{bmatrix} \tag{28}$$

It is easily shown that the rate on bonds increases, and the rate on loans decreases, when banks shift from bonds to loans:

$$\frac{dR_2}{d\gamma_3} > 0, \qquad \frac{dr_3}{d\gamma_3} < 0.$$

In this case, however, the rate on capital may either increase or decrease. For example, suppose the changes in the rate on bonds and loans offset each other and leave the demand for cash unaffected. The decrease in the loan rate increases borrowers' demand for capital. The increase in the bond rate decreases wealth-owners' demand for capital. If, at the initial rate on capital, the increased demand of borrowers for capital more than offsets the decreased demand of wealth owners, the rate on capital must decrease to clear the market. If the decreased demand of wealth owners more than offsets the increased demand of borrowers, then the rate on capital must increase to clear the market. That is, the attempted shift from bonds into loans by banks is contractionary if borrowers' demand for loans (and hence capital) is relatively inelastic, if at the same time wealth owners are sensitive to increases in the bond rate.

The usual presumption is that a shift in the demand of banks from bonds to loans is expansionary. This view is consistent with our results if certain assumptions are made about the relative size of the demand elasticities of the various assets. The usual explanation emphasizes the effect of the shift in demand on the volume of indirect demand for capital. Furthermore it is usually implicitly assumed that the demand for loans is quite elastic, so that increases in the indirect demand for capital are likely to be greater than the decreases in the direct demand for capital which result from the increases in the bond rate. At the same time, it is typically assumed that banks' demand for currency reserves is relatively insensitive to the loan rate as compared to the bond rate. If the demand for loans is relatively elastic and any increase in banks' demand for currency in response to decreases in the loan rate is small, the shift in bank portfolios will be expansionary.

The precise condition indicating whether the rate on capital increases or decreases when the demand for cash is affected by the changes in the bond and loan rates is shown in Table 3.

Changes in the Reserve Requirement on Banks

Changes in the legal reserve requirement directly affect the equilibrium rates on the various assets. We are also interested in knowing the way they alter the "effectiveness" of monetary control. As was argued in the introduction to this section, this involves an evaluation of the way in which a change in the level of a reserve requirement affects the response of the rate on capital both to open market operations and to various disturbances.

Here we will first demonstrate that an increase in a legal reserve requirement will indeed be contractionary. We will then investigate the more difficult question of how a permanent increase in the reserve requirement (or in its average level) affects the response of the rates of return to the shifts of demand which we have already discussed.

Thus far, it has not mattered whether banks' demand for currency reflects transactions and precautionary needs, or whether it is due to a legal reserve requirement, or both. In the remainder of this section we will assume that a legal reserve requirement, k, exists and that it affects the demand of banks for currency, bonds, and loans:

$$c = c(R_2, r_3;\ k)$$
$$b = b(R_2, r_3;\ k) \tag{29}$$

We will assume that an increase in the legal reserve requirement always increases banks' demand for cash and decreases (or leaves unaffected) their demand for bonds and loans:

$$\frac{\delta c}{\delta k} > 0, \qquad \frac{\delta b}{\delta k} \leq 0, \qquad -\frac{\delta(b + c)}{\delta k} \leq 0.$$

The Effect of Increasing the Reserve Requirement on the Rates of Return.[23] The effect of increasing the reserve requirement on the various rates may be found by differentiating the equation system 22 with respect to k. This leads to the following system of equations:

$$J_2 \begin{bmatrix} \dfrac{dR_0}{dk} \\ \cdot \\ \cdot \\ \cdot \\ \dfrac{dR_n}{dk} \end{bmatrix} = -D_3 \begin{bmatrix} \dfrac{\delta c}{\delta k} \\ \dfrac{\delta b}{\delta k} \\ \dfrac{-\delta(b + c)}{\delta k} \\ 0 \\ \cdot \\ \cdot \\ \cdot \\ 0 \end{bmatrix} \tag{30}$$

---

[23] The analysis and results which follow may be applied equally well to a change in banks' preferences which results in an increase in their demand for cash and an associated reduction in their demand for bonds and/or loans.

where J_2 is the Jacobian in equation 23. It is easily shown that an increase in the "reserve requirement" raises the rate of return on all of the assets.

$$\begin{bmatrix} \dfrac{dR_0}{dk} \\ \cdot \\ \cdot \\ \cdot \\ \dfrac{dR_n}{dk} \end{bmatrix} > 0 \qquad (31)$$

With a given currency supply, a higher reserve requirement must curtail the public's holdings of currency or deposits or both. An increase in the return on some competing assets is required to induce the public to behave in this way. An increase in the rate on any one asset will lead to increases in the rates on others by virtue of their gross substitutability.

The Effects on the Responsiveness of the System. The effects of open market sales of bonds and three different shifts in demand on the rates of return have previously been investigated. In each case, certain changes in the rates of return are necessary to restore the equilibrium after some initial "disturbance" occurs. These changes in the rates are given implicitly in systems of equations having the following form:

$$J_2 \begin{bmatrix} \dfrac{dR_0}{d\gamma} \\ \cdot \\ \cdot \\ \cdot \\ \dfrac{dR_n}{d\gamma} \end{bmatrix} = -\left[\dfrac{\delta X}{\delta \gamma}\right] \qquad (32)$$

where γ may represent S_2, γ_1, γ_2, or γ_3, and $[\delta X/\delta \gamma]$ is the vector of partial derivatives of the excess demand equations with respect to γ. The effect of increases in the reserve requirement on the response of the rates to any one of the parameters $(S_2, \gamma_1, \gamma_2, \gamma_3)$ may be found by differentiating this system with respect to k.

After some simplification this gives:[24]

---

[24] This analysis applies for any "disturbance" for which the size of the initial disequilibrium in the various markets is not affected by changes in k. If changes in k do alter the initial disequilibrium we should include a term $\delta^2 x/\delta \gamma \delta k$ on the right hand side of this system.

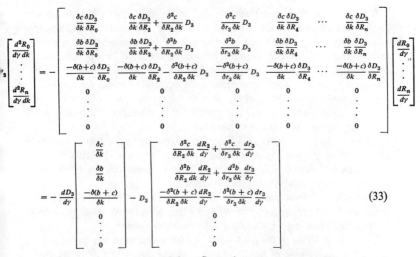

The second term on the right reflects the consequences of increasing k on the responsiveness of banks' portfolio demand to changes in the rates of return on bonds and loans. Unfortunately, this effect on the second derivatives $d^2R_i/d\gamma dk$ is ambiguous, even in the case of open market operations. Of course, if the portfolio demand of banks does not respond to rate changes, or more generally, if:

$$c(R_2, r_3; \ k) = c^1(R_2, r_3) + c^2(k)$$

this term will be zero. In the remainder of this section we will make that assumption.

In that case, except for the multiplication of the right hand side by the change in the volume of bank deposits which results from a change in the parameter, this system is identical to equation 30. It follows that whether an increase in reserve requirement increases or decreases the response of the rates to open market operations or shifts in demand depends solely upon whether they increase or decrease the volume of bank deposits.

$$\text{sign} \begin{bmatrix} \dfrac{d^2R_0}{d\gamma \, dk} \\ \cdot \\ \cdot \\ \cdot \\ \dfrac{d^2R_n}{d\gamma \, dk} \end{bmatrix} = \text{sign} \ \dfrac{dD_3}{d\gamma} \qquad (34)$$

If an open market operation or a shift in demand results in a decrease in the volume of bank deposits, an increase in the reserve requirement causes a smaller increase (or larger decrease) in the response of the various rates to the open market operation or shift in demand. This is intuitively reasonable. With a larger reserve requirement any decrease in the volume of deposits causes a larger reduction in the demand of banks for currency and a smaller reduction in their demand for bonds and loans. This is relatively expansionary in the same way that a reduction in a reserve requirement would be. On the other hand, if bank deposits increase in response to a shift in demand, a larger reserve requirement means a larger absorption of currency by banks and a smaller increase in their demand for bonds and loans. This is relatively contractionary in the same way that an increase in the reserve requirement is.

In the case of open market sales of bonds we know that the volume of bank deposits decreases. Hence, we know that open market sales of bonds increase the rates less with a larger reserve requirement.[25]

Each of the shifts in demand which we have discussed has ambiguous effects on the volume of bank deposits. Hence, the effect of increasing the reserve requirement on the response of the system is also ambiguous. The ambiguity in the sign of $dD_3/d\gamma$ reflects the fact that in each of the three cases the rate on bonds and the rate on capital may move in opposite directions. This is always the case with a decrease in the demand for bonds and an increase in the demand for capital. In such instances the question of whether the volume of bank deposits increases or decreases depends on the relative sensitivity of the demand for deposits to these two rates.

If an increase in the demand for loans results in a decrease in the rate on bonds (the rate on capital always falls), then the volume of deposits increases. In that case, the impact of the shift in demand is less expansionary with a larger reserve requirement. Similarly, when banks shift from bonds to loans, the rate on capital may rise with the bond rate, resulting in a decrease in the volume of deposits. In this case, the rates on bonds and capital rise less in response to the shift in demand with a larger reserve requirement.

These results are summarized in Table 4.

5 REGULATION OF THE DEPOSIT RATE AT COMMERCIAL BANKS

Introduction

Commercial banks are subject to regulations which prevent the payment of interest on demand deposits and place a ceiling on rates paid on time

---

[25] It should be remembered that we have assumed that the rate paid on bank deposits is fixed. When the deposit rate is free to rise it is likely to induce an increase in the volume of deposits which reverses these results. For a more complete discussion of this point see Chapter 3, or Brainard, *op. cit.*

Table 4 The Effect of Increasing the Reserve Requirement on the Response of the System

Parameter	Condition	$\dfrac{dR_0}{dy}$	$\dfrac{dR_2}{dy}$	$\dfrac{dD_3}{dy}$	$d\left(\dfrac{dR_i}{dy}\right)\big/dk$
S_2 Open market sale of bonds		+	+	−	
γ_1 Demand for bonds down, demand for capital up		−	+	− for $\dfrac{\delta D_3}{\delta R_0}=0$; + for $\dfrac{\delta D_3}{\delta R_2}=0$	
γ_2 Demand for loans up, indirect demand for capital up	$\left(\dfrac{\delta D_1}{\delta R_0}+c\dfrac{\delta D_3}{\delta R_0}\right)\dfrac{\delta b}{\delta r_3} > \left(\dfrac{\delta D_2}{\delta R_0}+b\dfrac{\delta D_3}{\delta R_0}\right)\dfrac{\delta c}{\delta r_3}$ $(\ \ ) < (\ \ )$	−	+	?	+
γ_3 Bank demand for bonds down, bank demand for loans up	$\dfrac{\dfrac{\delta c}{\delta r_3}\,D_3}{\dfrac{\delta L_3}{\delta r_3}} < \dfrac{\left(\dfrac{\delta D_1}{\delta R_2}+c\dfrac{\delta D_3}{\delta R_2}+\dfrac{\delta c}{\delta R_2}\,D_3\right)}{\dfrac{\delta D_0}{\delta R_2}}$ $(\ \ ) > (\ \ )$	+	+	?	−

and savings deposits. A number of monetary economists have objected to these regulations on the grounds that they interfere with the efficient allocation of resources. This position is based on the welfare implications of a discrepancy between the marginal cost of deposits and the "price" which depositors are charged.[26] Our model is not suitable for an analysis of the efficiency of allocation and such an analysis will not be attempted. It has also been suggested that the effectiveness of monetary policy would benefit from removal of the regulations on the various deposit rates. Is monetary restriction more deflationary (i.e., does it produce a larger increase in the rate of return on capital) when the deposit rate is fixed or when it is flexible?[27] Do deposit rate regulations increase, or decrease, the response of the system to disturbances?

This section will examine the consequences of deposit rate regulation on the effectiveness of monetary policy in a world with a variety of financial assets and intermediaries. It will then sketch briefly the results of the Tobin-Brainard paper and contrast them with what one obtains when greater detail is included in the model. Before we begin this task, however, we will discuss briefly the determination of deposit rates at banks and the possibility of deposit-currency complementarity.

The Deposit Rate Function

Suppose that regulations fixing the maximum rate payable on demand, time, and savings deposits are eliminated. One would then expect that competition for deposits by commercial banks would cause the deposit rates to be related to the rates of return on assets which are held in the portfolios of banks and to respond to changes in these rates. This suggests that it would be appropriate to write:

$$R_3 = f(R_2, r_3),$$

where

$$\frac{\delta f}{\delta R_2}, \frac{\delta f}{\delta r_3} > 0. \tag{35}$$

Even without deposit rate regulations, of course, the behavior of the banking industry would not be perfectly competitive. Various characteristics which differentiate the liabilities of individual banks (service, location, etc.) would remain. An increase of 1 % in the rate of return on the assets in the portfolios of banks is not likely to result in an increase of 1 % in the rate paid on the associated deposits. The greater the degree of

---

[26] See, for example, Milton Friedman, *A Program for Monetary Stability* (New York: Fordham University Press, 1960).

[27] This question was explored in Chapter 3, in a simpler version of the model presented here.

competition among banks, the greater the change in deposit rate which would be expected from a given change in the bond or loan rate.

In the earlier sections of this chapter we assumed that the existence of rate regulations prevented any adjustment of the deposit rates in response to changes in the rates of return on bank portfolios, i.e., we assumed that they were exogenously fixed. This is undoubtedly an overstatement of the influence of rate regulations. Even if the nominal rate paid were fixed by regulation, banks could alter the attractiveness of their deposits by adjusting their service charges, and by providing various non-pecuniary returns to depositors (air-conditioned buildings, gifts of alarm clocks, etc.). Of course, in the case of time and savings deposits, the present regulations do not in fact fix the rate paid by banks but rather the maximum rate payable. By no means do all banks actually pay this maximum rate. If "the" deposit rate in our model is taken to mean some sort of average of the rates paid by banks, then it may respond to competitive pressures even though the ceiling does not. Another reason that the existing rate regulations are not equivalent to fixing the deposit rates is that the ceiling rate itself is not entirely exogenous. During periods of generally high interest rates, the Federal Reserve is subject to pressures to increase the ceiling in order to "enable banks to compete more effectively for funds." Although historically the ceiling rates were seldom changed, there has recently been some suggestion of greater flexibility on the part of the Fed.

These considerations suggest that it may be appropriate to regard the deposit rate as functionally related to the rate of return on banks' portfolios even in the presence of deposit rate regulations. However, one would expect the deposit rate to adjust more rapidly, and more completely, in their absence. Accordingly, we will assume that a deposit rate function like equation 35 applies with or without deposit rate regulation, but with the responsiveness of the deposit rate to changes in rate of return on earning assets depending upon the degree of deposit rate competition.

$$R_3 = f(R_2, r_3; \; \lambda)$$

where λ represents the "degree of rate competition."

Removal of rate regulations, increases in the ceiling rate, or other changes which increase rate competition among banks are represented by increases in λ.[28] Increases in the "degree of rate competition" are assumed to increase the response of the deposit rate to changes in bond and loan rates:

$$\frac{\delta^2 f}{\delta R_2 \, \delta \lambda}, \; \frac{\delta^2 f}{\delta r_3 \, \delta \lambda} > 0. \tag{37}$$

[28] One would expect an increase in the ceiling rate to increase the level of the "deposit rate" as well as increase its responsiveness to changes in the rate of return on earning assets. That is, increases in the ceiling rate shift the deposit rate function upwards.

Substitutes and Complements

In all the models discussed in this chapter there are two sources for the demand for currency.[29] One is the *direct* demand of the public. The other is the reserve requirement of banks; in effect the public's demand for deposits creates a fractional *indirect* demand for currency. The basic assumption about the portfolio behavior of wealth owners is that assets are substitutes for one another. Essentially the same assumption is applied to the behavior of borrowers. That is, a rise in the interest rate of asset "A" introduces, *ceteris paribus*, an increase in desired holdings of "A" and a decrease, or at most no change, in desired holdings of every other asset. This means, among other things, that the direct demand of the public for currency is assumed to decline or at most not to rise in response to an increase in the rate offered on bank deposits. But clearly an increase in this interest rate also increases the demand for bank deposits. Thus, the demand for bank reserves, i.e., for currency, increases indirectly.

It is certainly conceivable, especially if the required reserve ratio is high, that the indirect effect of an increased deposit rate outweighs the direct effect. In that event currency and deposits are, taking account of both the public and the banks, *complements* rather than substitutes. This possibility is the simplest example of a very general phenomenon. Even though the substitution assumption applies to the portfolio choices of each economic agent separately, it is possible that assets will be complements in the system as a whole. This can happen whenever the public and intermediaries hold the same assets (currency, or government bonds, or other securities), or whenever one intermediary holds the liabilities of another intermediary as assets.

In the regimes which we have discussed thus far this complication cannot arise because the deposit rate is taken as fixed. The question of whether deposits and currency are complements or substitutes becomes an important one as soon as changes in the deposit rate are allowed. In simple models, for example in the model described in Chapter 3, a number of policy questions hinge on its answer. In addition, extreme complementarity can lead to instability of the system. While the changes in rates necessary to restore equilibrium in the unstable cases are frequently startling, they are, of course, essentially uninteresting. In this section we will assume stability. The restriction which this places on the partial derivatives of the demand functions provides us with the additional information we need (in the complements case) to obtain results.[30]

---

[29] This paragraph and the one which follows is adapted with minor modifications from the author's paper with James Tobin, Chapter 3.

[30] See Appendix to this chapter.

The Effect of Increasing Rate Competition in the General Model

How would an increase in rate competition alter the responsiveness of the system to open market operations and disturbances? We will first investigate this question in our most general regime. Although the complexity of this regime prevents us from obtaining definite qualitative results, our analysis will serve to clarify the issues on which the answer to the foregoing question depends.

Consider the regime with capital, currency, bonds, banks and $(n - 3)$ intermediaries:

$$
\begin{aligned}
D_1(\ ) + c(\ )D_3(\ ) &= S_1 \\
D_2(\cdot) + b(\ )D_3(\ ) &= S_2 \\
(1 - (b + c))D_3(\ ) - L_3(\ ) &= 0 \\
R_3 &= f(r_3;\ \lambda) \\
\left. \begin{aligned}
D_i(\ ) - L_i(\ ) &= 0 \\
R_i = r_i - m_i
\end{aligned} \right\}\ i &= 4, \ldots, n
\end{aligned}
\tag{38}
$$

To simplify matters we have assumed that the deposit rate does not respond to changes in the bond rate.[31] Except for the endogenous deposit rate this is the same as the regime of pages 110 to 112.

Differentiating this system to obtain the effect of changing some parameter (e.g., S_2, γ_1, γ_2, γ_3, k) gives:

$$
J_3 \begin{bmatrix} \dfrac{dR_0}{d\gamma} \\ \cdot \\ \cdot \\ \cdot \\ \dfrac{dr_n}{d\gamma} \end{bmatrix} = -\left[\dfrac{\delta X}{\delta \gamma} \right]
\tag{39}
$$

where J_3 is the Jacobian obtained by differentiating the system of equations 38 with respect to the rates. $[\delta X/\delta \gamma]$ represents the vector of partial derivatives of these equations with respect to the parameter. The effect of increasing the responsiveness of the deposit rate to changes in the loan rate is then found by differentiating equation 39 with respect to λ:

$$
J_3 \left[\dfrac{d^2 R_i}{d\gamma\, d\lambda} \right] = -\dfrac{\delta(J_3)}{\delta \lambda} \left[\dfrac{dR_i}{d\gamma} \right].
\tag{40}
$$

---

[31] In the case of open market operations allowing the deposit rate to respond to changes in the bond rate would not alter our results since in that case the bond and loan rates move in the same direction.

But since

$$\frac{\delta(J_3)}{\delta\lambda} = \frac{\delta f_1}{\delta\lambda}\begin{bmatrix} 0 \cdots 0 & \vdots & \frac{\delta X}{\delta R_3} & \vdots & 0 \cdots 0 \\ \cdot & & \cdot & & \cdot \\ \cdot & & \cdot & & \cdot \\ \cdot & & & & \\ 0 \cdots 0 & \vdots & & \vdots & 0 \cdots 0 \end{bmatrix}$$

where $f_1 = \delta f/\delta r_3$, we find that 40 reduces to:

$$J_3\left[\frac{d^2 R_i}{d\gamma\, d\lambda}\right] = -\frac{\delta f_1}{\delta\lambda}\frac{dr_3}{d\gamma}\begin{bmatrix} \dfrac{\delta D_1}{\delta R_3} + c\,\dfrac{\delta D_3}{\delta R_3} \\[2mm] \dfrac{\delta D_2}{\delta R_3} + b\,\dfrac{\delta D_3}{\delta R_3} \\[2mm] (1 - (b+c))\,\dfrac{\delta D_3}{\delta R_3} \\[2mm] \dfrac{\delta D_4}{\delta R_3} \\ \cdot \\ \cdot \\ \cdot \\ \dfrac{\delta D_n}{\delta R_3} \end{bmatrix}$$

Except for multiplication of the right hand side by $(\delta f/\delta\lambda)(dr_3/d\gamma)$ this equation system is identical to the one obtained by differentiating the system with respect to the level of the deposit rate ceiling (or with respect to an upward shift in the deposit rate function) on banks. Hence,

$$\text{sign}\left[\frac{d^2 R_i}{d\gamma\, d\lambda}\right] = \text{sign}\left[\frac{dR_i}{d\bar{R}_3}\right]\frac{dr_3}{d\gamma} \tag{41}$$

where $dR_i/d\bar{R}_3$ represents the change in R_i with respect to an increase in the rate ceiling, or an upward shift in the deposit rate function. Whether increased deposit rate competition strengthens or weakens the response of some rate of return to disturbances (or to open market operations) depends on two simpler, but related, questions. First, does the disturbance raise or lower the loan rate? Second, what is the effect of an increase in the deposit rate ceiling (or an upward shift in the deposit rate function) on that rate? It is frequently possible to tell how a disturbance affects the loan rate.[32] In those cases the entire question hinges on the effect of

---

[32] For example, we know how the loan rate is affected by open market operations and two of the three disturbances discussed in Section 4.

increasing the deposit rate ceiling. Unfortunately, in this regime, there is no simple condition indicating whether such an increase raises or lowers a particular rate. We are primarily interested in what happens to the responsiveness of the rate of return on capital. Increasing deposit rate competition decreases the response of the rate on capital to open market operations if exogenous increases in the deposit rate are expansionary, and increases its response if they are contractionary.

In the case of disturbances matters are complicated by the general indeterminacy of their effect on the loan rate. Of the three shifts in demand discussed previously, two had unambiguous effects on the loan rate (see Table 3). An increase in the demand for loans increases the loan rate and decreases the rate on capital. Hence, if exogenous increases in the deposit rate are expansionary, this shift is more expansionary with a flexible deposit rate, i.e., the rate on capital is more responsive to this "disturbance" with a flexible deposit rate. A shift in the demand of banks from bonds to loans always decreases the loan rate. Hence, if exogenous increases in the deposit rate are expansionary, the effect of this shift will be less expansionary (or more contractionary) with a flexible deposit rate. A shift in wealth-owners' demand from bonds to capital may either increase or decrease the rate on loans and hence the response of the rate on capital to this disturbance may be either increased or decreased.

These results suggest that the desirability of removing deposit rate restrictions will depend, among other things, on an empirical judgment as to the relative importance of various types of "disturbances." If, for example, shifts in loan demand are thought to be the most important factor contributing to cyclical fluctuations (and it is assumed that exogenous deposit rate increases are expansionary), then on stabilization grounds we would prefer a fixed to a flexible deposit rate. A fixed deposit rate gives the monetary authority smaller adjustments to make and a more potent tool to make them. If, on the other hand, shifts in banks' portfolios make an important contribution to economic fluctuations, deposit rate flexibility may be an automatic stabilizer.

Summary of Earlier Results

The question of how increasing deposit rate competition alters the effectiveness of monetary control was discussed in Chapter 3, the Tobin-Brainard paper. The analysis there differed from the analysis above in two major respects. First, the model used was an extremely simple one. There were no bonds, no non-bank intermediaries, and banks were assumed to hold a fixed proportion of their portfolio in currency. Second, the analysis was restricted to the way in which increasing deposit rate competition altered the response of the system to increases in the money supply; no disturbances were considered. The greater simplicity of that model made it possible to give a particularly simple condition for the consequences of increased deposit rate competition. We will sketch briefly the Tobin-Brainard results so that we may examine the way in which they are altered when greater detail is introduced into the model.

In the model used in Chapter 3, private wealth is the sum of the currency supply and the capital stock. Wealth owners divide their holdings among currency, bank deposits, and capital. Banks are subject to a legal reserve requirement and allocate fixed proportions of their deposits to currency reserves and loans. Borrowers hold that part of the capital stock which is not directly held by wealth owners.

In the earlier paper, two regimes were considered; one with a fixed deposit rate, and the other with the deposit rate equal to a fixed fraction $(1 - c)$ of the loan rate. A comparison was then made of the effect of increasing the supply of currency in these two regimes. By introducing the deposit rate function of equation 36 we obtain a regime for which both of these earlier regimes are special cases. Equilibrium in this new model may be represented by the following three equations:

$$D_1(\ ) + cD_3(\ ) = S_1$$

$$(1 - c)D_3(\ ) - L_3(\ ) = 0 \tag{42}$$

$$R_3 = f(r_3; \bar{R}_3, \lambda), \qquad \frac{\delta f}{\delta \bar{R}_3} > 0.$$

The proposition which we have demonstrated above in equation 41 applies to this regime as well. Hence we know that:

$$\text{sign} \begin{bmatrix} \dfrac{d^2R_0}{dS_1\,d\lambda} \\[2mm] \dfrac{d^2r_3}{dS_1\,d\lambda} \end{bmatrix} = \text{sign} \begin{bmatrix} \dfrac{dR_0}{d\bar{R}_3} \\[2mm] \dfrac{dr_3}{d\bar{R}_3} \end{bmatrix} \frac{\delta f_1}{\delta \lambda} \frac{dr_3}{dS_1} \tag{43}$$

As in the more complicated model of equation 38 we know that an increase in the supply of currency will decrease the loan rate, and hence

$$\left(\frac{\delta f_1}{\delta \lambda} \frac{dr_3}{dS_1} \right) < 0.^{33}$$

However, in this model the effect of increasing the ceiling rate hinges on a relatively simple condition.

---

[33] Open market operations cannot be considered in this regime as there are no bonds. Increases in S_1 are effectively open market purchases of capital.

Table 5 The Effect of Increasing Deposit Rate Competition (assuming exogenous increases in the bank deposit rate are expansionary)

Parameter	$\dfrac{d^2 R_0}{d\gamma\, d\lambda}$	Responsiveness of R_0 Increased $(+)$ Decreased $(-)$
S_2 Open market sale of bonds	$-$	$-$
γ_1 Demand for bonds down, demand for capital up	?	?
γ_2 Demand for loans up, indirect demand for capital up[a]	$-$	$+$
γ_3 Bank demand for bonds down, bank demand for loans up[a]	$+$	If $\dfrac{dR_0}{d\gamma_3} < 0,\ -$ If $\dfrac{dR_0}{d\gamma_3} > 0,\ +$

[a] These results refer to the regime analyzed on pages 114 to 118.

The effect of an increase in the regulated deposit rate is obtained by differentiating the system of equations 42 with respect to $\bar{R}_3$:

$$
\begin{bmatrix}
\dfrac{\delta D_1}{\delta R_0} + c\,\dfrac{\delta D_3}{dR_0} & 0 \\[2ex]
(1-c)\dfrac{\delta D_3}{dR_0} - \dfrac{\delta L_3}{\delta R_0} & -\delta L_3 \\ & \overline{\delta r_3}
\end{bmatrix}
\begin{bmatrix}
\dfrac{dR_0}{d\bar{R}_3} \\[2ex]
\dfrac{dr_3}{d\bar{R}_3}
\end{bmatrix}
= -
\begin{bmatrix}
\dfrac{\delta D_1}{\delta R_3} + c\,\dfrac{\delta D_3}{\delta R_3} \\[2ex]
(1-c)\,\dfrac{\delta D_3}{\delta R_3}
\end{bmatrix}
\dfrac{\delta f}{\delta \bar{R}_3}
\quad (44)
$$

Solving these two equations, it is easily shown that whether an increase in the regulated deposit rate increases or decreases the required rate of return on capital depends upon whether deposits and currency are complements or substitutes.

$$
\text{sign}\,\frac{dR_0}{d\bar{R}_3} = \text{sign}\left(\frac{\delta D_1}{\delta R_3} + c\,\frac{\delta D_3}{\delta R_3}\right)
\quad (45)
$$

If they are substitutes, an increase in $\bar{R}_3$ will be expansionary. In this case an increase in the deposit rate will reduce the demand for currency.

Therefore the rate on capital, R_0, which balances the supply and demand for currency will be lower. If, on the other hand, currency and deposits are complements, an increase in the deposit rate will require an increase in the rate on capital.[34]

It follows that whether increased deposit rate competition increases or decreases the response of the rate on capital to changes in the currency supply also hinges on whether currency and deposits are substitutes or complements. If currency and deposits are substitutes, an increase in the deposit rate is expansionary $(dR_0/d\bar{R}_3 < 0)$, it opposes and weakens monetary expansion $d^2R_0/dS_1 \, d\lambda > 0$. But if they are complements, the reverse is true. Flexibility in the deposit rate reinforces and strengthens quantitative monetary control.

The Consequences of Complicating the Model with Bonds, Variable Reserves, and Non-Bank Intermediaries

We have just shown that with a restricted menu of assets the consequences of increasing deposit rate competition for the effectiveness of monetary actions depends solely on whether currency and deposits are complements or substitutes. Which of the various complications included in the general model account for the ambiguity of results we found on page 128? Bonds, portfolio flexibility, and non-bank intermediaries alter the conditions for which greater deposit rate competition increases (or decreases) the effectiveness of monetary actions to the extent that they alter the conditions under which deposit rate increases are contractionary (or expansionary). We will discuss each of these modifications of the simple system in turn.

The Addition of Bonds. First, let us consider a regime where wealth owners may hold bonds in their portfolios as well as cash, capital, and the deposit liabilities of banks.[35] Even if bonds are not available to banks, their presence in the system is sufficient to alter the conditions for which exogenous increases in the deposit rate are contractionary, and hence the way in which increasing deposit rate competition alters the response of the system to changes in parameters.

---

[34] Not surprisingly, it can also be shown that in the substitutes case the loan rate decreases in response to an increase in the regulated deposit rate. However, in the complements case the effect on the loan rate is ambiguous. The increase in the deposit rate stimulates the supply of loans, while the increase in the rate of return on capital stimulates the demand for them. Consequently the loan rate necessary to equate the supply and demand for loans may be either higher or lower than its initial value.

[35] It should be remembered that bonds are meant to be government securities and not corporate securities used to finance holdings of capital. Inclusion of corporate bonds is analytically equivalent to the inclusion of a nonbank financial intermediary with a competitively determined deposit rate. See page 110.

In this regime the effect of exogenous increases in the deposit rate are found by solving the following system of equations:

$$
\begin{bmatrix}
\dfrac{\delta D_1}{\delta R_0} + c\dfrac{\delta D_3}{\delta R_0} & \dfrac{\delta D_1}{\delta R_2} + c\dfrac{\delta D_3}{\delta R_2} & \left(\dfrac{\delta D_1}{\delta R_3} + c\dfrac{\delta D_3}{\delta R_3}\right)f_1 \\[3mm]
\dfrac{\delta D_2}{\delta R_0} & \dfrac{\delta D_2}{\delta R_2} & \dfrac{\delta D_2}{\delta R_3}f_1 \\[3mm]
(1-c)\dfrac{\delta D_3}{\delta R_0} - \dfrac{\delta L_3}{\delta R_0} & (1-c)\dfrac{\delta D_3}{\delta R_2} & (1-c)\dfrac{\delta D_3}{\delta R_3}f_1 - \dfrac{\delta L_3}{\delta r_3}
\end{bmatrix}
\begin{bmatrix}
\dfrac{dR_0}{d\bar{R}_3} \\[3mm] \cdot \\ \cdot \\ \cdot \\[3mm] \dfrac{dr_3}{d\bar{R}_3}
\end{bmatrix}
= -
\begin{bmatrix}
\dfrac{\delta D_1}{\delta R_3} + c\dfrac{\delta D_3}{\delta R_3} \\[3mm]
\dfrac{\delta D_2}{\delta R_3} \\[3mm]
(1-c)\dfrac{\delta D_3}{\delta R_3}
\end{bmatrix}
$$

$$(46)$$

Since the determinant of the Jacobian is negative, it is easily seen that the qualitative effect of increases in the deposit rate on the rate of return on capital are given by:

$$
\operatorname{sign}\frac{dR_0}{d\bar{R}_3} = \operatorname{sign}
\begin{vmatrix}
\left(\dfrac{\delta D_1}{\delta R_3} + c\dfrac{\delta D_3}{\delta R_3}\right) & \left(\dfrac{\delta D_1}{\delta R_2} + c\dfrac{\delta D_3}{\delta R_2}\right) \\[3mm]
\dfrac{\delta D_2}{\delta R_3} & \dfrac{\delta D_2}{\delta R_2}
\end{vmatrix}
\tag{47}
$$

In the "substitutes case" an increase in the deposit rate continues to be expansionary. In the "complements case," however, it no longer follows that an increase in the deposit rate will necessarily result in an increase in the rate on capital. This ambiguity reflects the fact that, in contrast with the simpler regime, the initial increase in the demand for currency $[(\delta D_1/\delta R_3) + c(\delta D_3/\delta R_3)]$ may be partially at the expense of the demand for bonds rather than wholly at the expense of the demand for capital. The smaller decrease in the direct demand for capital may be more than offset by the increase in the indirect demand as banks increase their loans in response to increases in the volume of their deposits. Condition 47 may be understood by considering whether the changes in the bond and loan rates, which are necessary to clear the bond and loan markets at the initial rate on capital, leave an excess demand or an excess supply of capital. Initially, after the exogenous increase in the deposit rate, there is an excess demand for currency (complements case), an excess supply of bonds, and considering both the direct and indirect demand, either an excess demand for or an excess supply of capital. If the bond rate adjusts so as to clear the bond market, and the loan rate adjusts so as to equate the indirect demand for capital with the supply of loans, the excess demand for capital is equal in magnitude but is opposite in sign to the excess demand for currency. The bond rate must increase by $-[(\delta D_2/\delta R_3)/(\delta D_2/\delta R_2)]$ to clear the bond market. This reduces the initial excess demand in the currency market by

$$- \left[\frac{\delta D_2/\delta R_3}{\delta D_2/\delta R_2} \left(\frac{\delta D_1}{\delta R_2} + c \frac{\delta D_3}{\delta R_2} \right) \right].$$

If this more than offsets the initial excess demand for currency

$$[(\delta D_1/\delta R_3) + c(\delta D_3/\delta R_3)]$$

we know there is, at this stage, an excess demand for capital.

$$\text{sign } \frac{dR_0}{d\bar{R}_3} = \text{sign } \left[- \frac{\delta D_2/\delta R_3}{\delta D_2/\delta R_2} \left(\frac{\delta D_1}{\delta R_2} + c \frac{\delta D_3}{\delta R_2} \right) + \left(\frac{\delta D_1}{\delta R_3} + c \frac{\delta D_3}{\delta R_3} \right) \right]$$

This is, of course, the same as condition 47.

Whereas in the simple model complementarity between deposits and currency always meant that increasing the deposit rate was contractionary, the possibility of substitution away from assets other than capital in regimes with a wider variety of assets makes this result less likely.

If banks, not only wealth owners, are allowed to hold bonds in their portfolios along with currency and loans, the results are further complicated. The initial decrease in the demand for bonds is less, since increased bank deposits lead to an increase in the demand of banks for bonds. If the decrease in the direct demand for bonds is relatively small, it is even possible for there to be an increase in demand for bonds (if bonds and deposits are complements). Suppose first that both currency and bonds are in the aggregate substitutes for deposits. It follows that initially the demand for capital, direct plus indirect, has increased. Although increases in the bond rate necessary to restore equilibrium in the bond market (at the initial rate on capital) decrease the excess demand for capital, we know that an excess demand remains after the bond market is cleared, since these increases in the bond rate serve only to increase the excess supply of currency. Similarly if bonds and currency are complements with deposits, the equilibrium rate on capital must increase. In the mixed cases, where currency and deposits are substitutes while bonds and deposits are complements (or vice versa) the results are not so obvious. When currency and deposits are substitutes but bonds and deposits are complements, there may be either an excess demand for or an excess supply of capital initially. If there is an excess demand, reductions in the bond rate which are brought about in order to clear the bond market will only reinforce the initial pressures for a reduction in the rate on capital. If there is initially an excess supply, reductions in the bond rate may not offset this initial condition, and an increase in the rate on capital may follow. Similar reasoning can be used to explain the possibility of decreases in the rate on capital when currency and deposits are complements but bonds and currency are substitutes. The precise condition on the sign of the derivative for the rate of return on capital with respect to increases in the deposit rate is given by:

$$\text{sign } \frac{dR_0}{d\bar{R}_3} = \text{sign} \begin{vmatrix} \dfrac{\delta D_1}{\delta R_3} + c\dfrac{\delta D_3}{\delta R_3} & \dfrac{\delta D_1}{\delta R_2} + c\dfrac{\delta D_3}{\delta R_2} \\[2ex] \dfrac{\delta D_2}{\delta R_3} + b\dfrac{\delta D_3}{\delta R_3} & \dfrac{\delta D_2}{\delta R_2} + b\dfrac{\delta D_3}{\delta R_2} \end{vmatrix} \tag{48}$$

Variation in Currency Reserves. In the simpler model (i.e. in the model in Chapter 3) it was assumed that banks hold a fixed proportion of their assets in currency. In fact, of course, banks are free to hold reserves in excess of the nominal reserve requirement, and vary these holdings in response to changes in the rates of return on alternative assets. Does the rate of return on capital respond more or less to an exogenous increase in the deposit rate with flexible or with fixed reserves? Suppose the currency demand of banks depends on the loan rate. In that case, whether induced changes in reserve holdings increase or decrease the response of the rate of return on capital depends upon whether or not the loan rate is moving in the same direction as the rate on capital. This is easily shown. When the reserve proportions respond to changes in the loan rate, the equation system 46 should be altered by the addition of terms in the third column. If we denote the Jacobian in equation 46 by J_4, the Jacobian for the case where the loan rate influences the demand of banks for currency reserves may be written:

$$J_4' = J_4 + \begin{bmatrix} 0 & 0 & \dfrac{\delta c}{\delta r_3} D_3 \\[2ex] 0 & 0 & 0 \\[2ex] 0 & 0 & -\dfrac{\delta c}{\delta r_3} D_3 \end{bmatrix}$$

where we use a prime (') to indicate the case in which reserve proportions are variable. But since:

$$J_4 \left[\frac{dR_i}{d\bar{R}_3} \right] = J_4' \left[\frac{dR_i'}{d\bar{R}_3} \right]$$

it follows that:

$$J_4 \left[\frac{dR_i}{d\bar{R}_3} - \frac{dR_i'}{d\bar{R}_3} \right] = \begin{bmatrix} 0 & 0 & \dfrac{\delta c}{\delta r_3} D_3 \\[2ex] 0 & 0 & 0 \\[2ex] 0 & 0 & -\dfrac{\delta c}{\delta r_3} D_3 \end{bmatrix} \left[\frac{dR_i'}{d\bar{R}_3} \right] \tag{49}$$

Restricting our attention to the relative magnitude of the response of the rate on capital to changes in the deposit rate we find:[36]

$$\text{sign}\left(\frac{dR_0}{d\bar{R}_3} - \frac{dR_0'}{d\bar{R}_3}\right) = -\text{sign}\,\frac{dr_3'}{d\bar{R}_3}\frac{\delta c}{\delta r_3}\left(\frac{\delta D_2}{\delta R_2} + b\,\frac{\delta D_3}{\delta R_2}\right) \qquad (50)$$

or

$$\text{sign}\left(\frac{dR_0}{d\bar{R}_3} - \frac{dR_0'}{d\bar{R}_3}\right) = \text{sign}\,\frac{dr_3'}{d\bar{R}_3}$$

If the loan rate decreases, banks have less incentive to economize on cash holdings. This is relatively contractionary. If the rate on capital decreases (in response to an exogeneous increase in deposit rate) under fixed reserves, it decreases less (or even increases) under flexible reserves. When the loan rate increases, just the opposite is true. The rate on capital decreases more or increases less, with variable reserves. When currency and bonds are both substitutes for deposits, we have already shown that the rates on capital and on loans both decrease unambiguously in response to exogenous increases in the deposit rate. Hence, in that case an increase in the deposit rate is less expansionary when reserves are variable. In every other case, it is possible for the loan rate to move in the opposite direction from the rate on capital. When that occurs, variation in reserves increases the magnitude of the response of the rate on capital.

The Influence of Non-Bank Financial Intermediaries.   One of the major arguments for the removal of restrictions on the interest paid on commercial bank deposits is that allowing banks to raise their deposit rate may prevent the (expansionary) movement of deposits to non-bank intermediaries during periods of tight money. How does the presence of non-bank financial intermediaries affect our conclusions about the way deposit rate flexibility alters the effectiveness of monetary actions? We have shown on page 128 that the presence of non-bank intermediaries alters the results only insofar as it alters the conditions under which the exogenous increases in the deposit rate are expansionary or contractionary. Even if the impact of deposit rate increases were to continue to depend on whether deposits and currency are substitutes or complements, explicit recognition of non-bank intermediaries might alter one's view. The presence of non-bank intermediaries (as in the case of bonds) provides an additional asset for which wealth owners may substitute bank deposits. The substitutes case, which seemed so plausible when the only assets for which the public may substitute bank deposits are currency and capital,

---

[36] In order to make the results comparable to those in the model used in Chapter 3 we assume f_1 in J_4 is zero.

may appear less so in the presence of the deposit liabilities of other intermediaries.

The substitutes assumption itself is no longer sufficient to guarantee that increases in the bank deposit rate will be expansionary. With non-bank intermediaries it is possible, even when deposits and currency are substitutes, for increases in the deposit rate to increase the required rate of return on capital. The demand for the deposits of non-bank intermediaries is in effect the supply of loans from non-bank intermediaries to borrowers. Hence, any reduction in the demand for these deposits is in effect a reduction in the indirect demand for capital. In order to explore the implications of this fact, consider the following simple model with two intermediaries plus currency and capital:

$$\begin{aligned} D_1(\ ) + cD_3(\ ) - S_1 &= 0 \\ (1 - c)D_3(\ ) - L_3(\ ) &= 0 \\ D_4(\ ) - L_4(\ ) &= 0 \end{aligned} \tag{51}$$

Following the usual procedure it may be shown that:

$$\operatorname{sign} \frac{dR_0}{d\bar{R}_3} = \operatorname{sign} \begin{vmatrix} \left(\dfrac{\delta D_1}{\delta R_3} + c\dfrac{\delta D_3}{\delta R_3}\right) & 0 & \left(\dfrac{\delta D_1}{\delta r_4} + c\dfrac{\delta D_3}{\delta r_4}\right) \\[2mm] (1-c)\dfrac{\delta D_3}{\delta R_3} & -\dfrac{\delta L_3}{\delta r_3} & \left((1-c)\dfrac{\delta D_3}{\delta r_4} - \dfrac{\delta L_3}{\delta r_4}\right) \\[2mm] \dfrac{\delta D_4}{\delta R_3} & -\dfrac{\delta L_4}{\delta r_3} & \left(\dfrac{\delta D_4}{\delta r_4} - \dfrac{\delta L_4}{\delta r_4}\right) \end{vmatrix} \tag{52}$$

In order to understand this condition, let us consider the borderline case between currency-deposit substitutability and currency-deposit complementarity. Under this assumption condition 52 becomes

$$\begin{aligned} \operatorname{sign} \frac{dR_0}{d\bar{R}_3} &= -\operatorname{sign} \begin{vmatrix} (1-c)\dfrac{\delta D_3}{\delta R_3} & -\dfrac{\delta L_3}{\delta r_3} \\[2mm] \dfrac{\delta D_4}{\delta R_3} & -\dfrac{\delta L_4}{\delta r_3} \end{vmatrix} \\[2mm] &= \operatorname{sign} \left\{ \frac{\delta D_4}{\delta R_3} - \left[(1-c)\frac{\delta D_3/\delta R_3}{\delta L_3/\delta r_3}\right] \frac{\delta L_4}{\delta r_3} \right\} \end{aligned} \tag{53}$$

The condition on the sign of $dR_4/d\bar{R}_3$ is the negative of this expression; when the rate on capital goes up, the rate on deposits and loans at the second intermediary must go down.

It is worth noting that when banks do not compete for the loans of the second intermediary ($\delta L_4/\delta r_3 = 0$), the rate on capital falls as the deposit rate increases $(dR_0/d\bar{R}_3) < 0$. This is true in the borderline case, and also, of course, in the substitutes case.

Condition 53 may be understood in the following way. Initially bank deposits are up by $\delta D_3/\delta R_3$ and the second intermediary's deposits are down by $\delta D_4/\delta R_3$. Assume first that banks lower their loan rates sufficiently to make loans of $(1 - c)(\delta D_3/\delta R_3)$. This requires a change in r_3 of

$$(1 - c)\frac{\delta D_3/\delta R_3}{\delta L_3/\delta r_3}.$$

The lower bank loan rate decreases the demand for loans from the second intermediary by an amount of

$$\left[(1 - c)\frac{\delta D_3/\delta R_3}{\delta L_3/\delta r_3}\right]\frac{\delta L_4}{\delta r_3}.$$

This reduction in loan demand at the second intermediary may be greater or less than its original loss of deposits. If it is smaller, the second intermediary will find it necessary to raise its rate to discourage borrowers and attract new depositors. If it is greater, it will lower its rate to enourage borrowers and further discourage depositors. Any reduction in the deposit-loan rate of the second intermediary which is necessary to clear its loan market will create an excess (total) demand for capital. To be sure, reductions in the volume of deposits at the second intermediary (reductions in the ultimate supply of loans by the second intermediary) are partially offset by increases in the direct demand for capital, and the indirect demand for capital financed by bank loans. But these increases in the demand for capital will be less than the reductions in indirect demand financed by the second intermediary, since part of the reduction in demand for the deposits of the second intermediary shows up as an increase in the demand for currency (direct and indirect). Consequently, the rate on capital must increase.

Condition 53 also indicates that in the complements case an increase in the deposit rate is not necessarily contractionary. If reductions in the bank loan rate do not significantly reduce the demand for loans from the second intermediary, the second intermediary will find it necessary to raise its deposit-loan rate, causing, among other things, an expansionary movement from currency to the indirect financing of capital.

6 CONCLUDING REMARKS

Needless to say, this study leaves unanswered a number of theoretical questions which are of interest to monetary economists. We have had little to say about the interaction of the capital and income accounts. Nor have we been concerned with the dynamics of the adjustment from one equilibrium to another.

This theoretical study should not end, however, without some mention of the fact that the problems that remain are empirical as well as theoretical. We have seen that the effects of certain policy measures depend on the relative elasticities of demand for various assets. Furthermore, we have found that structural changes affect the response of the system to different disturbances differently. Consequently, an empirical judgment must be made as to the relative prominence of the various disturbances.

It is hoped that this study has clarified the logical connection between certain empirical judgments and answers to policy questions, and in so doing, has suggested and encouraged empirical research. While theoretical results may stimulate empirical research, the latter may in turn support restrictive assumptions which will make certain theoretical problems tractable.

APPENDIX

Most of the results reported in this chapter are obtained by brute force application of Cramer's rule. Typically, this involves a determination of the sign of the determinant of a matrix J_i and the signs of the cofactors of its elements. Several basic propositions about matrices are frequently useful.

Proposition 1. Let A be an $n \times n$ indecomposable matrix with $a_{ii} > 0$; $a_{ij} \leq 0$, $i \neq j$; $\sum_i a_{ij} \geq 0$ for all j and with strict inequality for at least one j. Then:

$$(i) \ |A| > 0$$
$$(ii) \ A^{-1} > 0; \ \text{cofactor} \ a_{ij} > 0; \ i, j = 1, \dots, n.$$

Property (i) is an immediate consequence of the fact that for $B = A[\text{diag}(1/a_{ii})]$, $|B| > 0$.[37] Property (ii) follows from the non-negativity of $C = (I - B)$ and the indecomposability of A (and hence C).[38]

---

[37] See for example Bear et al., "Elementary Proofs of Propositions on Leontief–Minkowski Matrices," *Metroeconomica*, XIV (1962), pp. 59–64.

[38] See for example F. Gantmacher, *The Theory of Matrices* (New York: Chelsea Publishing Company, 1960) pp. 51–52.

Proposition 2.   Let J be a matrix formed by replacing the first column of A above with a vector of non-positive elements $[y_i]$ with at least one $y_i < 0$.

Then:

  (i) $|J| < 0$.

  (ii) The elements in the first row of J^{-1} are strictly negative.

Property (i) follows from development of $|J|$ by the first column. Property (ii) is immediate.

Results of Section 3

By virtue of the gross substitution assumption, J_1 (and J_2) meet the conditions on J in Proposition 2 above. Hence, by Cramer's rule, the sign of dR_i/dS_2 is opposite that of the determinant of the matrix obtained by substitution of the right hand side of equation 17 (equation 23) in the ith column of J_1 (J_2). This determinant may be developed by adding the first row to the second and expanding by the ith column. Since the cofactors of the first row are positive (even after addition of the first row to the second) dR_i/dS_2 is positive.

Results of Section 5

When the deposit rate at banks is allowed to vary, the matrix of partial derivatives of the demand equations with respect to the rates need no longer exhibit the properties of J in Proposition 2 above. In Section 5 positive off-diagonal elements in the Jacobian J_3 may arise from either currency-deposit or bond-deposit complementarity. In order to obtain results in the cases with deposit rate flexibility we will assume stability of the system. Stability of the system requires $|J_3| < 0$. The proof that stability depends on the sign of $|J_3|$ is as follows:

Assume that excess demand for an asset leads to a fall in the rate on that asset.[39]

$$\dot{R}_i = -K_i A_i(R_0, \ldots, R_n), \qquad i = 0, 2, \ldots, n \qquad \text{(A-1)}$$

where the $K_i > 0$ are speeds of adjustment, which by choice of units may be taken as unity. A_i is the excess demand function for the ith asset.

We can approximate A_i in the neighborhood of equilibrium by the linear expression:

$$A_i = \sum_j a_{ij}(R_j - R_j^e) \qquad i = 0, 2, \ldots, n \qquad \text{(A-2)}$$

---

[39] For simplicity we assume that the deposit rate equations for intermediaries always hold. A dot over a symbol indicates differentiation with respect to time.

where a_{ij} is the partial derivative of excess demand for the ith asset with respect to the jth rate and $R_j{}^e$ is the equilibrium R_j.

Substituting equation A-2 into equation A-1 we find:

$$[\dot{R}_i] = -A[R_i - R_i{}^e]$$

where $A = [a_{ij}]$.

Stability of this system requires that the characteristic roots of $-A$ have negative real parts. But the determinant of $-A$ is equal to the product of the roots of $-A$. Hence $|-A|$ is negative if n is odd and positive if n is even. (Complex roots must appear in pairs as complex conjugates.) Since $|-A| = (-1)^n |A|$, $|A|$ must be positive. By adding the last $(n - 1)$ rows of $|J_3|$ to the first it can be seen that $|J_3| = -|A|$. Hence stability requires $|J_3| < 0$.

5

Monetary Policy, Debt Management, and Interest Rates: A Quantitative Appraisal*

ARTHUR M. OKUN

INTRODUCTION

Discussions appraising the effectiveness of monetary policy in recent years have been frequent, intense, and illuminating; but they have rarely been quantitative. It is the purpose of this chapter to advance quantitative measures of the effect of monetary and debt-management actions on interest rates. The numerical estimates advanced below are necessarily speculative and highly tentative. They are drawn from time-series data of the United States postwar economy and they are subject to all the limitations of statistical manipulation on highly intercorrelated and autocorrelated time-series variables. They do, however, represent a possible partial answer to the needs of monetary economists for a more specific assessment of the potentialities of monetary and debt-management instruments. Theoretical discussions can help to tell us whether curves should be drawn steep or flat; the exponents and disparagers of the

* SOURCE: Reprinted from *Stabilization Policies*, prepared for the Commission on Money and Credit (Englewood Cliffs, N.J.: Prentice-Hall, Inc., 1963), pp. 331–380. Reprinted by permission of Prentice-Hall, Inc., © 1963. This chapter was prepared for and financed by the Commission on Money and Credit. The research was done at the Cowles Foundation for Research in Economics at Yale University. I wish to thank Charlotte Phelps, Karen Hester, and Wilma Heston for their able assistance with the empirical work presented below.

central bank's role can debate such matters to the benefit of the profession and the policy-maker. But the issues are quantitative—an appraisal of the effectiveness of monetary policy should estimate the changes in macroeconomic variables that will be achieved by central bank actions. Quantitative measures of effectiveness offer something to debate, discuss, and refine; qualitative appraisals of effectiveness may depend heavily on preferences about the definitions of the word "effective."

MONETARY POLICY IN KEYNESIAN THEORY

The Keynesian model of short-run income determination provides a clear specification of the way in which central bank instruments affect the level of output. A change in the volume of money alters the rate of interest so as to equate the demand for cash with the supply; the change in interest affects the level of investment; the change in investment has a multiplied effect on equilibrium income. The present chapter is an empirical study of the first link in this chain of effects, i.e., the relationship between money and interest. In the Keynesian model, the central bank is assumed to fix the supply of money, while the public's demand for money depends on income and interest, as expressed in the liquidity preference function. In the world of the model, a single homogeneous earning asset is available to the public as an alternative to cash. The yield required to induce the appropriate demand for the earning asset relative to zero-yielding cash depends on the supply of money relative to income. Thus, when the central bank alters the volume of money, it affects the rate of interest.

The liquidity preference function is expected to display a negative relationship between the demand for money and the rate of interest. In the *General Theory*, this negative slope is explained primarily by inelastic expectations regarding interest rates.[1] The public allegedly feels that, when bond prices are low relative to their historical averages, they are more likely to rise and less likely to fall farther. Thus, when bond yields are high, the chance that interest returns will be canceled by capital losses appears smaller, and bonds are more attractive. Tobin has shown that aversion to capital-value risk is sufficient to account for a negatively sloped liquidity preference function, even if there are no expected capital gains or losses.[2] A higher yield on bonds compensates the investor for

[1] John Maynard Keynes, *The General Theory of Employment, Interest and Money* (New York: Harcourt Brace, 1936), pp. 201–202.

[2] James Tobin, "Liquidity Preference as Behavior Towards Risk," *Review of Economic Studies*, XXV (February 1958), pp. 65–86, reprinted in Cowles Foundation Monograph 19, *Risk Aversion and Portfolio Choice* (New York: John Wiley and Sons, 1967), Chap. 1.

taking greater risk in holding an expanded volume of bonds. The rate of interest on a financial claim equates the attractiveness, on the margin, of safe zero-yield cash and the risky earning asset as portfolio components. When monetary policy alters the relative supplies of the earning asset and of cash, the equilibrium yield on the earning asset is changed. Furthermore, when income rises while the supply of cash is constant, more money is demanded for transactions purposes, and the interest rate must increase to maintain the required demand for earning assets.

This theoretical world supplies an instructive approximation to reality, and it is amenable to empirical verification. The rate of interest, according to liquidity preference theory, should be positively related to the level of income and negatively related to the supply of money. These hypotheses have been tested statistically any number of times and they have been confirmed.[3] There is no need for a further test of the qualitative relationships: if one found opposite results at this stage, suspicion would be cast on his empirical procedures rather than on the theory. The quantification of the relationships, however, deserves much additional study. For this purpose, the simple theoretical world is not so easily translated into operational terms. It must be adapted in a number of ways to yield estimates of relevant magnitudes.

FEDERAL RESERVE AND TREASURY ACTIONS

In the first place, the institutional factors governing public control of the monetary system must be duly recognized. In the theoretical world, the central bank simply and directly controls the supply of money. In reality, public control over the volume of money is imperfect and indirect. The Federal Reserve System and the Treasury have particular instruments of monetary and debt policy at their disposal. These actions have complex

[3] See the following:

A. J. Brown, "Interest, Prices, and the Demand Schedule for Idle Money," *Oxford Economic Papers* (May 1939), pp. 46–69;

M. Kalecki, "The Short-term Rate of Interest and the Velocity of Cash Circulation," *Review of Economics and Statistics*, XXIII (May 1941), pp. 97–99;

James Tobin, "Liquidity Preference and Monetary Policy," *Review of Economics and Statistics*, XXIX (May 1947), pp. 124–131;

A. M. Khusro, "Investigation of Liquidity Preference," *Yorkshire Bulletin of Economic and Social Research*, IV (January 1952), pp. 1–20.

Henry Allen Latané, "Cash Balances and the Interest Rate—A Pragmatic Result," *Review of Economics and Statistics*, XXXVI (November 1954), pp. 456–460;

Andrew C. Stedry, "A Note on Interest Rates and the Demand for Money," *Review of Economics and Statistics*, XLI (August 1959), pp. 303–307;

Martin Bronfenbrenner and Thomas Mayer, "Liquidity Functions in the American Economy," *Econometrica*, XXVIII (October 1960), pp. 810–834.

effects on balance sheets. A review of these actions can assist the construction of an appropriate empirical framework for the evaluation of monetary policy instruments as determinants of interest rates.

When the Federal Reserve System purchases Government securities on the open market, it reduces the volume of interest-bearing federal debt held by the private sector and increases the volume of zero-yielding demand obligations (deposits in the Federal Reserve and currency) of the government. This exchange of demand obligations for marketable term securities will normally increase the volume of money in the community. The maximum potential increase in money is easily calculated as the amount of the open-market purchase divided by the percentage reserve requirement on the demand deposits of member banks. But the actual increase may differ substantially from the maximum potential: any induced rise in currency holdings of the public, any increase in excess reserves of commercial banks, any induced reduction in member bank borrowing from the Federal Reserve will make the actual fall short of the maximum. The resulting increase in money is the outcome of private actions and is not subject directly to control by public authority.

Another important instrument of Federal Reserve policy is the setting of the required reserve ratio for deposits of member banks. Changes in reserve requirements have no direct impact on the balance sheets of economic units. They alter the volume of demand deposit liabilities that can be supported by a given quantity of member bank reserves. When the Federal Reserve lowers reserve requirements, there is a determinate possible maximum increase in the supply of money. As in the case of open-market transactions, the actual expansion is likely to differ from the potential, as banks and their customers make choices which are not directly subject to Federal Reserve control.

The discount rate is the cost to member banks of borrowing from the Federal Reserve. Changes in the discount rate induce movements in the volume of member bank reserves to the extent that the amount of borrowing changes. Again, the commercial banks, rather than the central bank, determine the resulting alteration in the stock of money.

The Federal Reserve may also alter the composition of its security-holdings by selling Government obligations of a given maturity and simultaneously purchasing an equal volume of bonds of a different maturity. In this case, there is a change in the term structure of the federal debt held in the private sector. Investors are induced to trade one type of Government obligation for another.

The debt-management actions of the Treasury have effects on balance sheets which are identical to the pair of Federal Reserve open-market transactions described above. When the Treasury retires one type of outstanding security at maturity and issues a new security in equal volume, it lengthens the term structure of the federal debt. The private sector holds an unchanged volume of federal interest-bearing obligations, but the disappearance of the old issue and the sale of the new one alters relative supplies of debt of different lengths. The mere passage of time shortens the debt in the absence of Treasury action.

The concept of debt management is usually applied to the handling of the maturity structure (and other characteristics) of a public debt of given size. It is thus distinguished from fiscal policy which may involve a change in the magnitude of the public debt over time through surplus or deficit operations. Fiscal actions do have distinct balance-sheet effects which are relevant to the determination of interest rates. If the Treasury markets additional new securities to the private sector with the intention of financing a deficit, the sale immediately raises private holdings of federal interest-bearing securities. It simultaneously lowers, by an equal amount, private holdings of federal demand obligations, since payment for the bonds reduces the volume of Federal Reserve deposits of member banks and currency. As the Treasury spends the proceeds of the borrowings the volume of member bank deposits and currency is restored. Treasury deficit-financing, like a Federal Reserve open-market sale, expands the volume of interest-bearing obligations held by the public. But while the Federal Reserve trades bonds for money, the Treasury, in effect, makes payments to the public with bonds, thus increasing the volume of government liabilities to the private sector. Treasury surplus-financing has opposite effects.

The open-market operations of the Federal Reserve and the debt management operations of the Treasury alter the composition of federal debts to the public. In principle, actions undertaken which have the same balance-sheet effects on the private sector can be viewed as identical whether they are carried out by the Treasury or by the Federal Reserve. The market has little reason to care whether a billion dollars of extra bonds are being offered by the Treasury or the central bank. The market does have every reason to try to anticipate future moves of the Treasury and the Federal Reserve. For this reason, there may be instances where a relatively small move by either agency could be given great significance as a harbinger of future actions. The quantitative effect of any transaction on interest rates may be ultimately dependent on how much it surprises the market and how it alters expectations. However, the effects on expectations are likely to be complicated and to depend on the specific circumstances surrounding each policy decision; they cannot be adequately handled by lumping actions of the Federal Reserve together and separately combining all actions undertaken by the Treasury. Consolidation of the

Federal Reserve and the Treasury appears to be the optimal strategy for evaluating monetary and debt policy.

The combined debts of the Federal Reserve and the Treasury to the public consist of non-interest-bearing demand obligations and interest-bearing dated obligations. The former category consists of cash assets; the components are Treasury and Federal Reserve currency held outside the federal government, and deposits of member banks and others (excluding the Treasury) in Federal Reserve banks. These cash obligations of the government are designated as federal demand debt. Federal demand debt is the foundation of the money supply—the currency items are themselves money, while the deposits in the Federal Reserve are the basis for the creation of demand deposits by the commercial banks. Open-market operations change the supply of demand debt and the supply of interest-bearing debt in opposite directions by equal amounts. Changes in reserve requirements may be viewed as shifting commercial bank demand functions for federal demand debt. Changes in the discount rate alter the price at which commercial banks can directly acquire federal demand debt by borrowing from the Federal Reserve. Treasury debt actions (and Federal Reserve open-market "swaps") alter the maturity composition of federal interest-bearing debt. Treasury surplus or deficit financing acts to alter the volume of federal interest-bearing debt.

The monetary authorities have direct control over the volume of private holdings of interest-bearing federal debt; because of member bank borrowing, they have less complete control over the quantity of demand debt; they have only imperfect and indirect control over the volume of money. The indirect route by which policy actions affect the money supply raises a problem of strategy in the explanation of how these actions influence interest rates. A quantitative explanation of interest rates that employs components of private balance sheets as independent variables does not provide a direct estimate of the way interest rates are affected by particular policy actions. Another quantitative link is needed to relate the private balance sheet items to the variables under policy control. For example, suppose the reduction in interest per billion dollar increase in the money supply is known; then the determination of the effect on interest of open-market purchase of $1 billion requires the further knowledge of how large an increase in the stock of money is induced by the purchase. A two-stage explanation emerges, running from policy action to private liquidity and then from private asset-holdings to interest rates. An alternative approach would seek to consolidate the two steps and relate interest rates to variables directly under public control, ignoring the money supply and other balance sheet items that are not completely controlled by public authority. The choice between these approaches will be discussed below.

THE MULTIPLICITY OF FINANCIAL ASSETS

The existence of a large variety of heterogeneous earning assets constitutes another important difference in reality from the world of the simple Keynesian model. All of the yields reported on the financial pages of the press are candidates for explanation. Presumably their yields are all interdependent and dependent on the supplies of each type of asset. In principle, this difficulty can be met. The liquidity preference function can be generalized into a set of demand curves for financial assets. Cash, bonds of various types, and equities compete for their shares in the portfolios of investors. Some pairs of these alternative securities are clearly close substitutes, and one would expect a change in the supply of one type to have substantial cross-effects on the yield of the other. In general, the demand for any type of asset can be expressed as a function of: (a) income; (b) wealth; (c) its own yield; and (d) the yield of related assets. From such a system, one could determine the yield of each asset from information on the supplies of all assets and the level of income. Similarly, for given changes in the supply of any asset, changes in yields could be estimated for all assets.

While the procedure can be readily described, the empirical formulation and estimation of such a general equilibrium system of financial markets is a huge task. It is far beyond the scope of this chapter. Certainly, everything depends on everything else in financial markets. However, progress can be made by focusing on a small set of key variables. Yields on marketable obligations of the federal government stand out as worthy of particular attention. In dollar volume, federal debt is far greater than any other single type of marketable claim in the postwar American economy. Furthermore, monetary policy deals in federal debts to achieve its objectives. All federal security issues share the exclusive property of being absolutely free of default risk; since the United States Government can print money, it can always meet its legal obligations to redeem matured securities for currency. Interest-bearing marketable claims on the Treasury differ among themselves only by having individual maturity dates. The interest rates on three-month Treasury bills and on long-term federal bonds stand at extreme ends of the maturity spectrum for governments. The principal emphasis of this chapter will be on these two interest rates.

Claims against private borrowers differ in degree of default risk from one another and from Governments. The differential in yield between any one of them and a government obligation of equal maturity will vary as the compensation required for assuming default risk is consistently revalued in financial markets. Despite the varying differentials, it will be shown below that the explanation of government yields accounts for the major portion of the variation in private yields as well.

The simple Keynesian theoretical model suggests that the yields on Governments should be related to the stock of money and the level of income. The general equilibrium view of financial markets suggests that the stocks of all other financial assets should be considered as possible determinants of the interest rates on federal debt. The approach adopted here is an intermediate one. There are strong *a priori* reasons for believing that the size and composition of the federal debt will have considerable influence on Treasury bond and bill yields; these supplies are therefore used as explanatory variables for the selected interest rates. On the other hand, the magnitudes outstanding of particular types of private obligations are excluded. These are potential substitutes for Governments and may well affect the government rate: an autonomous change which doubled the supply of corporate AAA bonds would be expected to raise government long-term yields. However, the volume of private assets is considered in this chapter only by the inclusion of total private wealth as a possible explanatory variable. Thus, income, the supply of money, the volume and composition of federal debt, and total wealth are the tentative explanatory variables for government interest rates. Other possible influences will be discussed subsequently.

INTEREST RATES AND MATURITY

The dependence of long and short rates on the term structure of the federal debt follows from theoretical reasoning. Only if bills and bonds could be viewed as perfect substitutes would their yields be independent of their relative supplies. In a world of perfect foresight, no investment costs, and complete shiftability, the long rate would be purely an average of future short-term rates;[4] arbitrage would guarantee that the two rates could not be affected by changes in the term structure of the public debt. Any modification of these extreme assumptions will, however, provide a role to the composition of debt.

Suppose that foresight is not perfect but that investors are risk-neutral and thus act purely to maximize expected return. Then each investor chooses between long and short securities by balancing the expected return on long bonds against the expected return on bills. If the relevant

---

[4] Friedrich A. Lutz, "The Structure of Interest Rates," *Readings in the Theory of Income Distribution* (Philadelphia: Blakiston, 1946), pp. 499–504; J. R. Hicks, *Value and Capital*, Second Ed. (Oxford: Clarendon, 1953), pp. 141–145; Joseph W. Conard, *An Introduction to the Theory of Interest* (Berkeley: University of California, 1959), pp. 290–301.

period is taken as the three-month lifetime of bills, the expected short yield is certain; it is simply the market interest rate on bills. The expected return on bonds, however, differs from the market interest rate by an expected capital gain on bonds over the three-month interval. People anticipating a rise in the long rate must deduct an expected capital loss in their estimates of the return from long securities. On the other hand, those investors who anticipate a decline in long rates will have expected returns greater than the current market long rate. The equilibrium market differential will then, in general, depend on the relative supplies of longs and shorts. On Figure 1, investors are ordered according to the size of

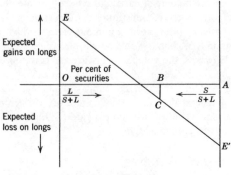

Figure 1

their expected capital gain (or loss) on bonds, expressed as a percentage per year. Those with the largest expected capital gain are farthest to the left; each investor is weighted by the magnitude of his demand for longs and shorts combined. The horizontal axis is scaled as fractions of the total outstanding supply of long plus short securities with the distance OA representing 100 per cent. Given the expected gain curve EE', if the outstanding securities are split into OB per cent of longs and BA per cent of shorts, the equilibrium market long rate must exceed the short rate by BC, just enough to offset the expected capital loss of the marginal long investor. People on the EC portion of the expectation curve will hold longs while those along CE' hold shorts. If the long-term fraction of the total security supply exceeded OB while the EE' curve was unchanged, a larger rate differential would be required. A smaller relative supply of longs would be associated with a smaller excess of the long rate over the short rate. The slope of the EE' curve depends on the extent to which investors differ in their estimates of future long rates. The greater the unanimity of opinion, the smaller the influence of relative supplies on the rate structure. So long as there are different views, even in the world of no risk-aversion and no investment costs, relative supplies do matter.

Once attitudes towards risk and costs of transactions are considered, additional reasons are found for the dependence of rates on relative supplies. At equal expected returns, longs and shorts would not be equally attractive to every investor; furthermore, individual investors might well choose to mix longs and shorts in their portfolios. Because a bill is always close to its maturity date, the price of a short security is unlikely to vary substantially; the bill offers little danger of capital loss and slight hope of capital gain. Capital-value risk is thus small for a bill but large for a long security. To a risk-averting investor, this would be a feature favoring the holding of short-term securities. On the other hand, an investor who continually held short securities would incur large transactions costs as he was forced to reinvest his proceeds each time his short holdings matured; the economy of investment costs favors the holding of long-term securities. Furthermore, each time the investor acquired a new crop of shorts, he would be subject to the whims of the market. At any point in time, he would be assured of the level of his interest income for only a brief interval in the future. The short portfolio has substantial *income risk*.[5] The holder of longs gains assurance of a steady flow of interest income over the long run by sacrificing safety on the market value of his portfolio in the near future. The security-holder who is able to stay with his holdings for a long period is thus encouraged to go into bonds. Hence, long-term securities typically are preponderant in the portfolios of universities and insurance companies. Because of their many differing features, short and long securities should be viewed as imperfect though close substitutes like tea and coffee; they are not well conceived of as perfect substitutes like nickels and dimes. Theoretical reasoning suggests that relative supplies will affect relative yields; only quantitative empirical research can determine how much of an effect will exist.

THE EMPIRICAL FRAMEWORK

The following decisions of strategy emerge from the discussion above:

1. The market yields of Treasury bills and of long-term Government bonds are the two key dependent variables to be investigated.

2. The balance sheets of the Treasury and the Federal Reserve System are to be consolidated; all other economic units are aggregated into a single private sector.

---

[5] Joan Robinson, "The Rate of Interest," *The Rate of Interest and Other Essays* (London: Macmillan, 1952), pp. 5–10.

3. The volume and composition of the interest-bearing federal debt should be treated as possible determinants of the yields on Governments.

4. Measures of income and wealth will also be included as potential explanatory variables.

5. Some measure of money supply is required as an explanatory variable. If the traditional notion of demand deposits plus currency is employed, a further link is needed to relate money to policy variables. Alternatively, use could be made of some measure of money supply directly controlled by public authorities.

Certain of these decisions require further implementation. The volume of federal interest-bearing debt is taken as the dollar maturity value of marketable issues held outside of government agencies and the Federal Reserve. (Savings bonds are thus omitted.) This total is divided into three categories:

S, issues maturing within one year,
I, issues maturing in one to five years, and
L, issues maturing in five years or more.

The classification depends only on the distance of a security to its maturity date at the particular point in time considered. It does not consider the original length-to-maturity of an existing issue. A bond may have a fifteen-year term when it is originally sold by the Treasury, but fourteen years later it is a short-term one-year obligation and presumably will be so evaluated in the market. Call provisions are uniformly ignored; the procedure which takes the term of an issue to run only to its call date when its price exceeds par is rejected because it makes maturity dependent on bond prices.

The principal limitation to this (or any other) categorization procedure is that it produces abrupt changes in the classes at discrete points in time. The aging of bonds is continuous; a bond changes character gradually when it moves toward its maturity date from 61 months away to 60 months and then to 59 months. But these two movements are reflected very differently in the data. As a 60-month issue, the security remains in the long category; at 59 months, it shifts into the intermediate class. A mean maturity variable (T) for the long category is introduced to mitigate this problem. The T variable expresses the mean length to maturity of all obligations with maturity dates 60 or more months away. Thus, when a security falls into the intermediate class with the passage of time, the reduced volume of the L group is potentially offset by the rise in T. Obviously, the mean maturity of the long category is increased by the disappearance of a 60-month issue from that class.

The income variable is designed to reflect private transactions demand for liquidity. Since government needs for cash balances should not be included, there is an argument for omitting government outlays from Gross National Product. However, government purchases from business require transactions balances in the private sector. For this reason, the income variable selected is Gross Private Product (GNP less compensation of government employees). Since state and local governments are part of the "private sector," the logic would argue that only federal compensation to employees should be deducted, but the quarterly data do not permit this distinction to be made.

The wealth variable is Net Private Wealth. It differs from National Wealth by including all government liabilities and excluding all assets of the government. This is the same wealth variable relevant to the Pigou effect; it is sometimes designated Patinkin wealth.[6]

The data employed are quarterly observations for the period 1946 to 1959. All stocks are measured at the end of the quarter. The Bill Rate is taken as the yield on newly-issued Treasury three-month bills during the last month of the quarter; the long rate is the average yield to maturity for the last month of the quarter on a group of long-term Government bonds due in more than ten years. The bonds included in the long-term rate index change occasionally, and the maturity length of the sample covered is not held constant; however, since all the components of the sample are very long issues, the variation in maturity does not seem important.

The functional forms by which interest rates are explained are all linear. There are strong reasons to believe that non-linearities will exist; the Keynesian liquidity preference function is usually drawn convex to the origin. It seemed that the most convenient way to introduce non-linearity was to transform the dependent variable from r to the reciprocal of r or to $(r + \text{constant})^{-1}$. The independent variables would then remain in linear form. However, experimentation with such transformations of the interest variables produced discouraging results and led to the decision to restrict the regression equation to linear forms. Thus, the equations explaining the long rate (r) and the bill rate (b) take the following form:

$$r(\text{or } b) = a_0 + a_1 \cdot \text{Money} + a_2 \cdot S + a_3 I + a_4 L + a_5 T + a_6 Y + a_7 W \tag{1}$$

An alternative approach assumes that interest rates are homogeneous of degree zero in all stocks and income: a doubling of income, wealth,

---

[6] James Tobin, "Asset Holdings and Spending Decisions," *American Economic Review*, XLII (May 1952), pp. 110–120.

all types of federal debt, and money would be expected to leave rates unaffected. This hypothesis leads to equations of the following type:

$$r(\text{or } b) = c_0 + c_1 \frac{\text{Money}}{Y} + c_2 \frac{S}{Y} + c_3 \frac{I}{Y} + c_4 \frac{L}{Y} + c_5 T + c_6 \frac{W}{Y} \quad (2)$$

The variables S, I, and L are the three categories of federal debt, while T is the maturity variable; Y and W represent income and wealth, as defined above. The money variable has not yet been defined. An obvious choice is the conventional definition of money, namely demand deposits adjusted plus currency outside of banks. An alternative choice was suggested by Gurley's study of liquidity in the postwar period.[7] There, Gurley explains interest rates by the volume of all liquid assets, appropriately weighted, in relationship to income. He argues that the demand for money may be reduced by expansion of the supply of non-monetary liquid assets; therefore the traditional liquidity preference function should be generalized to include money-substitutes. Interest rates are determined by the supply of liquidity relative to income, as in the original Keynesian view; but, according to Gurley, liquidity must be measured as a weighted total of all liquid assets, not merely media of exchange. The resulting view of the liquidity function is that the rate of interest depends on the volume of all liquid assets, appropriately weighted in relation to the level of income.

Liquid assets are defined as "claims held by nonfinancial sectors of the economy that are ... fixed in price and redeemable into money on demand."[8] Gurley adopts a weight for all non-monetary liquid assets (N) equal to one-half the weight for money (M'), where money is given its usual meaning of adjusted demand deposits plus currency. The measure of aggregate liquidity is thus $Q = (M' + N/2)$, and the aggregate liquidity-income ratio is taken as the ratio of Q to Gross National Product (Y_g). Gurley's empirical support for his thesis rests on the close negative relationship found between Q/Y_g and the interest rate in annual postwar United States data. The relationship holds for both the yield on corporate BAA bonds and the prime commercial paper rate.

Empirical explorations with the Gurley liquidity ratio were disappointing, however. In the quarterly data for 1946 to 1959, the ratio of money to income (M'/Y_g) provides a better explanation of both the long government rate and the Bill Rate than the ratio Q/Y_g. The addition of one-half

---

[7] John G. Gurley, "Liquidity and Financial Institutions in the Postwar Economy," *Study of Employment, Growth, and the Price Levels*, prepared for the U.S. Congress, Joint Economic Committee (Washington: U.S. Government Printing Office, 1960).
[8] *Ibid.*, p. 3.

the volume of non-monetary liquid assets worsens the fit. Calculated results for the long rate are:

$$r = \frac{-5.3Q}{Y_g} + 6.4; \qquad R^2 = .56 \qquad (3)$$

$$r = \frac{-7.4M'}{Y_g} + 5.5; \qquad R^2 = .66 \qquad (4)$$

For the short rate, the findings are:

$$b = \frac{-9.6Q}{Y_g} + 8.3; \qquad R^2 = .60 \qquad (5)$$

$$b = \frac{-12.7M'}{Y_g} + 6.4; \qquad R^2 = .62 \qquad (6)$$

When the ratio of non-monetary liquid assets to income (N/Y_g) is used as a second independent variable with M'/Y_g to explain r and b, positive coefficients surprisingly emerge for N/Y_g: the implication is that, for any given M'/Y_g, interest rates will be higher for higher N/Y_g. There is no obvious reason why an expansion of non-monetary liquid assets should raise interest rates. It could mean that N responds to the strength of demand for money—money-substitutes increase in volume when liquidity preference is particularly strong. Alternatively, it might be a spurious result; the positive coefficient is statistically significant only in the equation for r. In any case, these data give no support to the view that the rapid postwar growth of non-monetary liquid assets has held down interest rates. On these grounds, the volume of nonmonetary liquid assets was discarded as a potential explanatory variable.

In addition to the conventional definition of money, consideration was given to other candidates for the money variable that are more directly controlled by public policy. The discussion above enumerated the various possible slippages between a central bank action and the resulting change in the supply of money. There is only one open link in the Federal Reserve's control over the volume of demand debt; that lies in possible changes in member bank borrowing from the Federal Reserve. Subject to its ability to offset autonomous fluctuations in borrowings, the monetary authority can regulate the volume of federal demand debt. On these grounds, one can take the volume of demand debt (M) in relation to the required reserve ratio (R) as a measure of the money supply permitted by the central bank. If there were no currency and no excess reserves and if all demand debt were utilized to back demand deposits of the private sector, the money supply would be M/R. This volume of money is a *maximum maximorum* relative to the government balance sheet. The actual supply will never reach M/R, but that magnitude can serve as one measure of potential money. Furthermore, if given fractions of demand debt were absorbed by excess reserves, currency, foreign deposits in the Federal Reserve, and backing against time deposits, it could still be argued that fluctuations in M/R were associated with proportionate changes in the volume of demand deposits. The M/R variable would be a good gauge of the conditions under which the monetary authority allowed commercial banks to create demand deposits for their customers.

The data suggest that currency has absorbed a variable proportion of demand debt over time in the postwar period. On these grounds, it may be preferable to view the demand for currency as exogenous, and to treat $(M - C)/R$ as potential demand deposits. Here, the actual volume of currency (rather than a zero volume) is taken as a benchmark; potential demand deposits are viewed as the portion of demand debt which is not absorbed in currency divided by the required reserve ratio. The concept of potential money which then emerges is the sum of potential demand deposits plus actual currency or $[(M - C)/R + C]$. Here, currency includes holdings of commercial banks since these absorb federal demand debt. In measuring M', currency in commercial banks is excluded.

Results are reported below with the money variable defined in three ways:

1. Currency plus demand deposits, i.e., the actual stock of money;
2. Demand debt divided by the required reserve ratio, i.e., maximum potential money;
3. Potential deposits plus actual currency, where potential deposits equal demand debt exclusive of currency divided by the required reserve ratio.

It was pointed out above that income could reasonably be treated as a separate independent variable, as in equation 1; or as a divisor of all the stock variables, as in equation 2. Empirical findings strongly suggest the use of the separate treatment. When the divided-through form was used, the reciprocal of income was highly significant statistically as an additional variable, carrying a negative coefficient. This led to the rejection of the homogeneity hypothesis. It implies that a doubling of income and of all stocks will affect interest rates; they are raised by this event. It is not clear why this should be the case—if anything, economies of scale in the handling of cash-balances lead to the possibility that rates would be reduced by an equiproportionate increase in income and all assets. The empirical results here imply the opposite behavior of interest rates. The assumption of homogeneity does not stand up empirically, and equation 2 is therefore the form adopted. An alternative possibility involves using the divided form, as in equation 1, with the addition of another independent variable, $1/Y$. While this form differs from equation 2 only slightly, it does not fit so well.

Further empirical experimentation showed that the wealth variable produced insignificant results. It was expected that the coefficient of wealth would be negative; larger wealth totals for given supplies of money and Government securities mean that claims on the federal government are a smaller fraction of private net worth. As such, a lower yield should be required to induce the holding of this volume of government debt. In general, the expanded size of portfolios has a wealth effect which should raise the demand for Governments and thus reduce their yield. The wealth variable, however, offered no assistance whatsoever in explaining the long rate. It did consistently have a negative coefficient in various formulations explaining the Bill Rate, but the coefficient was never as large as twice its standard error. Because it could not meet conventional criteria for statistical significance, the wealth variable was dropped. Theoretically, it is a relevant variable. Its failure may be attributable to a number of factors. Wealth is highly correlated with income, for one thing. Secondly, the empirical formulation does not consider the changing composition of wealth, which may overshadow the growth of the total.

The three-way categorization of federal interest-bearing marketable debt (S, I, and L) also ran into difficulties. The coefficient of I (one- to five-year intermediate-term issues) proved quite unstable with respect to the choices of functional form and auxiliary variables. In certain cases, it exceeded substantially the coefficients of both S and L; in others, it was the smallest of the three by far. Much more reasonable and more stable results were obtained when I was combined with S to form just two categories of federal debt: $(S + I)$ represents those issues maturing within five years, and L is the category of those having five or more years to run. The judgment was therefore made to present all results in terms of this two-way classification.

Because of varying seasonal demands for liquidity combined with stock variables that are not seasonally adjusted, suspicion arose that a seasonal factor would distort the regression equations. Tests showed that this suspicion was well-founded in the case of the Bill Rate, but not for the long rate. Consequently, a quarterly seasonal dummy variable was inserted into all equations explaining the Bill Rate. In effect, there is a separate intercept for each quarter of the year. In the first quarter, $Q_1 = 1$ while Q_2 and Q_3 are set equal to zero. In the second quarter, Q_2 alone has a unity value. In the fourth quarter, Q_1, Q_2, and Q_3 are all equal to zero.

It was repeatedly found that T, the mean maturity of long debt, was not significant in explaining b although it was typically a significant explanatory variable for r. It is not surprising that a change in the age composition of long-term Government bonds will affect the yield of a given long-term issue but will not noticeably influence the Bill Rate. On these grounds, T was retained in the r equations but dropped from the b equations.

EMPIRICAL RESULTS

At last, fitted equations are given in Table 1; there are three pairs, using the alternative "money" variables. The actual money supply (M') is the least successful in explaining the Bill Rate by a wide margin. The coefficient of determination in equation 10 is .819, in contrast with .899 and .904 for equations 11 and 12, respectively. M' is not significant in explaining r, even though equation 7 nearly matches equations 8 and 9 in terms of R^2. The goodness of fit criterion offers no grounds for choosing between the two potential money variables: maximum potential money is superior by a slight margin in explaining the long rate, while potential demand deposits plus actual currency wins by an equally small margin in the Bill Rate equation. The standard errors of estimate (σ_u) are about one-third of 1 percentage point for the Bill Rate and only half as large for the long-term interest rate. The coefficient of determination is higher for the long rate; the variance of r is smaller and a larger percentage of that variance is explained by the selected independent variables.

As expected, the coefficients of $(S + I)$, L, T, and Y are positive, and each of the money variables has a negative coefficient. The quarterly dummy variables in the b equations indicate that the Bill Rate would rise substantially in the third and fourth quarters if additional cash was not provided to meet seasonal demands for greater liquidity. This is reasonable, and corresponds with the adjustment factors used to eliminate seasonality from official time-series for currency.

Surprisingly, the coefficient of $(S + I)$ exceeds that of L in each of the r equations; this means that an increase in the supply of long-term debt would raise the long rate by less than an equal increase in the supply of bills or other short-term securities. The difference between these coefficients is trivial—both by statistical criteria and in terms of the magnitudes of economic effects. An increase of $1 billion in the supply of long-term securities (with average maturity for the L category) coupled with a decrease of $1 billion of shorts produces an estimated decline of 0.002 or 0.003 percentage points in the yield on long-term bonds. The calculated effect is miniscule and its direction cannot be taken seriously.

Table 1 Alternative Equations Explaining Bond and Bill Yields

Equation	Dependent Variable	Type of Money Variable	"Money"	$S + I$	L	T	Y	Constant	Q_1	Q_2	Q_3	R^2	σ_u
7	r	M'	−0.0072 (0.0084)	+0.0159 (0.0040)	+0.0138 (0.0023)	+0.0047 (0.0028)	+0.0091 (0.0016)	−1.92 (1.14)	—	—	—	.929	0.158
8	r	$\dfrac{M}{R}$	−0.0066 (0.0021)	+0.0219 (0.0042)	+0.0197 (0.0029)	+0.0046 (0.0023)	+0.0105 (0.0014)	−2.21 (0.69)	—	—	—	.935	0.152
9	r	$\dfrac{M-C}{R} + C$	−0.0127 (0.0058)	+0.0168 (0.0037)	+0.0141 (0.0022)	+0.0045 (0.0024)	+0.0096 (0.0014)	−1.31 (0.95)	—	—	—	.929	0.158
10	b	M'	−0.0976 (0.0483)	+0.0217 (0.0115)	+0.0139 (0.0070)	—	+0.0252 (0.0068)	−3.93 (5.49)	−0.83 (0.34)	−0.76 (0.31)	−0.49 (0.28)	.819	0.459
11	b	$\dfrac{M}{R}$	−0.0370 (0.0051)	+0.0576 (0.0074)	+0.0410 (0.0068)	—	+0.0227 (0.0025)	−1.57 (0.65)	−0.62 (0.14)	−0.47 (0.13)	−0.21 (0.13)	.899	0.340
12	b	$\dfrac{M-C}{R} + C$	−0.1067 (0.0139)	+0.0287 (0.0066)	+0.0128 (0.0045)	—	+0.0241 (0.0025)	+6.37 (1.31)	−0.80 (0.15)	−0.72 (0.14)	−0.35 (0.13)	.904	0.331

The result is further qualified by the positive coefficient on the maturity variable, T; a lengthening of the federal debt is estimated to increase the long rate insofar as it raises the mean maturity of issues with more than five years to run. Thus, a sale of 10-year bonds by the Federal Reserve coupled with a purchase of an equal volume of 20-year bonds has an estimated positive influence on r. If this is the case, surely a sale of bills accompanied by a purchase of 10-year bonds should have a similar effect. Perhaps, in retrospect, the inclusion of a mean maturity variable for short and intermediate securities would have helped to isolate this effect. Despite all these necessary qualifications, a principal conclusion of this study is that the long rate is relatively insensitive to changes in the maturity composition of the public debt. This finding, discussed in detail below, emerged consistently with a variety of functional forms and alternative sets of independent variables that were used to explain bond yields.

Standard errors of the coefficients in Table 1 are shown in parentheses below the estimated coefficients; as presented, most of the estimates differ significantly from zero at the 1 per cent level. However, many possible variables—like wealth—were discarded when they did not pass standard tests of statistical significance. Since statistical significance was one of the criteria employed in the selection of explanatory variables, it is hardly surprising that most of the survivors passed this test. The "mining" of the data through experimentation detracts from the statistical evaluation of the results. This is no catastrophe, however, since the study is designed to develop optimal point estimates rather than to test hypotheses.

Further attempts were made to refine the results shown in Table 1. A number of lagged stock variables and first differences in stocks were tested as possible additional explanatory variables. The use of end-of-quarter stocks in the equations of Table 1 implies that the bond market adjusts immediately and completely to the supplies which are offered to the public. On the other hand, in most qualitative discussions of the behavior of interest rates, the bond market is viewed as imperfect by financial experts.

References to the "thinness" of the bond market imply that a large increase in the supplies of securities will raise yields sharply in the process of being absorbed by bond-holders. An "overshoot" theory of interest rate determination emerges; a given new issue will raise yields initially by more than will be maintained when the issue is safely committed to portfolios. Indeed, if investors are exceedingly reluctant to trade securities and concentrate mainly on the allocation of new cash-inflow in their investment decisions, the flow of net new issues—rather than the total existing stock—would be the principal determinant of interest rates. To the extent that there is general reluctance to review portfolios or to engage in trading because of transactions costs, net new issues would be expected to influence yields.

In this event, changes in stocks of securities should bear positive coefficients when they are inserted into the equations of Table 1 as additional independent variables. In fact, quarterly changes in the volume of federal long debt (ΔL) and other debt [$\Delta(S + I)$] are not significant in explaining either r or b. These are not ideal variables; they record changes in $(S + I)$ and L due to certain issues crossing the 60-month dividing line between maturity categories as equivalent to changes attributable to open-market operations, Treasury new issues, and maturing securities. As an alternative, gross new issues of Governments by the Treasury was tried with a similar lack of success. Nor did the inclusion of new corporate issues with the new Governments improve the results. Gross new issues also is a faulty variable; it omits open-market actions and ignores the volume of maturing securities. Still, the consistency of negative findings with the various flow variables is striking.

It would be most rash to conclude that the bond market is and has been sufficiently perfect in the postwar era to make "thinness" a myth. A more reasonable view is that the imperfection of the market is not evident in the data because the monetary authorities have confined themselves to rather modest quarterly flows of net new issues and net acquisitions in the open market. The Federal Reserve and the Treasury have kept their net transactions in any quarterly period small relative to the size of the outstanding public debt. Partly because the monetary authorities subscribe to an overshoot theory of the bond market, no large sudden shifts are observed in the volume of federal debt. If larger shifts occurred, perhaps evidence of thinness would emerge. In private discussion of these findings, my colleague Henry Wallich suggested the following analogy. The monetary authorities have consistently viewed the bond market as thin ice and they have therefore skated with great care. According to the data, they have never fallen through the ice. Yet, it cannot be justifiably concluded that the ice is solid and the caution gratuitous.

Pressing the skating analogy a bit further, one does not even find evidence that the ice cracked or showed any warning signs in the postwar period. Perhaps, therefore, the skaters could afford to display more boldness while watching carefully for indications of danger. If, however, the ice of the bond market would suddenly break under the rash skater with no warning, any counsel of relaxed caution would be misguided.

Other experiments with the equations of Table 1 were directed toward the incorporation of cyclical influences. Suppose that the levels of Gross Private Product were identical in two quarters five years apart and that the combined Treasury-Federal Reserve balance sheets were also identical for these two periods. Each of the equations presented in Table 1 would estimate identical values of *r* (or of *b*) for these two quarters. Obviously, however, the later period would be marked by depressed economic activity and widespread unemployment. With continued secular advances in productivity and the labor force, constant output would be associated with increasing slack over time. On *a priori* grounds, one might well believe that interest rates on Government securities would be lower in the later, depressed period because unfavorable expectations and slump psychology would raise demands for relatively safe assets. Such a possible effect could be investigated if secular and cyclical changes in income are distinguished.

This distinction was most successfully accomplished by the inclusion of a variable reflecting the full-employment level of output in addition to the actual output variable. If full employment is taken to mean a 4 per cent rate of unemployment, the potential level of GNP at full utilization can be estimated through an adjustment of actual GNP for any excess or shortfall of the unemployment rate from 4 per cent. Each percentage point difference in unemployment is associated with a much more than proportionate difference in GNP because hours worked per man, the size of the labor force, and man-hour productivity all vary with the level of resource utilization. Statistical analysis, recently conducted by the Council of Economic Advisers, suggests that on the average, a 3.2 per cent increment in GNP accompanies a 1 percentage point decrement in the unemployment rate.[9] This yields the following estimate of potential GNP (*P*):

$$P = \text{actual GNP} \cdot [1 + 0.032 \ (\text{actual unemployment percentage} - 4)].$$

When both actual and potential output variables are included, the potential variable reflects secular forces, leaving the actual variable free to register cyclical factors. For any given potential output, actual Gross Private Product shows the strength of private demand in the economy.[10]

Table 2 shows the results obtained when *P* is added to the independent variables of equations 8, 9, 11, and 12. These were the equations of Table 1 that used M/R and $[(M - C)/R + C]$ as money variables. The coefficients of *P* are all negative as hypothesized; for given *Y*, the more

---

[9] Council of Economic Advisers, "The American Economy in 1961: Problems and Policies," *Hearings on the January 1961 Economic Report of the President*, Joint Economic Committee (Washington: U.S. Government Printing Office, 1961), pp. 327–329, 373–377.

[10] There is a possible objection to the inclusion of government payrolls in the potential variable when it is excluded from actual *Y*, but the alternative of constructing a concept of potential Gross Private Product seemed even less appealing.

Table 2 Alternative Equations Explaining Bond and Bill Yields with Inclusion of Potential GNP

Rate	Money Variable	Coefficients											
		"Money"	$S + I$	L	T	Y	P	Constant	Q_1	Q_2	Q_3	R^2	σ_u
Eq. 13 r	$\dfrac{M}{R}$	−0.0051 (0.0027)	+0.0223 (0.0042)	+0.0192 (0.0030)	+0.0046 (0.0023)	+0.0119 (0.0022)	−0.0018 (0.0021)	−2.41 (0.73)	—	—	—	.936	0.152
Eq. 14 r	$\dfrac{M-C}{R}+C$	−0.0080 (0.0064)	+0.0195 (0.0040)	+0.0153 (0.0023)	+0.0045 (0.0024)	+0.0045 (0.0022)	−0.0032 (0.0019)	−1.99 (1.02)	—	—	—	.933	0.155
Eq. 15 b	$\dfrac{M}{R}$	−0.0218 (0.0064)	+0.0601 (0.0069)	+0.0342 (0.0066)	—	+0.0345 (0.0042)	−0.0161 (0.0048)	−3.65 (0.85)	−0.43 (0.14)	−0.31 (0.13)	−0.09 (0.13)	.916	0.313
Eq. 16 b	$\dfrac{M-C}{R}+C$	−0.0705 (0.0152)	+0.0431 (0.0064)	+0.0181 (0.0041)	—	+0.0363 (0.0038)	−0.0160 (0.0040)	+1.69 (1.65)	−0.58 (0.14)	−0.50 (0.14)	−0.21 (0.12)	.928	0.289

slack in the economy, the lower interest rates will be. In equations 15 and 16, P is significantly negative. The coefficient of determination of .916 in equation 15 may be compared with the .899 for equation 11, which is identical in all respects except for the inclusion of P. The R^2 of .928 for equation 16 similarly corresponds to a value of .904 for equation 12. The explanation of b is substantially improved by the inclusion of P.

The explanation of r is, in contrast, assisted only slightly by the P variable. The estimated coefficients of P in equations 13 and 14 do not differ significantly from zero, although the decision is a close one in equation 14. The rise in R^2 over the corresponding equations of Table 1 is trivial. On empirical grounds, P has fully earned a place in the b equations but not in the r equations. Yet, from analytical reasoning, the cyclical effect should emerge in long as well as short yields.

The coefficient of Y is increased by the inclusion of P. This is a plausible finding; a rise in Y now represents purely a cyclical increase at a point in time with a greater impact on expectations. However, the estimated coefficients of the money variables are uniformly lowered in absolute value by the inclusion of P and this is a less plausible finding. In particular, the money coefficients in both r equations are no longer statistically significant, in contrast with the results in Table 1. No analytical support can be invoked to explain why the inclusion of P should reduce the estimated effect of a change in demand debt on the long rate.

These considerations leave doubt as to whether the equations of Table 1 or those of Table 2 should be accepted as the basic estimates. My judgment calls for a sacrifice of symmetry in following the empirical results by employing equations 15 and 16, which include P, for b, and using equations 8 and 9, excluding P, for r.

The cyclical-secular distinction was also aimed at eliminating the significantly positive serial correlation of residuals that occurred for the equations of Table 1. That objective was not achieved; positive autocorrelation remains in the equations of Table 2. If r (or b) is above the value estimated by the equation in one quarter, it is likely to exceed its calculated value again in the next quarter. The serial correlation coefficients run in the neighborhood of one-half. Also, there is positive covariance of the r and b residuals; when the long rate is above its estimated value, the Bill Rate also tends to have a positive error.

Nevertheless, the equations trace the cyclical patterns of interest rates quite well over the period of observation. Table 3 shows the actual and estimated movements during selected periods of recession and expansion. The estimated changes are based on equations 9 and 16, which use $[(M - C)/R + C]$ as the money variable. The estimated changes are

Table 3 Changes in Interest Rates for Selected Periods: Actual and Estimated

	Actual Change	Estimated Change	Estimated Changes Attributed To		
			"Money" $\frac{M - C}{R} + C$	Publicly Held Marketable Debt (S, I, L, T)	Aggregate Economic Activity (Y, P)
Recession periods					
Short rates (b):					
53-II to 54-II	−1.58	−1.55	−0.54	−0.19	−0.82
57-II to 58-II	−2.43	−1.94	−0.98	−0.02	−0.94
Long rates (r):					
53-II to 54-II	−0.58	−0.29	−0.10	−0.09	−0.10
57-II to 58-II	−0.39	−0.25	−0.18	+0.03	−0.10
Expansion periods					
Short rates (b):					
54-II to 55-II	+0.88	+0.98	−0.05	+0.14	+0.89
54-II to 57-II	+2.69	+2.20	−0.22	+0.69	+1.73
58-II to 59-II	+2.37	+2.58	+0.49	+0.79	+1.30
Long rates (r):					
54-II to 55-II	+0.27	+0.39	−0.01	+0.09	+0.31
54-II to 57-II	+1.03	+0.92	−0.04	+0.21	+0.75
58-II to 59-II	+0.90	+0.79	+0.09	+0.24	+0.46

divided into three categories: those resulting from changes in the money variable; those attributable to changes in the volume and structure of publicly held marketable debt; and those stemming from changes in actual output and, for the case of b, in potential output. The only weak spot in these estimates is the underestimate of the decline in r during recessions, and, even there, the order of magnitude is not out of line.[11]

In the two periods of recession, income changes accounted for roughly half the estimated decline in rates. The other half is attributable to changes in the money variable and in the structure and volume of marketable debt—in this sense, policy accomplished about half of the estimated reductions in yields. Most of the increase in rates during the 1954 to 1957 expansion is attributable to the rise in aggregate activity, but changes in money and public debt also pushed rates upward, especially after mid-1955. In 1958 and 1959, the money and debt variables subject to policy control accounted for a substantial part of the rise in rates. In this sense, policy was actively—not just passively—tight.

ESTIMATED EFFECTS OF POLICY

The equations set forth above provide estimates of the effects on interest rates of hypothetical policy actions that might be undertaken by the monetary authorities. Table 4 presents these estimates for six actions and for a change in Y. For certain of the actions, the estimated changes in rates depend on the initial values of some of the variables. Therefore, a benchmark period must be adopted for specific calculations. The fourth quarter of 1959 was selected, and values of the relevant variables in that quarter are shown in the table. The effects are estimated with the assumptions that income, currency-holdings in the private sector, and member-bank borrowings are constant, i.e., that they are not altered by the policy action. These restrictions will be relaxed subsequently. In the last example, the change in Y is supposed to occur instantaneously and to be independent of any action of the Treasury or Federal Reserve.

Two sets of estimates for each rate are shown in Table 3, corresponding to the two money variables M/R and $[(M - C)/R + C]$. The estimates for r are based on equations 8 and 9 of Table 1; those for b rely on equations 15 and 16 of Table 2, including the potential GNP variable. Open-market sales or "swaps" can also be interpreted as Treasury new issues or refundings. Changes in reserve requirements are shown separately for increases and decreases, since the legal reserve ratio enters the equations nonlinearly. In all other cases, a reversal of the action (e.g., from sale

---

[11] A few sample calculations suggest that the equations were much less successful in tracing the cyclical movements of rates during 1960 and 1961.

Table 4 Estimated Effects on r and b of Hypothetical Policy Actions (Percentage-Point Change)

Example	Estimated Change in r		Estimated Change in b	
	Equation 8 (M/R)	Equation 9 $\left(\dfrac{M-C}{R}+C\right)$	Equation 15 (M/R)	Equation 16 $\left(\dfrac{M-C}{R}+C\right)$
A—An open market sale of $1 billion of bills, notes, or other short-term issues	+0.064	+0.099	+0.202	+0.501
B—An open market sale of $1 billion of 20-year bonds	+0.073	+0.106	+0.176	+0.476
C—A rise in reserve requirements by one percentage point	+0.135	+0.096	+0.447	+0.537
D—A decline in reserve requirements by one percentage point	−0.154	−0.110	−0.509	−0.610
E—Retirement of $1 billion of 5-year bonds and simultaneous issue of $1 billion of 20-year bonds	+0.020	+0.019	0	0
F—Retirement of $1 billion of bills or certificates and simultaneous issue of $1 billion of 20-year bonds	+0.010	+0.007	−0.026	−0.026
G—A rise in Y of $1 billion	+0.010	+0.010	+0.034	+0.036

Variables in 1959-IV: $M = 51.8$; $C = 32.6$; $R = 0.154$; $L = 42.3$; $T = 150.5$.

to purchase) simply changes the sign of the estimated effect without altering its magnitude.

A sample calculation is offered herewith for any reader who might wish to roll his own. Consider the effect on b of a $1 billion open-market sale of shorts, as estimated by equation 16. The sale raises outstanding $(S + I)$ by $1 billion and lowers M by $1 billion. The estimated effect of the $\Delta(S + I)$ is 0.0431 percentage points, applying the coefficient of $(S + I)$. The ΔM must be divided by the required reserve ratio, 0.154, to get the decline in $[(M - C)/R + C]$. Then that figure, -6.494, multiplied by the relevant coefficient, -0.0705, has a product of $+0.4578$. The 0.501 figure shown in the table is the sum of 0.0431 and 0.4578.

One obvious matter of interest is the consistency of the two sets of estimates for each rate, based on the alternative money variables. These are distressingly far apart for the effects of open-market actions on the Bill Rate. A sale of \$1 billion of bills (Example A) is expected to raise the bill yield by 20 basis points according to equation 15, while 50 basis points is the estimate from equation 16. On the other hand, the two estimates of the effects on r resulting from open-market sales are fairly close together and so are the pairs of estimated effects due to changes in reserve requirements.

Intuitive feelings about the magnitude of effects on rates are so rare and so weak that it is difficult to get a subjective judgment on the plausibility of these estimates. A few economists have told me that the estimated effects of monetary actions on the long rate seem surprisingly small to them.[12] To achieve a decline in r of 1 percentage point, the Federal Reserve would have to buy an estimated \$9 billion of bonds according to equation 9, and nearly \$14 billion according to equation 8. Alternatively, reserve requirements would have to be cut by some 6 percentage points to attain the same objective. The estimated elasticity of r with respect to potential demand deposits and currency (as of the end of 1959) was under one-half, which does seem small. In contrast, the estimated elasticity of r with respect to Y was slightly greater than unity.

The much greater volatility of short-term rates is clearly reflected in the estimates. Changes in reserve requirements and open-market sales are expected to have three to five times as much effect on bill yields as on long-term yields. The short rate can be altered by 1 percentage point through a 2-point change in reserve requirements, for example. According to equation 16, the elasticity of b with respect to the money variable was more than two, while its income-elasticity exceeded three.

Comparison of Examples A and B reveals that an open-market sale of very long securities has an estimated effect on r only about 10 per cent greater than an equal sale of bills. Similarly, sales of shorts affect b only slightly more than do equal sales of bonds. As a result, the estimated changes in the cases of trades (Examples E and F) are uniformly small. Since T was not included in the b equations, a change in the maturity composition of the long category has a zero estimated effect on the Bill Rate. A comparison of Examples E and F for the long rate reveals incredible results, which occur because the coefficients of $(S + I)$ were

---

[12] Arthur Broida of the Board of Governors of the Federal Reserve System offered helpful comments and criticisms on these matters.

slightly greater than those of L in the r equations. Certainly no one can believe that the long rate is increased to a greater extent when very long securities are sold to acquire five-year bonds than when the very longs are traded in exchange for bills. The important conclusion is that both examples have small effects. Example G shows that income changes lead to an estimated Δb that is over three times the corresponding Δr. When Examples A and F are compared, it appears that an open-market purchase of bills of $100 to $160 million is required to hold r constant when Y rises $1 billion. The corresponding estimates for holding b constant in that event is $70 to $170 million.

The results of Table 4 reveal the limitations of a linear function. Since the estimated effect of an open-market purchase of bills is simply proportional to the volume of the purchase, large purchases could have estimated effects which would turn rates negative.

Interest rates influence the level of income and yet here Y is treated as an exogenous variable. As a result, the estimated regression coefficients are biased. To remove the bias would require the construction and estimation of a complete aggregative econometric model, a task which is obviously beyond the scope of this chapter.

Thus far, member bank borrowings have been taken as constant regardless of monetary policy. However, suppose the Bill Rate rises as a result of sales of securities by the monetary authorities. If the discount rate was unchanged, there would be increased incentive for borrowing by member banks. Any increase in borrowing would raise federal demand debt and thereby modify the increase in rates. The net effect of a sale on demand debt would then be less than the amount of the sale. The quarterly data for 1946 to 1959 confirm the hypothesis that member bank borrowings (B) are positively related to the Bill Rate and negatively related to the discount rate (d):

$$B = 0.188 + 0.487b - 0.306d; \qquad R^2 = .535 \qquad (17)$$
$$(0.118) \quad (0.120) \quad (0.152) \qquad \sigma_u = 0.249$$

Borrowings rise by an estimated $487 million for each percentage point increase in b, with d constant.

This result can be used to adjust the estimates shown in Table 4. Since additions to B are increases in M, the amount by which b is altered by a unit change in M (denoted as a_M) is also the effect on b of a unit change in B. So Δb^* (adjusted for changes in B) will differ from Δb, as shown in Table 4, by $a_M \Delta B$; $\Delta b^* = \Delta b + a_M \Delta B$. In turn, from equation 17, ΔB is estimated as 0.487 times the true (or adjusted) Δb^*. Therefore,

$$\Delta b^* = \frac{\Delta b}{1 - 0.487 a_M} \qquad (18)$$

With the legal reserve ratio equal to 0.154, the value of a_M derived from equation 15 is -0.142 (or $-0.1218/0.154$), while equation 16 gives a value of a_M of -0.458. The final conclusion is that, for estimates based on equation 15, $\Delta b^* = 0.935\,\Delta b$; while, for those derived from equation 16, $\Delta b^* = 0.818\,\Delta b$. Induced borrowing by member banks acts as a stabilizer on interest rates. According to the equation which uses $[(M - C)/R + C]$ as the money variable, they are a rather important influence, curtailing changes in the Bill Rate by nearly one-fifth. The M/R equation attributes much less influence to the induced change in borrowings.

By the same reasoning, a correction for the estimates of Δr is required. Even though borrowings are assumed to depend solely on short rates, any change in B affects r. The adjusted change in r (Δr^*) from any event is:

$$\Delta r^* = \Delta r + 0.487 a_M' \,\Delta b^*, \tag{19}$$

where Δr is the estimate made on the assumption of constant B; a_M' is the estimated effect of a unit ΔM on r; and Δb^* is the adjusted change in the Bill Rate due to the event in question. The estimated adjustment from equation 8 is:

$$\Delta r^* = \Delta r - 0.021\,\Delta b^*. \tag{19a}$$

The adjustment from equation 9 is:

$$\Delta r^* = \Delta r - 0.040\,\Delta b^*. \tag{19b}$$

One further adjustment is in order for the estimated effects of a change in Y from equations employing $[(M - C)/R + C]$ as the money variable. To the extent that the demand for currency may be viewed as a pure transactions demand, it is reasonable to take C as independent of interest rates, but it cannot be independent of Y. By raising transactions demand for money, an increase in Y should expand C. In fact, the data confirm this hypothesis:

$$C = 23.68 + 0.0185\,Y; \qquad R^2 = .774; \qquad \sigma_u = 0.753 \tag{20}$$
$$(4.40) \quad (0.0014)$$

The expansion in C, in turn, has a multiplied effect in reducing potential demand deposits and therefore lowers $[(M - C)/R + C]$ for given M. It should reinforce the effect of an increase of Y in raising interest rates. However, the income-effect on C, while highly significant in statistical terms, is very small—less than \$20 million per \$1 billion increase in Y. Hence, this adjustment makes very little difference in the estimated effect of a change in Y.

Table 5 repeats the examples of Table 4 with the estimates adjusted for changes in borrowings and currency. Except for reducing somewhat the

Table 5 Estimated Effects on r and b of Hypothetical Policy Actions—Adjusted for Estimated Changes in Borrowings and Currency (Percentage-Point Change)

Example	Estimated Change in r		Estimated Change in b	
	Equation 8	Equation 9	Equation 15	Equation 16
A—An open market sale of $1 billion of bills, notes, or other short-term issues	+0.060	+0.083	+0.189	+0.410
B—An open market sale of $1 billion of 20-year bonds	+0.070	+0.090	+0.165	+0.389
C—A rise in reserve requirements by one percentage point	+0.126	+0.088	+0.418	+0.439
D—A decline in reserve requirements by one percentage point	−0.144	−0.090	−0.476	−0.499
E—Retirement of $1 billion of 5-year bonds and simultaneous issue of $1 billion of 20-year bonds	+0.020	+0.019	0	0
F—Retirement of $1 billion of bills or certificates and simultaneous issue of $1 billion of 20-year bonds	+0.010	+0.007	−0.024	−0.021
G—A rise in Y of $1 billion	+0.010	+0.010	+0.032	+0.030
H—A rise in the discount rate by one percentage point	+0.013	+0.025	+0.043	+0.140

wide gap between the alternative estimates of Δb in a few cases, the adjustment does not alter the results of Table 4 markedly. Table 5 also includes estimated effects of a change in the discount rate. According to equation 17, a rise in the discount rate of 1 percentage point will reduce B and hence M by $306 million. The table shows the resulting changes estimated for b and r. Again, the two estimates are far apart quantitatively but they agree in attributing little potency to the discount rate as an instrument of monetary policy. An open-market sale of $250 million has about as large an estimated influence as an increase of 1 percentage point in the discount rate. Of course, the discount rate may have an important influence on expectations by signaling the attitude of the Federal Reserve System. Such effects would not be reflected in the estimates shown. Furthermore, the Federal Reserve reacts to rates and the level of borrowings in deciding whether to change the discount rate. If the observations reflect high values of d that result from high levels of B, the true deterrent effect of the discount rate on borrowing would be underestimated by the regression equation. It is precisely because d has frequently followed b rather than leading it, that the discount rate was not employed as an explanatory variable for *b*. The Federal Reserve System obviously controls the discount rate but it has apparently used this instrument at times to follow the bill market. As a result it is particularly difficult to quantify the causal influence of the discount rate on the bill market.

INTEREST RATES ON PRIVATE ASSETS

The monetary authorities are dealers in federal debt, but their actions influence yields of private assets. In fact, monetary policy affects aggregate demand for output by altering the cost and availability of funds to private borrowers. The relative importance of changing rates and changing availability need not be evaluated here. Even if availability was all important, changes in interest rates on marketable securities would be an unfailing symptom of variations in the tightness of financial markets. Hence, regardless of the mechanism by which monetary actions ultimately influence the demand for output, the effect of policy on private interest rates is a matter of importance.

Interest rates on key private assets are related to one another and to government yields in Table 6. No attempt is made here to explain these other yields by their basic stock and flow determinants. Table 6 is designed to show the extent to which various rates have moved together in the postwar years. Fourteen interest rates are considered, and those make up both the rows and columns of the table. Entered in the table are the simple correlation coefficients among various pairs of yields for 55 quarterly observations from 1946 through the third quarter of 1959. Since each rate is, of necessity, perfectly correlated with itself, all the diagonal elements of the matrix are unity. Because the correlation of y with x is identical to the correlation of x with y, only half of the off-diagonal elements need to be filled.

The concept of an interest rate structure gets support from the close relationships among corporate bonds, municipal bonds, prime commercial paper, larger bank loans, and Governments. Generally, the correlation coefficients between pairs of these yields exceed 0.8. On the other hand, both dividend and earnings yields on common stocks typically show negative correlations with the yields of debt issues. Yields on preferred stock and the rate on small bank loans ($1,000 to $10,000) display relatively low correlations with most other rates but a surprisingly close relationship to each other.

Table 6 also points to the rate on long-term Governments as the pivotal yield in the interest structure. Every one of the eleven private yields is more closely related to the long rate than to the Bill Rate. This would have been

Table 6 Simple Correlations Among Various Interest Rates (Based on 55 Quarterly Observations from 1946-I to 1959-III)

	(1)	(2)	(3)	(4)	(5)	(6)	(7)	(8)	(9)	(10)	(11)	(12)	(13)	(14)
1.	1	.855	.714	.556	.220	−.501	.852	.213	.641	.743	.816	.955	.841	−.463
2.		1	.938	.824	.476	−.604	.863	.486	.829	.880	.910	.868	.930	−.631
3.			1	.959	.732	−.470	.887	.731	.913	.901	.877	.736	.815	−.584
4.				1	.826	−.315	.812	.823	.896	.847	.790	.589	.705	−.482
5.					1	.090	.654	.948	.757	.631	.511	.223	.265	−.175
6.						1	−.358	−.025	−.364	−.447	−.521	−.544	−.621	.825
7.							1	.658	.882	.895	.890	.847	.723	−.498
8.								1	.839	.716	.598	.262	.257	−.329
9.									1	.978	.936	.694	.673	−.583
10.										1	.983	.792	.764	−.624
11.											1	.861	.825	−.649
12.												1	.851	−.520
13.													1	−.531
14.														1

(Data sources given in Appendix Table A-1)

1. Treasury bills
2. Long-term U.S. bonds
3. Corporate Aaa bonds
4. Corporate Baa bonds
5. Dividend yields—preferred
6. Dividend yields—common
7. Prime commercial paper

8. Bank loan rate $1–10 thousand
9. Bank loan rate $10–100 thousand
10. Bank loan rate $100–200 thousand
11. Bank loan rate $200 thousand and up
12. Discount rate
13. High grade municipals
14. Earnings/price ratio—common stocks

expected for corporate and municipal bonds, but it seems surprising for short-term private debts like bank loans. Even the prime commercial paper rate maintains the unanimity, although by an insignificant margin. And the negative relationship with common stock yields is close for the long rate. These findings suggest that, if monetary policy influences the long rate in the ways indicated in earlier sections of this chapter, it will also alter yields on private assets. This conclusion gives a causal interpretation to the correlations of Table 6, implying that other yields have moved because of changes in the government yield. The data, of course, show only association and not causation. It could be argued that common forces have typically acted in the same direction on yields of both government and private debt, but that concerted monetary policy actions to alter government yields would not be transmitted to private securities. This argument requires an answer; for example, the negative correlation between equity returns and the government rate is clearly not causal. The usual *a priori* view is that a tightening of monetary policy depresses equity prices, thus raising their yield just as it raises the yield on Governments. The data are, however, dominated by the fact that cyclical forces change the relative demands for equities as opposed to claims. When profits and the price level seem headed upwards, investors will accept lower current returns on common stock and will demand higher compensation for holding bonds. But the Federal Reserve would not promote bullishness on Wall Street by making a large open-market sale of Governments.

While a non-causal interpretation must be supplied for the negative correlation between equity and debt yields, that does not discredit the positive relationship among yields of debt issues. Marked changes in the relative preferences of investors among claims are far less likely to occur. If they did happen during the postwar period, the positive correlations shown in Table 6 are smaller than those that would emerge solely from autonomous changes in supplies. It seems reasonable to use the high positive correlations to approximate the effects of a change in the government yield attributable to public policy. Then, the slopes of simple regressions of various private yields on Governments can be used to estimate the change in other interest rates accompanying a given change in r.

These slopes are shown in Table 7. In each case, the long-government rate is the independent variable and a private rate is dependent. The coefficients in the table show the estimated change in the private rate accompanying a change in r of 1 percentage point. The estimated changes for corporate and municipal bonds are about equal to Δr; those for large bank loans and commercial paper are about one and a half times as large. Only for small bank loans and yields on preferred stock is the slope much

Table 7 Estimated Slopes of Regressions of Various Interest
Rates on Long-Term U.S. Bond Yield

Yield	Slope on r
Corporate Aaa	0.961
Corporate Baa	1.018
Dividend yields—preferred	0.470
Prime commercial paper	1.577
Bank loan rate $1–10 thousand	0.692
Bank loan rate $10–100 thousand	1.124
Bank loan rate $100–200 thousand	1.398
Bank loan rate $200 + thousand	1.567
High grade municipals	1.40

(55 quarterly observations from 1946-I to 1959-III.)

below unity. These results suggest that changes effected in the yield of
long-term Governments will be transmitted without diminution to private
rates.

CONCLUSIONS: SUMMARY OF EMPIRICAL FINDINGS

1. The interest rates on long-term Government bonds (r) and Treasury
bills (b) are both positively related to the following independent variables:

$(S + I)$ The volume of federal debt with maturity of less than five
years held outside government agencies and the Federal
Reserve System.

L The volume of federal debt with maturity of five years or
more held outside government agencies and the Federal
Reserve System.

Y Gross Private Product, i.e., GNP minus government
payrolls.

In addition, r is positively related to the mean maturity (T) of long debt.
Quarterly dummy variables affect b significantly, reflecting a seasonal
pattern, but they do not influence r. The Bill Rate is negatively affected
by deficiencies in aggregate demand as reflected by a potential GNP
variable used in conjunction with actual output; the same effect was
expected but could not be empirically established for the long rate.

Two alternative "money" variables are negatively related to both
r and b. One of these consists of federal demand debt divided by the legal
revenue ratio (M/R); it represents the hypothetical maximum volume of

money that could exist with the given combined balance-sheets of the Treasury and Federal Reserve System in the absence of currency, time-deposits, and excess reserves. The other "money" variable takes the actual volume of currency outside the Treasury and Federal Reserve and adds to that the remainder of demand debt divided by the legal reserve ratio. The resulting variable is the sum of actual currency plus potential demand deposits, where the potential would be reached only if time deposits and excess reserves were both zero.

2. Both of the hypothetical money variables are more successful in explaining interest rates than is the actual volume of money. Furthermore, the addition of private near-monies to the money supply does not aid the explanation of rates. The hypothetical variables reflect the conditions established by the monetary authorities under which commercial banks can create demand deposits. There is little ground for choice between M/R and $[(M - C)/R + C]$ on either analytical grounds or criteria of empirical success.

3. The resulting equations account for 92 to 93 per cent of the variance of b and r in 56 quarterly observations covering 1946 to 1959. The residuals of the equations, however, display significant positive auto-correlation.

4. Net private wealth was expected to influence rates negatively, but the data did not confirm this hypothesis.

5. Changes in stocks of the public debt and flows of new securities could not be established as influences on b and r. This finding undoubtedly depends on the relatively small magnitudes of quarterly changes in the postwar period. Nevertheless, extreme views—or extreme fears—that attribute great imperfection to the Government bond market get no support from the evidence.

6. As expected, the Bill Rate is much more sensitive than the long rate to given changes in federal debt and in the level of income.

7. Open-market purchases and sales and changes in reserve requirements have very substantial estimated effects on b. The long rate is much less sensitive, but it can be altered significantly by major actions of monetary policy. In a few cases, the effect of a given action estimated from the M/R equation differs substantially from the estimate relying on $[(M - C)/R + C]$. It is obviously important whether an open-market sale of \$1 billion is likely to raise b by 20 or 40 basis points. Yet, neither estimate can be rejected on the grounds of subjective implausibility. If 20 and 40 seem equally sensible to monetary economists, one must conclude that the profession has done very little quantitative thinking in this area. Much more needs to be done to refine the highly tentative and speculative estimate advanced above.

8. The estimated effects of open-market actions are very similar, whether they are conducted by means of bills or of long bonds. The sale of very long bonds will produce an estimated increment in r only about 10 per cent higher than that associated with an equal sale of bills. Similarly, a bill sale has only a slightly larger estimated influence on b than an equal sale of bonds.

9. The effects of changes in the discount rate can be evaluated only insofar as they alter the volume of member bank borrowings. The discount rate appears to be a rather weak instrument of monetary policy in contrast with changes in reserve requirements or with open-market sales and purchases. The estimate does not reflect any impact of the discount rate on expectations. Still, there is no apparent reason why a movement in the discount rate should be a more dramatic signal to investors than altered reserve requirements or large open-market actions.

10. It is estimated that changes effected in the yield of long-term U.S. bonds are transmitted without diminution and without any substantial time-lag to corporate bonds, municipal bonds, and most bank loan rates.

CONCLUSIONS: IMPLICATIONS FOR THEORY AND POLICY

According to the empirical findings of this study, the long rate, the short rate, and the differential between them are all determined principally by the balance sheet of the monetary authorities, the legal reserve ratio, and the level of income. When the demand debt of the federal government is large relative to interest-bearing government debt and to the level of income, financial markets reflect the ease of monetary policy in low rates of interest for both short-term and long-term Government securities and in a large excess of the long rate over the short rate. A smaller volume of demand debt, more interest-bearing debt or higher income raises the yields of all Government securities, but has a particularly strong effect on the short rate. Thus, greater tightness reduces the excess of r over b. The rate differential fluctuates widely; it depends principally on the over-all tightness of financial markets. This is shown schematically in Figure 2.

The greater sensitivity of b to the degree of tightness makes $(r - b)$ dependent on the over-all state of financial markets. If monetary conditions are sufficiently stringent, the Bill Rate is estimated to lie above the long rate. To account for the much greater volatility and sensitivity of the short rate, one must invoke inelastic expectations concerning future rates. If any change in the short rate altered expected future short rates by an equal amount, there could scarcely be a consistently smaller change in the long rate. The expected returns from longs and shorts would be kept in equilibrium only by an equally large change in the long rate. If, however, there are inelastic expectations, expected short rates through the future are altered by only a fraction of the current change in the short rate, and then the long rate should display a smaller change. Yet the *a priori* case for inelastic expectations is not compelling.[13] Nor is there any means of obtaining direct evidence on this score. All one can say is that inelastic expectations would account satisfactorily for the greater volatility of the short rate and they are the only basis of an adequate explanation. Culbertson has advanced an interesting alternative non-expectational explanation.[14] He argues that short rates may be more

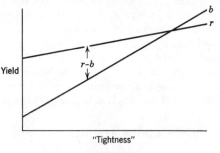

Figure 2

volatile because the volume of outstanding private short-term debt declines by a far greater proportion in a recession than does long-term debt. Hence, if many investors have strong preferences for holding short-term claims, they will accept much smaller returns on those short assets which are available. Because no adequate quarterly series of private debts by maturity category could be assembled, no direct test of the Culbertson thesis was made in this study. But Culbertson's emphasis on relative supplies of long and short private debt seems inconsistent with the small significance that relative supplies of long and short public debt had in my results. Furthermore, Culbertson's explanation would not account for the finding that b is much more sensitive than r to given changes in the volume of federal demand debt. In my judgment, the explanation must rest on inelastic expectations of future interest rates.

The insensitivity of the rate differential to relative supplies of longs and shorts suggests that the expectation curve shown back in Figure 1 should be drawn flat. Investors cannot differ greatly in their best guesses about future long rates, for, if they did, relative supplies would play a greater

---

[13] See Hicks, *op. cit.*, pp. 262, 281.
[14] John M. Culbertson, "The Term Structure of Interest Rates," *Quarterly Journal of Economics*, LXXI (November 1957), pp. 485–517.

role. Furthermore, one can infer that, to a substantial group of investors, bills and bonds are very close substitutes. This group presumably does not have a strong intrinsic preference for shorts versus longs and is willing to alter the maturity composition of portfolios in response to small changes in the yield differential, given the state of market expectations. I cannot identify this important group of arbitragers. This is one of the many areas where my results need to be investigated and appraised at a microeconomic level.

The slight significance attributed to relative supplies suggests that changes in the maturity structure of federal debt will not have dramatic effects on the rate structure. The managers of the debt will reduce $(r - b)$ if they retire long bonds and issue bills, but the magnitude of the estimated effects is small. By the same reasoning, these findings imply that controversy over recent monetary policy has vastly exaggerated the importance of "bills only" as a determinant of the structure of interest rates. If the results of this chapter are anywhere near the mark, *how much* the Federal Reserve buys (or sells) is far and away more important than *what* issue it chooses to deal in. This does not mean that "bills only" was wise policy, or that it was foolish policy. It does imply that it was not a policy of overwhelming significance. The furor over whether the Federal Reserve tied one hand behind its back in adopting "bills only" has obscured the crucial issue of how it used the hand that was unquestionably free.

Monetary policy can alter both long and short rates. While the redirection of a given open-market action between longs and shorts will not accomplish much, large purchases (or sales) and changes in reserve requirements can have decisive effects. The long rate is not easily moved, however. To alter the long rate substantially as an aid to stabilization policy, the Federal Reserve System must be prepared to take strong measures in varying the magnitude of its security holdings and the legal reserve ratio. Vigor is indispensable in the conduct of effective monetary policy.

APPENDIX

Notes to Table A-1: Based on Descriptions of Series in Business Statistics, 1959 ed., U.S. Department of Commerce

Column 1: Yield on Short-Term U.S. Government Bills (Source: Federal Reserve Bulletin). Yield on 3-month bills. Data for 1946

Table A-1 Yields on Financial Assets

		(1)	(2)	(3)	(4)	(5)	(6)	(7)	(8)
		Short-term U.S. Bills	Long-term U.S. Bonds	High Grade Municipal Bonds	Corporate AAA Bonds	Corporate BAA Bonds	Dividend Yields		
							Preferred Stock	Common Stock	Discount Rate
Year	Quarter								
1946	1	0.375%	2.09%	1.49%	2.47%	2.94%	3.45%	3.42%	0.50%
	2	0.375	2.16	1.55	2.49	3.03	3.46	3.41	1.00
	3	0.375	2.28	1.75	2.58	3.10	3.57	4.24	1.00
	4	0.375	2.24	1.97	2.61	3.17	3.76	4.41	1.00
1947	1	0.376	2.19	2.02	2.55	3.15	3.72	4.80	1.00
	2	0.376	2.22	1.92	2.55	3.21	3.76	5.09	1.00
	3	0.791	2.24	1.92	2.61	3.23	3.72	5.21	1.00
	4	0.948	2.39	2.35	2.86	3.52	4.07	5.41	1.00
1948	1	0.997	2.44	2.52	2.83	3.53	4.12	5.58	1.25
	2	0.998	2.41	2.26	2.76	3.34	4.04	5.30	1.25
	3	1.087	2.45	2.46	2.84	3.45	4.20	6.06	1.50
	4	1.153	2.44	2.26	2.79	3.53	4.15	6.78	1.50
1949	1	1.162	2.38	2.21	2.70	3.47	4.07	6.88	1.50
	2	1.158	2.38	2.28	2.71	3.47	3.98	7.22	1.50
	3	1.061	2.22	2.22	2.60	3.37	3.85	6.39	1.50
	4	1.102	2.19	2.13	2.58	3.31	3.88	6.58	1.50
1950	1	1.138	2.27	2.07	2.58	3.24	3.81	6.40	1.50
	2	1.174	2.33	2.09	2.62	3.28	3.85	6.35	1.50
	3	1.315	2.36	1.88	2.64	3.21	3.85	6.45	1.75
	4	1.367	2.39	1.77	2.67	3.20	3.89	6.89	1.75
1951	1	1.422	2.47	1.87	2.78	3.23	4.00	6.66	1.75
	2	1.499	2.65	2.22	2.94	3.49	4.17	6.79	1.75
	3	1.646	2.56	2.05	2.84	3.46	4.16	6.03	1.75
	4	1.731	2.70	2.10	3.01	3.61	4.28	5.56	1.75
1952	1	1.658	2.70	2.07	2.96	3.51	4.16	5.54	1.75
	2	1.700	2.61	2.10	2.94	3.50	4.04	5.48	1.75
	3	1.786	2.71	2.33	2.95	3.52	4.12	5.63	1.75
	4	2.126	2.75	2.40	2.97	3.51	4.11	5.14	1.75
1953	1	2.082	2.89	2.61	3.12	3.57	4.23	5.36	2.00
	2	2.231	3.13	2.99	3.40	3.86	4.47	5.60	2.00
	3	1.876	3.01	2.88	3.29	3.88	4.30	5.76	2.00
	4	1.630	2.79	2.59	3.13	3.74	4.20	5.54	2.00
1954	1	1.053	2.53	2.38	2.86	3.51	4.04	5.07	1.75
	2	0.650	2.55	2.48	2.90	3.49	4.05	4.74	1.50
	3	1.007	2.52	2.29	2.89	3.47	3.98	4.31	1.50
	4	1.174	2.59	2.33	2.90	3.45	3.93	4.09	1.50
1955	1	1.335	2.78	2.45	3.02	3.48	4.01	4.18	1.50
	2	1.432	2.82	2.48	3.05	3.51	3.98	3.71	1.75
	3	2.086	2.92	2.63	3.13	3.59	4.06	3.76	2.25
	4	2.564	2.91	2.71	3.15	3.62	4.05	3.92	2.50
1956	1	2.310	2.93	2.69	3.10	3.60	4.01	3.68	2.50
	2	2.527	2.93	2.75	3.27	3.75	4.17	3.82	2.75
	3	2.850	3.21	3.07	3.56	4.07	4.39	4.04	3.00
	4	3.230	3.40	3.44	3.75	4.37	4.63	3.90	3.00
1957	1	3.140	3.26	3.32	3.66	4.43	4.46	4.16	3.00
	2	3.316	3.58	3.75	3.91	4.63	4.69	3.79	3.00
	3	3.578	3.66	3.90	4.12	4.93	4.79	4.27	3.50
	4	3.102	3.30	3.47	3.81	5.03	4.49	4.58	3.00
1958	1	1.354	3.25	3.45	3.63	4.68	4.42	4.35	2.25
	2	0.881	3.19	3.26	3.57	4.55	4.28	3.98	1.75
	3	2.484	3.75	3.96	4.09	4.87	4.58	3.54	2.00
	4	2.814	3.80	3.84	4.08	4.85	4.63	3.17	2.50
1959	1	2.852	3.92	3.76	4.13	4.85	4.48	3.28	3.00
	2	3.247	4.09	4.04	4.46	5.04	4.79	3.09	3.50
	3	3.998	4.26	4.13	4.52	5.18	4.80	3.13	4.00
	4	4.572	4.27						4.00

		(9)	(10)	(11)	(12)	(13)	(14)	(15)	(16)
		Prime Commer-cial	Bank Rates of 19 Cities Size of Loan (thousands of dollars)				Common Stock		Earnings Price Ratio
Year	Quarter	Paper	1–10	10–100	100–200	200 and over	Price per Share	Earnings per Share	
1946	1	0.75%	4.10%	3.10%	2.30%	1.70%	$ 52.00	$ 1.32	2.54%
	2	0.75	4.20	3.10	2.20	1.70	53.70	3.22	6.00
	3	0.81	4.00	3.10	2.10	1.70	44.38	3.97	8.95
	4	1.00	4.40	3.20	2.10	1.80	46.03	5.61	12.19
1947	1	1.00	4.30	3.10	2.50	1.80	45.67	4.74	10.38
	2	1.00	4.10	3.10	2.60	1.80	45.93	4.93	10.73
	3	1.06	4.10	3.10	2.40	1.80	45.85	5.39	11.76
	4	1.19	4.10	3.20	2.50	1.80	47.34	6.22	13.13
1948	1	1.38	4.20	3.30	2.50	2.10	46.60	6.35	13.63
	2	1.38	4.49	3.47	2.70	2.16	50.77	6.85	13.49
	3	1.56	4.53	3.58	2.92	2.29	46.87	7.25	15.47
	4	1.56	4.50	3.58	2.97	2.34	46.33	7.65	16.51
1949	1	1.56	4.62	3.64	2.89	2.42	46.21	6.60	14.28
	2	1.56	4.63	3.70	3.04	2.44	43.48	6.00	13.80
	3	1.38	4.62	3.64	2.98	2.31	48.16	6.75	14.01
	4	1.33	4.53	3.61	2.98	2.35	52.28	7.05	13.49
1950	1	1.31	4.45	3.54	2.94	2.31	53.76	6.59	12.26
	2	1.31	4.50	3.65	2.94	2.39	55.56	8.66	15.59
	3	1.66	4.51	3.63	2.95	2.34	61.27	9.44	15.41
	4	1.72	4.60	3.37	3.10	2.57	64.46	9.08	14.09
1951	1	2.04	4.68	3.88	3.27	2.76	67.40	7.62	11.31
	2	2.31	4.73	3.93	3.32	2.81	66.75	7.42	11.12
	3	2.19	4.74	3.99	3.36	2.78	74.09	6.36	8.58
	4	2.30	4.78	4.05	3.49	3.03	74.24	8.09	10.90
1952	1	2.38	4.85	4.16	3.66	3.24	75.63	6.79	8.98
	2	2.31	4.90	4.21	3.72	3.29	77.01	6.61	8.58
	3	2.31	4.91	4.22	3.74	3.27	74.58	6.76	9.06
	4	2.31	4.88	4.21	3.77	3.29	80.89	8.54	10.56
1953	1	2.36	4.89	4.25	3.75	3.32	77.64	7.26	9.35
	2	2.75	4.98	4.38	3.91	3.53	74.28	7.76	10.45
	3	2.74	5.01	4.40	3.93	3.54	72.09	7.76	10.76
	4	2.25	4.98	4.39	3.96	3.57	77.06	8.08	10.48
1954	1	2.00	4.99	4.37	3.94	3.52	85.53	7.97	9.32
	2	1.56	4.97	4.35	3.89	3.37	94.34	8.49	9.00
	3	1.31	4.99	4.32	3.82	3.32	102.88	7.63	7.42
	4	1.31	4.92	4.29	3.84	3.31	115.64	9.43	8.15
1955	1	1.69	4.93	4.29	3.83	3.30	117.61	9.70	8.25
	2	2.00	4.92	4.29	3.83	3.30	133.41	10.80	8.10
	3	2.54	4.98	4.44	3.99	3.56	138.21	9.94	7.19
	4	2.99	5.01	4.52	4.14	3.75	145.67	11.60	7.96
1956	1	3.00	5.05	4.55	4.13	3.74	155.90	10.75	6.90
	2	3.38	5.18	4.69	4.34	3.97	151.11	10.50	6.95
	3	3.50	5.30	4.86	4.52	4.19	145.06	8.70	6.00
	4	3.63	5.32	4.90	4.63	4.20	150.74	11.45	7.60
1957	1	3.63	5.38	4.94	4.59	4.21	141.98	11.12	7.83
	2	3.79	5.37	4.94	4.61	4.23	155.23	10.65	6.86
	3	4.00	5.67	5.29	5.01	4.69	138.73	9.40	6.78
	4	3.81	5.66	5.29	5.01	4.71	128.38	9.90	7.71
1958	1	2.33	5.55	5.10	4.75	4.29	134.17	7.35	5.48
	2	1.54	5.45	4.88	4.40	3.95	144.74	7.30	5.04
	3	2.93	5.45	4.90	4.47	4.00	161.34	8.10	5.02
	4	3.33	5.49	5.06	4.68	4.33	177.75	10.70	6.02
1959	1	3.35	5.53	5.09	4.74	4.32	174.47	10.30	5.90
	2	3.83	5.68	5.33	5.06	4.72	187.48	11.60	6.19
	3	4.63	5.91	5.65	5.43	5.15	184.64	8.00	4.33

181

represent average rates on issues announced within the period; thereafter, on new bills issued within the period. Data are for last month of the quarter.

Column 2: Yield on Long-Term U.S. Government Bonds (Source: Federal Reserve Bulletin). The data are averages of daily figures computed, beginning with April 1953, on the basis of the closing bid quotations on the over-the-counter market; prior thereto, on the basis of the mean of the closing bid and asked quotations. The series includes bonds as follows: Beginning April 1953, fully taxable marketable bonds due or callable in 10 years and over; from April 1952 through March 1953, fully taxable marketable bonds due or first callable after 12 years; prior thereto, bonds due or first callable after 15 years. Data are for the last month of the quarter.

Column 3: Yield on High Grade Municipal Bonds (Source: Standard and Poor's Corporation). The series is an arithmetic average of yields to maturity of 15 high-grade domestic municipal bonds. The yields are based on Wednesday closing prices and the monthly figures are averages of the four or five weekly figures for the month. Data are for the last month of the quarter.

Columns 4 and 5: Yields on Corporate AAA and Corporate BAA Bonds (Source: Moody's Investors Service). These averages were set up in 1928 to include 10 bonds of each rating for each group (railroad, public utility, and industrial). There has not uniformly been a full set of 10 bonds in some rating classifications because of the limited number of suitable issues. On September 1, 1958 there were 6 AAA and 10 BAA bonds in the railroad group; 10 AAA and 10 BAA bonds in the public utility group; and 7 AAA and 10 BAA bonds in the industrial group.

Occasional substitutions in the bond list have been made. Suitable adjustments (usually small), which are gradually amortized, are introduced to prevent such substitution from impairing the comparability of the series. No convertible or other unusual issues are included. The average maturity on September 1, 1958, was 25 years.

Averages are computed as follows: A daily yield based on the closing price for each individual bond is first computed and then unweighted arithmetic averages of these yields are compiled for the different rating classifications. The monthly series are averages of daily figures. Data are for the last month of the quarter.

Column 6: Dividend Yields on Preferred Stocks (Source: Standard and Poor's Corporation). Yields are computed for each of 14 high-grade noncallable issues (15 prior to April 1948), including public utility as well as industrial preferred stocks. The group yield is currently determined from the average of the 8 median yields (formerly 9). The indexes are based on one price weekly (as of Wednesday's close) with the monthly index computed from the average of the four or five weekly indexes of the month. Data are for last month of the quarter.

Columns 7, 14, and 15: Dividend Yields, Price per Share and Earnings per Share of 125 Industrial Common Stocks (Source: Moody's Investors Service). Dividends are at annual rates (without adjustment for seasonal variation) and are determined at the end of each month on the basis of each company's most recent declaration. These dividends are multiplied by the number of each company's common shares outstanding and the products are added to obtain aggregate values which are divided by the total number of shares outstanding, free from the effects of stock splits and stock dividends, to obtain per share figures.

Individual stock prices at the end of each month are used as a basis for deriving per-share prices. Earnings are net after taxes and contingencies less preferred dividend requirements (whether actually paid or not). Data represent quarterly earnings—partly estimated—at annual rates. There is no adjustment for seasonal variation. The method of computing price per share is similar to the method of computing dividends per share described above.

Yields are obtained by dividing per-share dividends by per-share prices.

Yield and price data are for the last month of the quarter. Earnings data are quarterly totals at annual rates.

Column 8: Discount Rate (Source: Federal Reserve Bulletin). Data are discount rate in effect on last day of quarter.

Column 9: Interest Rate on Prime Commercial Paper, 4 to 6 Month Maturity (Source: Federal Reserve Bulletin). Beginning with 1951, the data represent averages of daily quotations; prior thereto the figures are averages of weekly prevailing rates. Data are for the last month of the quarter.

Columns 10, 11, 12, and 13: Bank Rates on Short-Term Business Loans in 19 Large Cities (Source: Federal Reserve Bulletin). Data represent averages of rates charged on loans maturing in 1 year or less to business in the specified cities.

Since June 1948 data were reported on forms that call for the amount of the loans and the interest rate actually charged for each new loan or renewal made in the first half of March, June, September, and December by a selected sample of banks (mainly large ones) in 19 leading cities.

Column 16. Column 15 is divided by Column 14.

Table A-2   Money Supply

Year	Quarter	(1) Member Bank Reserves	(2) Other Deposits	(3) Currency Outside Government	(4) Federal Demand Debt	(5) Required Reserve Ratio	(6) Excess Reserves	(7) Member Bank Borrowings	(8) Currency Outside Banks	(9) Demand Deposits Adjusted
1945	4	15,915	1308	28,515	45,738	0.183	1364	334	26.5	75.9
1946	1	14,853	1212	27,879	43,944	0.183	971	683	26.1	75.0
	2	16,123	1250	28,245	45,618	0.183	867	119	26.5	79.5
	3	15,910	1069	28.507	45,486	0.183	824	141	26.5	81.4
	4	16,139	822	28,952	45,913	0.183	862	193	26.7	83.3
1947	1	15,264	971	28,230	44,465	0.183	739	153	26.1	80.4
	2	16,112	881	28,297	45,290	0.183	741	114	26.0	82.5
	3	16,784	842	28,567	46,193	0.183	884	98	26.3	84.1
	4	17,899	961	28,868	47,728	0.183	939	262	26.5	87.1
1948	1	16,639	1000	27,781	45,420	0.190	732	304	25.6	81.5
	2	17,389	859	27,903	46,151	0.196	765	97	25.6	82.7
	3	19,986	843	28,118	48,947	0.216	768	328	25.7	83.9
	4	20,479	1189	28,224	49,892	0.216	782	139	25.7	85.8
1949	1	19,118	1154	27,439	47,711	0.216	579	208	25.1	81.1
	2	17,867	940	27,493	46,300	0.202	616	130	25.0	82.2
	3	15,947	1050	27,412	44,409	0.176	685	192	24.9	83.1
	4	16,568	1517	27,600	45,685	0.176	773	52	25.0	86.7
1950	1	15,657	1133	27,042	43,832	0.176	600	253	24.6	83.2
	2	15,934	1431	27,156	44,521	0.176	640	51	24.6	85.4
	3	16,709	1374	27,161	45,244	0.176	603	140	24.5	88.0
	4	17,681	1460	27,741	46,882	0.176	851	283	25.0	93.2
1951	1	19,014	1323	27,119	47,456	0.196	524	374	24.4	89.0
	2	19,020	1261	27,809	48,090	0.196	561	211	25.0	89.5
	3	19,391	1127	28,288	48,806	0.196	669	195	25.4	92.0
	4	20,056	889	29,206	50,151	0.196	815	551	26.3	98.1
1952	1	19,733	845	28,473	49,051	0.196	1130	138	25.7	94.8
	2	19,381	845	29,026	49,252	0.196	700	189	26.0	95.8
	3	20,066	881	29,419	50,366	0.196	1094	282	26.6	96.4
	4	19.950	1005	30,433	51,388	0.196	858	1703	27.5	101.5
1953	1	19,322	878	29,754	49,954	0.196	605	924	26.9	97.4
	2	19,561	703	30,125	50,389	0.196	1154	281	27.1	97.2
	3	19,309	864	30,275	50,448	0.183	564	318	27.5	97.7
	4	20,160	916	30,781	51,857	0.183	813	211	27.8	103.3
1954	1	19,194	857	29,707	49,758	0.183	732	175	26.9	96.7
	2	19,011	922	29,922	49,855	0.180	839	138	27.1	98.1
	3	18,676	883	29,985	49,544	0.170	588	78	26.9	101.2
	4	18,876	871	30,509	50,256	0.170	621	243	27.4	106.7
1955	1	18,283	798	29,800	48,881	0.170	490	652	26.7	102.4
	2	18,066	822	30,229	49,117	0.170	490	402	27.1	103.2
	3	18,423	764	30,422	49,609	0.170	483	888	27.2	104.9
	4	19,005	956	31,158	51,119	0.170	683	753	27.9	109.8
1956	1	18,799	748	30,339	49,886	0.170	572	1196	27.2	104.4
	2	18,443	977	30,715	50,135	0.170	595	756	27.5	105.0
	3	18,831	610	30,768	50,209	0.170	503	705	27.4	105.4
	4	19,059	758	31,790	51,607	0.170	704	641	28.5	110.8
1957	1	18,629	615	30,585	49,829	0.170	609	819	27.4	105.2
	2	18,399	757	31,082	50,238	0.170	546	1003	27.8	105.6
	3	19,034	598	31,073	50,705	0.170	547	1100	27.8	105.5
	4	18,532	602	31,834	50,968	0.170	652	781	28.9	109.1
1958	1	18,532	644	30,666	49,842	0.163	688	164	27.4	104.6
	2	18,784	689	31,172	50,645	0.154	668	99	27.8	105.7
	3	18,147	653	31,245	50,045	0.154	593	433	27.9	108.1
	4	18,504	663	32,193	51,360	0.154	656	790	28.7	115.5
1959	1	18,192	695	31,250	50,137	0.154	458	600	27.9	110.3
	2	17,640	657	31,914	50,211	0.154	457	876	28.3	110.7
	3	17,760	760	31,848	50,368	0.154	220	721	28.5	111.4
	4	18,174	1039	32,591	51,804	0.154	464	928	29.4	115.4

Notes to Table A-2:   (Source: All data are taken from the Federal Reserve Bulletin)

Column 1: Member Bank Reserves (Millions of Dollars). "Statement of Condition of the Federal Reserve Banks." Data as of the end of the quárter.

Column 2: Other Deposits in Federal Reserve Banks (Millions of Dollars). Sum of "Foreign deposits" and "Other deposits."

Column 3: Currency Outside the Government (Millions of Dollars). Currency in circulation outside the Treasury and Federal Reserve Banks. Data as of the end of the quarter.

Column 4: Federal Demand Debt (Millions of Dollars). Sum of Columns 1, 2, and 3.

Column 5: Reserve Requirements Index. Weighted average of reserve requirements for central reserve city banks, reserve city banks, and country banks on net demand deposits at the end of the quarter. The weights are 0.32 (central reserve city banks), 0.40 (reserve city banks), and 0.28 (country banks).

Column 6: Excess Reserves (Millions of Dollars). Excess reserves of all member banks, average of daily figures for last week of the quarter.

Column 7: Borrowings (Millions of Dollars). Borrowings at Federal Reserve banks of all member banks, average of daily figures for last week in last month of the quarter. Figure for the fourth quarter of 1945 is monthly average.

Column 8: Currency Outside Banks (Billions of Dollars, not Seasonally Adjusted). Data as of last Wednesday of quarter.

Column 9: Demand Deposits Adjusted (Billions of Dollars, not Seasonally Adjusted). Data as of last Wednesday of quarter.

Notes to Table A-3

Columns 1 to 4: U.S. Government Debt (Millions of Dollars). All marketable direct public securities, excluding those held by federal agencies and trust funds and the Federal Reserve Banks. Classified according to maturity.

Sources: *Treasury Bulletin* 1946 through first quarter of 1953; *Federal Reserve Bulletin* second quarter of 1953 through fourth quarter of 1959. Beginning with the September 1953 issue of the *Federal Reserve Bulletin*, the basis for classifying bonds with optional call dates was changed from a first call to a final maturity date.

Column 1, S. Short-term U.S. Government Debt-securities maturing within one year.

Column 2, I. Intermediate-term U.S. Government Debt—securities maturing from one to five years.

Column 3, (S + I). Sum of Columns 1 and 2.

Column 4, L. Long-term U.S. Government Debt—securities maturing in five years or more.

Table A-3   Federal Debt, Income, and Wealth

		(1)	(2)	(3)	(4)	(5)	(6)	(7) Government Pay-rolls	(8)	(9) Net National Wealth	(10)
Year	Quarter	S	I	(S + I)	L	T	Y_g		Y		W
1946	1	46,077	16,259	62,336	104,975	191.6	198.0	24.9	173.1	584.4	740.1
	2	39,187	18,320	57,507	101,413	189.8	206.3	20.2	186.1	598.3	749.3
	3	38,025	12,604	50,629	103,037	188.3	217.1	18.8	198.3	649.8	796.1
	4	31,715	16,635	48,350	98,496	187.8	221.2	18.5	202.7	700.9	842.4
1947	1	28,277	18,591	46,868	96,528	187.2	226.0	17.9	208.1	736.4	872.8
	2	28,295	15,557	43,852	97,441	184.2	230.0	17.4	212.6	758.9	890.2
	3	30,958	17,689	48,647	92,456	188.9	235.6	16.9	218.7	807.7	933.9
	4	27,886	21,615	49,501	88,310	187.5	245.1	17.4	227.7	843.5	964.5
1948	1	33,701	15,667	49,368	85,392	184.5	249.5	17.7	231.8	867.4	985.1
	2	32,981	14,995	47,976	85,474	181.5	257.7	18.1	239.6	888.3	1002.7
	3	28,935	25,255	54,190	75,108	189.4	264.0	19.2	244.8	914.8	1025.9
	4	30,382	27,340	57,722	70,825	190.7	265.9	20.0	245.9	928.4	1036.3
1949	1	28,215	29,170	57,385	70,826	189.3	259.8	20.1	239.7	935.7	1044.9
	2	32,860	31,499	64,359	65,945	198.6	256.4	20.3	236.1	934.1	1044.7
	3	35,747	30,450	66,197	65,938	195.6	258.8	20.6	238.2	923.5	1035.4
	4	36,709	36,669	73,378	57,608	209.6	257.0	21.0	236.0	932.0	1045.3
1950	1	32,792	40,323	73,115	58,263	206.6	265.8	21.0	244.8	957.4	1067.6
	2	25,362	49,207	74,569	56,937	208.5	274.4	21.2	253.2	981.9	1089.0
	3	33,940	37,668	71,608	57,106	207.2	293.2	22.4	270.8	1034.8	1138.8
	4	30,379	40,420	70,799	55,568	205.4	304.3	24.3	280.0	1067.1	1168.1
1951	1	27,348	41,358	68,706	53,743	202.4	317.8	26.4	291.4	1105.7	1204.8
	2	29,387	40,407	69,794	44,462	186.2	326.4	28.2	298.2	1133.6	1230.7
	3	30,592	39,667	70,259	44,437	183.2	333.8	30.2	303.6	1147.4	1242.6
	4	33,692	38,563	72,255	44,381	180.2	338.1	30.8	307.3	1164.6	1257.8
1952	1	33,985	37,640	71,625	44,870	175.5	341.0	32.1	308.9	1184.5	1277.1
	2	33,339	37,649	70,988	44,085	171.2	341.3	32.9	308.4	1199.6	1291.6
	3	39,108	30,450	69,558	48,125	160.3	347.0	33.4	313.6	1204.6	1296.0
	4	42,071	30,479	72,550	48,052	157.2	358.6	33.6	325.0	1214.1	1305.0
1953	1	44,035	27,532	71,567	47,177	155.8	364.5	33.7	330.8	1227.6	1319.7
	2	48,921	25,726	74,647	44,482	167.2	368.8	34.0	334.8	1242.6	1335.9
	3	50,735	28,864	79,599	44,462	164.2	367.1	33.9	333.2	1253.6	1348.1
	4	56,088	23,020	79,108	46,056	159.5	361.0	33.9	327.1	1259.3	1355.1
1954	1	48,392	16,902	65,294	56,519	146.3	360.0	34.0	326.0	1267.8	1363.5
	2	43,736	21,453	65,189	56,583	144.3	358.9	34.3	324.6	1280.8	1376.4
	3	43,829	25,783	70,612	55,603	142.4	362.0	34.6	327.4	1291.2	1386.7
	4	43,342	26,382	69,724	59,694	138.8	370.8	34.8	336.0	1306.3	1401.7
1955	1	34,399	30,182	64,581	61,464	145.6	384.3	35.1	349.2	1325.9	1419.7
	2	32,224	34,216	66,440	61,436	142.6	393.0	36.1	356.9	1349.7	1441.9
	3	39,335	30,382	69,717	62,175	143.5	403.4	36.2	367.2	1371.9	1462.5
	4	39,467	36,320	75,787	58,443	145.4	408.9	36.6	372.3	1401.9	1491.0
1956	1	37,329	35,481	72,810	58,450	142.4	410.6	37.1	373.5	1432.4	1517.5
	2	37,545	30,410	67,955	58,349	139.4	415.0	37.7	377.3	1464.3	1545.4
	3	42,814	28,874	71,688	56,111	139.2	421.0	38.5	382.5	1488.2	1565.3
	4	45,416	39,940	85,456	44,998	153.3	430.0	38.9	391.1	1518.2	1591.3
1957	1	45,700	40,875	86,575	44,975	150.3	437.7	39.4	398.3	1546.5	1617.0
	2	49,649	37,923	87,942	40,237	157.4	442.4	39.9	402.5	1584.0	1651.9
	3	50,395	41,843	92,238	40,211	154.1	447.8	40.7	407.1	1610.3	1675.6
	4	51,705	43,334	95,039	38,576	159.0	442.3	40.7	401.6	1629.6	1692.3
1958	1	50,045	38,276	88,321	44,420	155.7	431.0	41.8	389.2	1639.6	1702.5
	2	43,873	38,492	82,365	52,226	148.0	434.5	42.9	391.6	1658.3	1721.4
	3	45,584	45,482	91,066	45,016	157.4	444.0	44.0	400.0	1667.1	1730.4
	4	50,900	46,741	97,641	44,977	154.4	457.1	44.3	412.8	1702.3	1765.9
1959	1	47,168	54,920	102,088	41,843	160.6	470.4	44.6	425.8	1734.4	1798.9
	2	51,341	51,253	102,594	42,389	157.2	484.8	45.4	439.4	1766.1	1830.9
	3	54,194	52,917	107,111	42,345	157.2	478.6	46.1	432.5	1782.6	1848.0
	4	58,765	53,176	111,941	42,285	150.5	483.5	46.7	436.8	1793.8	1859.9

Column 5, T.   Maturity of U.S. Government Debt due in five years or more (in months) (Source: Calculations from *Federal Reserve Bulletin*). Maturity is a weighted average of the maturity of marketable direct public securities outstanding at the end of each quarter which are due in five years or more.

Column 6, Y_g.   Gross National Product, seasonally adjusted quarterly totals at annual rates, current prices, (billions of dollars) [Source: *U.S.*

Income and Output (1946–1955) *Survey of Current Business*, July 1959 and May 1960 (1956–1959)].

Column 7, Government Payrolls. Government Civilian and Military Salaries and Wages, seasonally adjusted quarterly totals at annual rates, current prices (billions of dollars) (Source: *Ibid.*).

Column 8, Y. Gross Private Product. Column 6 less Column 7.

Column 9, Net National Wealth: U.S. Net National Wealth (Goldsmith), current prices (billions of dollars). The quarterly series was constructed by interpolating a quarterly series on net private domestic investment derived from U.S. Department of Commerce data into annual estimates of total national wealth excluding military wealth constructed by Goldsmith. Goldsmith's estimates of wealth from 1945 to 1958 were taken from an unpublished table. The estimates pertain to the end of the year. The figures for wealth in 1959 were extrapolated according to a formula given below.

The first step in the interpolation was to compute quarterly net private domestic investment in constant dollars. To do this, it was necessary to construct a constant dollars depreciation series to deduct from gross private domestic investment in constant dollars. The depreciation series was constructed by deflating capital consumption allowances by a weighted average of the new construction and producers durable equipment implicit price deflators. A weight of 0.6 was assigned to the new construction deflator, and a weight of 0.4 was assigned to the producers durable equipment deflator.

The second step was to express net investment in each quarter as a per cent of net investment during the year; for example, investment in the first quarter of 1947 was divided by net investment in 1947.

The third step was to apply the percentage of annual investment per quarter to Goldsmith's estimates of the annual increment to wealth in constant dollars. For example, Commerce data shows that 25 per cent of net investment in 1947 occurred in the first quarter. Therefore it is estimated that 25 per cent of the increment in real Goldsmith wealth between December 1946 and December 1947 occurred in the first quarter of 1947.

The final step was to convert the quarterly wealth series from constant dollars to current dollars. To do this it was necessary to construct a quarterly wealth deflator. This was done by taking the first difference of the capital consumption allowance deflator; expressing the first difference as a per cent of the change in the deflator over one year; computing a Goldsmith wealth deflator (wealth in current dollars divided by wealth in constant dollars); taking the first difference of the Goldsmith wealth deflator (annual increment in the price of wealth); and applying the percentage of annual increase in the capital consumption allowance deflator per quarter to the annual increase in the Goldsmith wealth deflator. For 1959 the Goldsmith wealth deflator was carried forward by the percentage change—quarter to quarter—of the capital consumption allowance deflator.

Column 10, W: U.S. Net Private Wealth in current prices (billions of dollars). Private wealth is defined as national wealth minus the net worth of the public sector. The quarterly series on private wealth was constructed by computing an annual (fourth quarter) series and making a straight line interpolation of annual increments in the net worth of the public sector.

Net worth of the public sector is equal to:

U.S. deposits in Federal Reserve and commercial banks

plus   Public assets
less   Net public debt
less   Gold certificates
less   Treasury currency.

(Sources: Net public debt, *Survey of Current Business*, July 1960; Gold certificates and Treasury currency, *Federal Reserve Bulletin*; U.S. deposits, *President's Economic Report for 1960*, Table D-40; Public Assets, Goldsmith, unpublished table, sum of public civilian structures, public producers durables, public land, and monetary metals.)

6

Determinants of Bond Yield Differentials: 1954 to 1959*

PETER E. SLOANE

INTRODUCTION

The theory of the structure of interest rates has traditionally been confined to an analysis of the difference between yields on short term and long term assets. This empirical study deals with differential yields at specific, long term maturities, but, in spite of this fact, the same general theoretical problems are encountered. Actually, it is not until uncertainty is introduced that the relevance of traditional theory is evident. With riskless securities and perfect certainty there would be no room for a study of risk premiums among assets of different quality, i.e., default risk. Once these conditions are relaxed, the subjective estimation of uncertain future conditions becomes equally paramount in determining whether the risk of holding longer term securities should be undertaken and in the choice among assets of equal maturity which are subject to varying degrees of risk with respect to interest and principal. Both decisions involve the confidence with which expectations are held. Choosing a longer term asset

* SOURCE: reprinted from *Yale Economic Essays*, Vol. 3, No. 1 (Spring 1963), pp. 3–55.

This topic was originally suggested and initial encouragement provided by Professor James Tobin. The carrying out and completion of the study relied heavily upon the good offices of Professors Arthur M. Okun and Harold W. Watts. I should like to express my sincerest appreciation for continued interest in spite of the press of other duties and for their invaluable comments and suggestions.

I should also like to thank my colleagues Donald Hester, Donald Snodgrass, and T. N. Srinivasan for their advice and opinions on specific points.

The Cowles Foundation has financed all the computational work undertaken. A final word of thanks should go to the staff of the Yale Computing Center.

involves the possibility that anticipations will not be realized and that on this account a loss will be taken; choosing a lower quality asset involves the same type of probability. In either case the investor will demand a premium to make an investment, the outcome of which is uncertain. A brief review of the existing theory, therefore, should serve as a useful background for consideration of the statistical analysis to follow.

In both the nonmonetary theory of Irving Fisher and the monetary theory of J. R. Hicks a first approximation of the long term rate is presented as the arithmetic average of the current and any anticipated, intervening short term rates. Abstracting from default risk, this assumption allows concentration upon *the* rate of interest since, once two or more short rates are known with certainty or with given expectations, the long rate can readily be calculated.[1] (As Hicks points out, the known and unknown rate can just as easily be reversed.[2]) In his "second approximation" Fisher allows variation in income streams due to size, composition, and time shape, but not until the "third approximation" does he allow for uncertainty. His partiality to neatly posited theory under controlled conditions is evident in his conclusion: "The second approximation gives a clear cut theory applicable to the clear cut hypotheses on which it is based. The third approximation cannot avoid some degree of vagueness."[3] Hicks, building his basic theory on the relative "moneyness" of various assets, attributes that part of interest paid beyond "pure" interest to default risk and uncertainty concerning the future course of interest rates.[4] The elasticity of expectations is introduced as a possible key element in the determination of the course of interest rates. However, most of the ensuing discussion is in terms of quite inelastic expectations, since Hicks concludes that this condition is usual.[5]

F. A. Lutz, in a synthesis of the theory and an extension of the implications of expectations with respect to the interest rate structure,[6] builds a

---

[1] Irving Fisher, *The Theory of Interest* (reprint; New York: Kelley & Millman, Inc., 1954), p. 70. J. R. Hicks, *Value and Capital* (London: Oxford University Press, 1939), pp. 145–46.

[2] Hicks, *op. cit.*, p. 260.

[3] Fisher, *op. cit.*, p. 227.

[4] Hicks, *op. cit.*, p. 163.

[5] Hicks, *op. cit.*, p. 282. The course of the statistical analysis will show how important this concept of elasticity is in explaining periods which are not normal and therefore may be given to a high degree of elasticity with respect to interest rate expectations.

[6] F. A. Lutz, "The Structure of Interest Rates," *Quarterly Journal of Economics*, LV (November 1940), pp. 36–63; reprinted in American Economic Association, *Readings in the Theory of Income Distribution* (Philadelphia: The Blakiston Company, 1946), Chap. 26, pp. 499–529.

model, initially, under conditions of (1) certainty, (2) zero transactions costs and (3) perfect shiftability. Dropping the last two assumptions, Lutz draws certain implications concerning the relationship of rates for borrowers and lenders before turning to the consideration of risk. Abstracting from default risk, he considers the risk associated with changes in interest rates. He concludes that there is no precision in calling the long rate an average of expected short rates, but rather that the relationship is a highly complex one bearing upon the whole pattern of expectations held by many different people operating in the market. The implication is that the greater stability of the long over the short rate cannot be explained simply by the fact that a change in the single, current short rate will have less and less effect on the average as the lengthening of the term under consideration involves the averaging of more and more short rates. He is, nevertheless, able to justify this characteristic of the long rate by an argument, very close to Hicks' inelastic expectations, which states that the market has no very definite expectations concerning future short rates which are well into the future. A second conclusion is that the over-all rate structure may exhibit either a rising, falling or horizontal trend depending upon whether short rates are expected to rise, fall or remain the same.

In a more recent article, J. M. Culbertson[7] attacks the expectational theories of Hicks and Lutz, resting his case upon the demand for and the supply of funds. "The behavior of rate structure does not seem explainable in terms of long run expectations, though near-term expectations can temporarily govern the behavior of rates."[8] He identifies demand factors as new issues, shifts in purposes of borrowing, Treasury debt management and supply factors as shifts in liquidity, relative lending costs, lender expectations, patterns of speculative activity, changes in monetary policy, etc. Again, the discussion centers around whether short rates exceed long rates and why, although interest rate interrelationships are also mentioned. If we have a world of perfect certainty or if expectations are inelastic, Culbertson's criticisms and conclusions are perhaps justified, but if the relationships he discusses do, in themselves, affect expectations throughout the interest rate structure, it is hardly wrong to assign high importance to the so-called expectational theories.

---

[7] J. M. Culbertson, "The Term Structure of Interest Rates," *Quarterly Journal of Economics*, LXXI (November 1957), pp. 485–517. See also L. S. Wehrle, "Culbertson on Interest Structure: Comment," and J. M. Culbertson, "Reply," *Quarterly Journal of Economics*, LXXII (November 1958), pp. 601–13.

[8] Culbertson, "The Term Structure of Interest Rates," *op. cit.*, p. 515.

J. W. Conard has done just this in his recent neo-classical synthesis.[9] Conard summarizes the implications of neo-classical theory of the interest rate structure in a world of certainty and perfect capital markets as: "for any defined period of time, however long or short, the expected net effective yield (including capital gains and losses) will be identical on all riskless securities regardless of their term."[10] With respect to expectations, neo-classical theory does not imply simple averaging of short rates but rather that investors seek to maximize returns on the basis of their expectations about future interest rates and changes in capital values. Only by adding considerations of risk and institutional factors can this theory be made realistic.

> The most fundamental fact which forces modification of the neoclassical theory is that of uncertainty. Some of the important consequences are these: (1) Expectations about conditions in the market for money and credit for the intermediate and long-term future are typically very vague or almost entirely unformed. Thus, long rates may be largely influenced by changes in short-term expectations and by considerations not described in neoclassical theory. (2) One of these other considerations is the fact that long-term securities offer more prospect of capital gain or loss than do shorts. The essential reason is that a simultaneous change in all expected short rates will cause a much larger change in long prices than in short prices, and a general change in expectations tends often to color the far as well as the immediate future, thus causing a similar if not an equal alteration in a substantial sequence of expected short rates. (3) A consequence of the more speculative character of longs is the tendency of institutions requiring a high degree of liquidity (e.g., banks and nonfinancial corporations) to hold very few longs. (4) Another consequence is that longs often yield more than shorts, partly as compensation for risk-taking. (5) A result of 3 and 4 is that the markets for securities of different term become partly segmented. An important consequence for the theory of interest is that there is no longer a single rate of interest even defined over short periods of time as there was in the unmodified theory. Thus securities of different term are no longer perfect substitutes for one another, and a rate determined by the theory of interest is no longer unambiguous.[11]

The actual modification of the theory to allow for uncertainty and institutional factors is left for a later book and further empirical research.

Empirical studies which are available have also been almost exclusively confined to the term structure of interest rates. The major work has been

---

[9] J. W. Conard, *Introduction to the Theory of Interest* (Berkeley: University of California Press, 1959). It is interesting to note, as will be amplified later, that neither empirical results of this study nor of Conard's tend to support the demand for and supply of loanable funds as being the dominant factors in determining interest rate structure. See Conard, *ibid.*, p. 338.

[10] *Ibid.*, p. 298.

[11] Conard, pp. 350–51.

under the auspices of the National Bureau of Economic Research and has involved research in the Corporate Bond market. Largely, this work has been of an historical nature to establish a basic yield curve representing, theoretically, the interest rate structure for the most risk free asset.[12] Utilizing these curves, studies of the Corporate Bond market were made in order to compare the "market rating" of bond quality to that of investment service ratings. The basic yield ("market rating") was found to vary more with the cycle than did agency ratings indicating that investors demanded and received a premium in excess of that justified by the *actual* risk of default.[13] A thorough analysis of the causative factors behind the differentials among various bond categories was deemed beyond the scope of these studies. The basic yield series for Corporate Bonds has been extended for the period 1952 to 1957 coupled with an analysis of the need for a thoroughgoing study of the entire structure of terms on which credit is extended and credit instruments transferred.[14] The only study concerned directly with yield differentials among monetary assets was of risk premiums on Corporate Bonds utilizing cross section analysis of a sample of firms. The basic conclusion was that risk of default and marketability are significant contributors to the average yield on particular bonds.[15]

Although the above review indicates that both theoretical discussion and empirical research have been confined almost exclusively to the consideration of the term structure of interest rates and have often imposed conditions involving risk free assets and perfect certainty, many of the theoretical implications drawn when these conditions are relaxed have bearing upon the interrelationships among yield curves in particular markets. Explanations of yield differentials among monetary assets fall under two general headings: (1) "pure" interest and (2) risk premium. The former breaks down into the consideration of transactions costs and the pattern of time preferences among individual investors. Under conditions of certainty or under conditions which allow close estimation of statistical probability based upon abundant empirical evidence, e.g., mortality tables, an investor may prefer a long term security for two basic

[12] D. Durand, "Basic Yields of Corporate Bonds 1900–1942," *Technical Paper No. 3* (National Bureau of Economic Research, June 1942); D. Durand and W. Winn, "Basic Yields of Bonds 1926–1947: Their Measurement and Pattern," *Technical Paper No. 6* (National Bureau of Economic Research, December 1947).

[13] W. Hickman, *Corporate Bond Quality and Investor Experience* (New York: National Bureau of Economic Research, 1958); W. Hickman, *The Volume of Corporate Bond Financing since 1900* (New York: National Bureau of Economic Research, 1953).

[14] D. Durand, "A Quarterly Series of Corporate Basic Yields 1952–1957 and Some Attendant Reservations," *Journal of Finance*, XIII (September 1958), pp. 348–56.

[15] L. Fisher, "Determinants of Risk Premiums on Corporate Bonds," *Journal of Political Economy*, LXVII (June 1959), pp. 217–37.

reasons: (1) transactions costs are reduced as only one security is purchased to be held for the entire time period involved and (2) a fixed, periodic return is received over the entire time period. (For the sake of clarity, let us assume that the *average*, certain return on the short term securities equals the return on the single long term security.) Typically, however, investors are pictured as having a strong time preference and demanding a premium for extending the average maturity of their asset holdings. In a world of riskless securities and perfect knowledge, this typical explanation does not seem rational. Only when the second explanatory element is introduced, involving the subjective estimation of the probabilities of default and of changes in capital values under conditions of uncertainty, can a consistent theory be approached. Portfolio selection involves the weighing of one element against the other as lower transactions costs and stability of income are evaluated against the probabilities that interest rates may rise or fall, plus the probability of default. It is this latter element, involving expectations and uncertainty, which is sorely in need of quantitative research as a first step in constructing an adequate theory of the entire interest rate structure.

It is the purpose of this study to isolate and analyze the determinants of the risk premium. To isolate the risk premium, analysis is confined to the Corporate and Federal Government Bond markets in which securities are readily substitutable and transactions costs are approximately equivalent throughout. Since bonds are classified by investment agencies according to default risk, it should be possible to construct yield curves for various homogeneous categories from the most risk free, or highest quality, to the lowest quality. By calculating the differential at specific maturities between the highest and lesser quality curves, it should then be possible to eliminate the last vestige of "pure" interest leaving only the existing risk premium.

That a risk premium must exist is evident from the fact that it is a function of the subjective estimation of the probability of (a) default with respect to interest and/or principal and (b) changes in capital values. Government Bonds, to all intents and purposes, enjoy zero default risk. All other bonds, even if the situation is reduced to one determined investor who contends that a chance remains that, e.g., AT & T may default, must yield slightly more. The presence of a risk premium may thus be explained by (a) above. Before continuing, another factor should be noted. Changes in capital values arise primarily from changes in the level of interest rates. In a period of unfavorable expectations when maximum safety is desired, interest rates on the whole would tend to fall (prices rise) as investors adjust the risk content of their portfolios. Among bonds of varying quality, however, the probability of default risk would increase more at the lower end of the quality spectrum, tending to set up an opposing force to the over-all drop in yields (rise in prices). It might be predicted, therefore, that under varying conditions, yields (prices) of lower quality bonds will exhibit a relative degree of stability when compared with those of higher quality bonds.

Once appropriate yield differentials have been compiled for use as dependent variables, the hypothesis to be tested is that the risk premium between closely substitutable assets is a function of two basic elements (1) the relative supplies of such assets and (2) the demand for such assets—demand based upon expectations concerning conditions in the financial markets and the economy in general. Among the primary questions to be answered with respect to the first element is whether stocks and flows of assets at specific maturities are significant determinants of the yield differentials. If so, yield curves will seldom show a smooth curvature; if not, it is logical to conclude that a smooth function based upon variables common to the entire maturity range is an adequate approximation. Other supply questions to be answered concern the impact of stocks and flows in general, covering bonds, competing assets, new issues, etc. Given the stock of bonds outstanding, the question becomes what changes in the risk premium result from changes in the money market, the equity market, and general economic conditions. The money market is the most closely attuned to changes in the interest rate structure; the equity market to changes in investor psychology and the relative attractiveness of equity versus debt; and existing economic conditions give a somewhat objective indication of default risk as corporate earnings respond to changes in business activity. Changes in any one of these areas affect expectations and also the availability of funds for the purchase of bonds. It is necessary to determine in what respect, if any, the analysis can support the contention that expectations must serve as the core of an adequate theory of the structure of interest rates.

THE BOND MARKET

Although the bond market offers a close approximation of the theoretical model desired, it is far from perfect and is extremely deficient in meeting the three basic criteria of an acceptable financial market—depth, breadth, and resiliency. It is a Walrasian-Hicksian affair.[16] Each weekday traders enter the market and cry bid prices (to buy) and ask prices (to sell). Sometimes only one trader appears in the market place and perhaps only a bid price is recorded that day; often no sale is consummated during the contracting period, and the traders retire until the next day. If failure to

---

[16] See Hicks, Chap. 9.

reach an equilibrium price persists for too long a period, the professional dealer enters the market and cries a price with the intention of adjusting the spread between bid and ask to a point which, in his opinion, more properly reflects existing market conditions. Finally, since the evaluation of risk is a highly subjective process based upon expected future conditions, actions of the monetary authorities and of the Treasury Department may temporarily influence prices especially during periods of exceptional uncertainty.

The above may lead to opinions that it is market imperfections which, in many cases, are the major contributory factor to the determination of yield differentials. However, with the degree of substitutability existing in the bond market and, therefore, the relatively favorable opportunities for arbitrage transactions, the primary effect of imperfections is merely to slow adjustments thus allowing one to minimize their impact by taking frequent observations over a period of time. It must again be noted that the size of the risk premium—especially that component which depends upon chances of capital gain or loss—is a function of subjective factors. By concentrating upon bonds, expectations concerning the general price level can be ignored, since monetary assets are all equally affected thereby; but expectations concerning the course of financial markets and general economic conditions are directly pertinent, and the normal diversity of opinion concerning them makes patent the high degree of uncertainty in any attempts to predict the future. Although taking observations over time should tend to reduce any impact due to imperfections in the market, this factor plus the fact that risk is strongly dependent upon highly diverse subjective evaluation means that any estimated equilibrium values of yield differentials can best be described in terms of a tendency or "normal" range.

THE DIFFERENTIAL

In order to calculate yield differentials—the dependent variable required for the purpose of statistical analysis—which most closely approximated the conditions outlined above, the first step was to choose bond categories which were homogeneous with respect to risk. The next step was to collect price data from which yield to maturity could be calculated and to plot these data against maturity for each bond category for a suitable time period. By fitting curves to the resultant scatters, it was then possible to construct a set of yield curves from which to calculate differentials for specific maturities.

The first category chosen was marketable U.S. Treasury Bonds. In the United States the prime securities consist of Federal Government obligations with the full taxing power of the central government behind them.

The quality of these bonds is based upon the fact that they are, as nearly as possible, completely free of default risk. Yield curves for these bonds were used as a base from which to calculate the dependent variables. Previous studies of bond yield differentials[17] have established a basic yield-maturity curve utilizing a visual fit of the lowest yielding (highest quality) bonds for the first quarter of each year from 1900 to 1947. The primary purpose in constructing basic yield curves as opposed to relying upon Treasury Bond yield curves was to allow historical research during a time when there were variations in the tax status of Government Bonds and a shift in listing from the New York Stock Exchange to the Over-the-Counter Market. The present analysis covers the period from 1954 to 1959 during which the status of Government Bonds was unchanged. It was therefore unnecessary to look further than this category for a basic yield. In order to get a sample of Corporate Bonds which were homogeneous with respect to risk, the specific categories chosen were Moody's Aaa and Baa bonds listed on the New York Stock Exchange. Moody's ratings are based upon the quality of Government securities and are the most widely consulted ratings by those who actively follow the bond market. Barring unforeseen shifts in industry solvency, such as occurred with respect to railroads after 1929, Moody's ratings have proved a stable and accurate indicator of the differences in default risk.[18] Aaa is the top quality rating while Baa is the minimum quality rating for investment purposes. The "Key to Moody's Ratings" defines each category as follows:[19]

Aaa

Bonds which are rated *Aaa* are judged to be of the best quality. They carry the smallest degree of investment risk and are generally referred to as "gilt edge." Interest payments are protected by a large or by an exceptionally stable margin and principal is secure. While the various protective elements are likely to change, such changes as can be visualized are most unlikely to impair the fundamentally strong position of such issues.

Aa

Bonds which are rated *Aa* are judged to be of high quality by all standards. Together with the *Aaa* group they comprise what are generally known as

---

[17] See D. Durand, "Basic Yields of Corporate Bonds 1900–1942"; D. Durand and W. Winn, "Basic Yields of Bonds 1926–1947: Their Measurement and Pattern"; and D. Durand, "A Quarterly Series of Corporate Basic Yields 1952–1957 and Some Attendant Reservations."

[18] See D. Durand and W. Winn, "Basic Yields of Bonds 1926–1947: Their Measurement and Pattern."

[19] *Moody's Industrial Manual* (New York: Moody's Investors Service, 1960), pp. v–vi.

high grade bonds. They are rated lower than the best bonds because margins of protection may not be as large as in *Aaa* securities or fluctuation of protective elements may be of greater amplitude or there may be other elements present which make the long term risks appear somewhat larger than in *Aaa* securities.

A

Bonds which are rated *A* possess many favorable investment attributes and are to be considered as higher medium grade obligations. Factors giving security to principal and interest are considered adequate but elements may be present which suggest a susceptibility to impairment sometime in the future.

Baa

Bonds which are rated *Baa* are considered lower medium grade obligations, i.e., they are neither highly protected nor poorly secured. Interest payments and principal security appear adequate for the present but certain protective elements may be lacking or may be characteristically unreliable over any great length of time. Such bonds lack outstanding investment characteristics, and in fact have speculative characteristics as well.

For the three categories—Government, Aaa Corporate, and Baa Corporate Bonds—monthly price data were collected over the six year period from 1954 to 1959 inclusive.[20] This postwar period was chosen as the longest feasible one during which both high and low interest rates prevailed and which was relatively free of changes in tax laws. Also, following the Treasury-Federal Reserve accord in 1951, the market was no longer subject to the influence of "pegged" rates for Government Bonds. Given these data, in theory one should find that two bonds with different coupons but the same quality rating and maturity have the same realized yield. In an attempt to assure at least an approximation of this result, only "straight" Corporate Bonds listed on the New York Stock Exchange, i.e., bonds not convertible into common stock or providing other special features such as warrants or voting rights, were included in the sample. However, a high degree of heterogeneity was found to exist in each category due to the appearance of new issues, the disappearance of maturing or called issues and changes in quality ratings. It was, therefore, necessary to include in the sample only those bonds outstanding in the pertinent category during the entire period under study. The result was

---

[20] All price and volume outstanding data were collected from one of the following sources: *Treasury Bulletin; Moody's Bond Record* (New York: Moody's Investors Service); *The Commercial and Financial Chronicle.*

monthly yield data for the six year period 1954 through 1959 for (1) 10–14 Government Bonds (2) 32 Aaa Corporate Bonds and (3) 27–31 Baa Corporate Bonds. Prices, from which yields to maturity were calculated, were taken as nearly as possible at the end of each month; where no actual sale information was available the midpoint between the bid and ask price was used. One further restriction was that during each annual period consideration was given only to those bonds maturing in six years or more; this accounts for the variation in sample size.

With reference to Treasury Bonds, except for two bonds in the first two maturity years, the sample consists of bonds subject to call at a specified date prior to maturity. (There were no noncallable bonds at maturities greater than seven years in 1954). The Treasury Department follows the convention of figuring yield to call date, rather than maturity date, whenever a callable bond sells above par. Although this condition was quite prevalent in 1954 and existed for one long term bond much of the following two years, it was felt that following the convention would not be feasible in a study dealing with specific maturities. Any error involved seems minimal since, in 52 instances of a total of 144 cases during 1954 when the convention would have applied, the average adjustment to yield would be minus 3.3 basis points (0.033 percentage points or an approximate error of 1.5 %) with a range of from 0 to 8 basis points. In 20 instances occurring in the case of a single long term bond during 1955 and 1956 the average adjustment would be minus 3.7 basis points (a 1.2 % error). Maturities on the bonds involved ran from 13 to 29 years with the call date five years in advance of final maturity. It seems dubious to suppose that an investor seeking a yield for such a lengthy period would count upon market conditions remaining the same and, therefore, immediately adjust his anticipated yield should the price exceed 100. Corporate Bonds are also, for the most part, subject to call, but the convention is not applied since the specific date is usually more nebulous than in the case of the Treasury Department. All yields, therefore, have been figured to final maturity.

The yield data, calculated as described above, were then plotted against maturity for the three bond categories for each of seventy-two months. The maturity for each bond was adjusted annually. For Government and Aaa Bonds yield curves were visually fitted to the resultant scatters; visual fitting was required since there is no accepted mathematical function to express the relation between yield and maturity and any attempt to obtain a smooth over-all curve would obviously dampen the sensitivity of the yield differential changes which are the subject of this study.

For the lower quality Corporate Bonds, however, a high degree of heterogeneity was found to exist within Moody's Baa classification. The fact that these bonds were less stable with respect to evaluation than Aaa's was anticipated, but the degree of their instability was not. A perusal of the "Key to Moody's Ratings" provides a clue as to why ". . . because of their very nature, rating changes are to be expected more frequently among bonds of lower ratings than among bonds of higher ratings . . . ."[21] If agency rating changes were the only variations which occurred, there would be no problem since only bonds which have retained the same rating for the entire six year study period have been used as a source for the basic data. However, the market also "rates" bonds in the sense that price and, therefore, yield reflect changes in investor attitudes toward particular securities. "As might be expected, the variables emphasized by the market in its rating system are quite similar to the ones stressed by the investment agencies and the compilers of legal lists . . . . The market · · · typically assigned top positions to the large, well secured, actively traded issues."[22] Hickman defined the market rating in much the same terms as the differential has been defined in this study—as the difference between the yield at market price and an equivalent point upon the National Bureau Basic Yield Curve.[23] He found a great deal of instability in this rating. "The market rating usually reflects changes in the credit standing of obligors more promptly than other ratings do . . . . The reason · · · is the extreme sensitivity, amounting almost to instability, of the market rating to changing conditions . . . ."[24] Both agency and market ratings, then, are based primarily upon (1) the extent to which earnings cover interest and other fixed charges and (2) the variability of those earnings—the market rating being more responsive to actual, or anticipated, changes. By definition, earnings variability is more prevalent among the lower rated bonds adding to the risk of investing in a bond already close to the margin of safety with respect to debt coverage. Therefore, it is to be expected that the investor will consider more carefully the current, ever changing, characteristics of a Corporate Bond in the Baa category.

Upon the hypothesis that there might be some consistent individual bond yield biases over the period from 1954 to 1959 due to variations in coverage of fixed charges and earnings among Baa Bonds, the following operation was performed. A second degree regression of yield versus maturity was estimated; the form of the equation was:

$$Y = a + b_1X_1 + b_2X_1^2 + c_1Z_1 + c_2Z_2 + \cdots + c_{11}Z_{11}.$$

---

[21] *Moody's Industrial Manual*, p. v.

[22] Hickman, *Corporate Bond Quality and Investor Experience*, p. 301.

[23] See Durand, and Durand and Winn. In this study the Treasury yield curve has been used as a basic yield curve as explained above.

[24] Hickman, *Corporate Bond Quality and Investor Experience*, p. 18.

The dependent variable was the mean yield for an individual bond during each of the twelve semi-annual periods. X_1 equaled the maturity of the bond; any bias due to maturity was minimized since years to maturity was changed annually for each bond. Z_1 was a dummy variable equal to one for the semi-annual period January through June 1959 and zero for every other period; Z_2 was a dummy variable equal to one for the semi-annual period July through December 1958 and zero for every other period; etc.

Table 1 B—Bond Adjustment Regression Results

$Y = 5.0258$	$+$	$0.027769 X_1$	$-$	$0.000503 X_1^2$
(0.13054)		(0.010429)		(0.000210)
				Calculated
Coefficients		Standard Error		Intercepts

Coefficients	Standard Error	Calculated Intercepts
$c_1 = -0.25629$	(0.11398)	4.77
$c_2 = -0.32830$	(0.11296)	4.70
$c_3 = -0.40830$	(0.11296)	4.62
$c_4 = -0.22376$	(0.11201)	4.80
$c_5 = -0.70755$	(0.11201)	4.32
$c_6 = -1.0208$	(0.11207)	4.01
$c_7 = -1.5122$	(0.11207)	3.51
$c_8 = -1.6124$	(0.11120)	3.41
$c_9 = -1.7008$	(0.11120)	3.33
$c_{10} = -1.7586$	(0.11038)	3.27
$c_{11} = -1.6679$	(0.11038)	3.36

$R^2 = 0.717$
$s_u = 0.041880$

The results were significant (0.01 level) and produced a family of parallel curves with different intercepts for each six month period. The constant term indicates the intercept for the last six months of 1959; the c coefficients indicate the factor to be subtracted from the constant term to derive the intercept for each of the semi-annual periods. The results of the regression and the calculated intercepts are shown in Table 1. To check whether the slope of the over-all regression was consistent for every six month period, an F-test was made utilizing the sums of squared residuals from independently run semi-annual regressions and from the over-all regression. The results ($F = 0.6693$ with 22/312 degrees of freedom) supported the null hypothesis that there was no significant difference in the slope of the yield curve for different periods. Adjustment factors were then computed as the difference between Y_c and Y_0, where Y_c equals the individual mean computed from the regression equation and Y_0 equals the actual six month mean yield for an individual bond. (See Appendix of this chapter.) The adjustment factors so calculated failed to exhibit the consistency necessary to eliminate the wide dispersion among the Baa Bonds. In some cases the "market" rating of an individual bond deteriorated, changing from plus to minus between 1954 and 1959; in others it improved, changing from minus to plus.

Investor confidence was not constant during the six years, and it is ultimately upon this factor that the market rating depends. "The market rating provides a sensitive yardstick for ranking issues in order of default risk at any given moment; but the yardstick is elastic expanding and contracting with investor confidence."[25] From 1954 to 1955 was a period of boom and steady improvement; from 1956 to 1957 was a period of leveling off; and from 1958 to 1959 was a period of recession and uncertainty. At the same time earnings experience for individual corporations varied. Baa bonds are largely comprised of railway bonds, and it is therefore proper to use a small sample of these as an illustration of changes in relative standings among individual bonds. Comparing three Class I (large) Railroads in the sample, numbers 29, 24, and 12 in the Appendix, against all Class I Railroads, the pattern is as follows:

Operating Record—Percentage of Gross Revenue Carried through to Net Operating Income before Federal Income Taxes[26]

	Class I Roads	Number 29	Number 24	Number 12
1954	11.7	21.1	9.2	11.0
1955	15.3	26.1	10.0	15.2
1956	13.9	23.5	8.1	11.8
1957	11.9	20.2	9.0	9.3
1958	10.5	18.5	9.3	4.0
1959	10.4	22.8	10.4	4.8

Debt coverage for the three roads showed changes of:

Number 29 $+30\%$
Number 24 -7%
Number 12 -52%

---

[25] *Ibid.*, p. 355.
[26] *Moody's Transportation Manual* (New York: Moody's Investors Service, 1960), p. a40.

Deviations from the regression ($Y_c - Y_0$) were of the following general pattern:

Relative Position		Pattern

It was this type of variation in relative market rating within the general Baa classification which had to be removed in order to consider changes in yield differentials ascribable to the quality rating as a whole. A further random sampling of the Baa bonds confirmed the fact that relative standing is a function primarily of earnings and debt coverage, and also that these market ratings are very responsive to changing aspects of the corporate balance sheet.

It was evident from the pattern of residuals in the Appendix that the six year period of the study could be roughly divided into three two-year periods—from 1954 to 1955, from 1956 to 1957, and from 1958 to 1959—and an average adjustment applied for each of the three periods. In almost every case there was a change in relative position during 1956 to 1957 as the economy leveled off and again from 1958 to 1959 as the economy turned down. From 1954 to 1955 and from 1958 to 1959 the market ratings showed some degree of stability and in every case, except five in the latter period, the adjustment factor shown for these periods is the same for the four six-month periods encompassed. The 1956 to 1957 period, however, does not exhibit the same degree of stability as re-evaluations took place at different times based upon the earnings trends of specific corporations. It was necessary, therefore, to estimate subjectively the cut off point for a particular market rating. In the case of bond

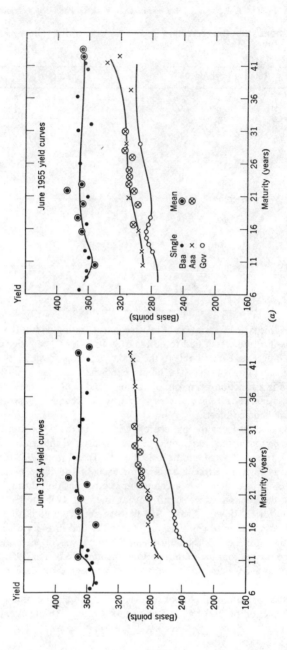

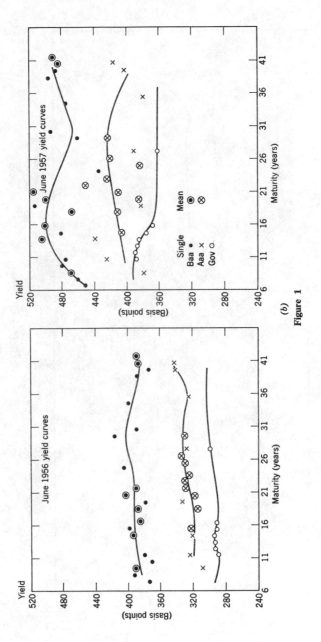

Figure 1

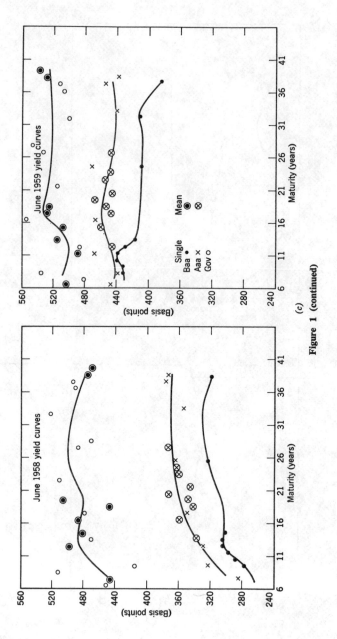

Figure 1 (continued)

number 5, for example, it was evident that a drastic re-evaluation took place in mid-1956 (see Appendix to this chapter). Inclusion of the first half of 1956 with the next three semi-annual periods would have called for a mean adjustment of −62 basis points during 1956 to 1957. The result would have been a vast overstatement of the market rating in the first half of 1956 and an understatement of it thereafter. It was deemed more appropriate to extend the initial division through the first half of 1956. In the case of bond number 9 the market rating did not change until 1957; in number 10 there was a drastic re-evaluation in the last half of 1957; number 20 lagged twice, not adjusting until the second half of 1956 and again in the second half of 1958, etc. The final Baa bond adjustment, therefore, was calculated predominantly as equal to

$$\frac{\sum (Y_c - Y_0)}{n}$$

for three two-year periods with $n = 4$. When necessary the middle period was varied and the appropriate value for n substituted in calculating the adjustment. Finally, the applicable adjustment factor, plus or minus, was applied to the monthly yield data. It was then possible visually to fit yield curves to the Baa scatter while still allowing significant variation from month to month.

Once three curves had been constructed for each of seventy-two months (see Figure 1), the dependent variables were measured as the absolute differences between a Corporate (Aaa or Baa) yield curve and a Government yield curve at twelve, sixteen and twenty-one years to maturity; a mean differential was also calculated for all bonds maturing in more than ten years. To test the hypothesis that the dependent variable should be expressed in percentage terms, the mean Treasury yield for bonds with more than ten years to maturity was inserted as an independent variable in the subsequent regression analysis. Since the yield on Government Bonds is the basic yield, the above hypothesis would mean that as the Government yield rose (price fell) the absolute difference between it and the Corporate yield must rise resulting in a higher percentage differential to offset any capital loss arising from selling Government and buying Corporate Bonds.[27] A positive sign for the coefficient would have supported this hypothesis; however, all results showed a negative relation. The dependent variable was defined, therefore, as the absolute differential between Corporate and Government yields.

---

[27] For an expression of this view see W. L. Smith, "On the Effectiveness of Monetary Policy," *American Economic Review*, XLVI (September 1956), p. 590.

THE INDEPENDENT VARIABLES

Having now defined the yield differentials, which are to serve as dependent variables, the next problem is to explain them. As mentioned above, the hypothesis to be tested is that the differential—the risk premium—is a function of two basic elements: (1) the relative supplies of closely substitutable assets and (2) expectations concerning conditions in the money market, the capital markets and the economy in general. This section presents the procedure followed in defining the independent variables.

The regression analysis undertaken was linear, of the form:

$$Y = a + b_1X_1 + b_2X_2 + b_3X_3 + b_4X_4 + b_5X_5.$$

Before discussing the variables which proved significant in the final analysis, however, it may be worthwhile to consider several which did not. The first independent variables considered involved the stock of bonds outstanding and changes in this stock, i.e., flows. Investment decisions and the evaluation of risk are made at a point in time in the face of a given stock of bonds outstanding and knowledge of the present and past rate of change in this stock. At the outset of the study it was desired to test for the impact of stocks and flows at specific maturity points as an indication of whether or not a smooth function can serve as an approximation for long term yield curves. The choice of maturities at which to calculate the dependent variables was dictated by the pattern of bonds outstanding since independent variables were to be used equal to the ratio, and the change in ratio, of volume outstanding (Corporate/Government) at specific maturities. (See Table 2.) Ratios were tested for (1) a three year range of outstandings with the maturity year of the differential as the midpoint (2) a four year range and (3) for all bonds over ten years from maturity. Also tested as separate variables were the Corporate and Government volumes for particular maturities. In all cases the signs of the coefficients—positive for the ratio, positive for the separate Corporate variable and negative for the Government—were consistent with the original hypothesis that a rise in the volume of Corporates outstanding would mean a higher yield (lower price) and an increased differential, while a rise in the volume of Governments outstanding would cause a drop in the differential. The results, however, were not significant, and the impact of this stock variable appears very weak, affecting the differential only to the extent of approximately one half basis point (0.005 %) for a 1 % change in the ratio. The explanation does not lie in any degree of constancy of volume outstanding at various points along the curve. In the 11 to 15 year range Government volume increased 32%, Aaa 100% and Baa 10%; in the 16 to 20 year range Governments fell from a positive amount to zero, Aaa increased 100% and Baa 60%. The ratios for all bonds with more than ten years to maturity rose from 0.11 in 1954 to 0.20 in 1959 in the case of Aaa/Governments and from 0.056 to 0.068 for Baa's. Any deficiency in variation of or magnitude of changes in the values of the

Table 2 Distribution of Volume Outstanding from 1954 to 1959

Maturity in Years	Aaa 54	55	56	57	58	59	Government 54	55	56	57	58	59	Baa 54	55	56	57	58	59
10	—	—	—	—	—	00	—	—	—	00	00	00	00	—	—	—	—	—
11	—	—	—	—	—	—	—	—	—	—	00	00	—	00	—	—	—	—
12	—	—	—	—	—	—	—	—	—	—	—	00	—	—	00	—	—	—
13	00	—	—	—	—	—	—	—	—	—	—	—	—	—	—	00	—	—
14	-0	00	—	—	—	—	00	—	—	—	—	—	—	—	—	0	—	—
15	—	00	00	—	—	—	—	00	—	—	—	—	—	—	—	—	—	—
16	—	—	00	00	—	—	00	—	00	—	—	—	—	—	—	—	—	—
17	—	—	—	00	00	—	00	00	-0	00	—	—	—	—	—	—	—	—
18	—	—	—	—	00	00	00	00	00	00	00	—	—	—	—	—	—	—
19	—	—	—	—	—	00	00	00	00	00	00	00	—	—	—	—	—	—
20	—	—	—	—	—	—	00	00	00	00	00	00	—	—	—	—	—	—
21	—	—	—	—	—	—	—	00	00	00	00	00	—	—	—	—	—	—
22	—	—	—	—	—	—	00	00	00	00	00	00	00	—	0	—	—	—
23	—	—	—	—	—	—	00	00	00	00	00	00	—	00	—	00	—	—
24	—	—	—	—	—	—	—	00	00	00	00	00	—	—	00	—	00	—
25	—	—	—	—	—	—	00	—	00	00	00	00	—	—	—	00	—	00
26	—	—	—	—	—	—	—	00	—	00	00	00	—	—	—	—	00	—
27	—	—	—	—	—	—	00	—	00	—	00	00	—	—	—	0	—	00
28	—	—	—	—	—	—	00	00	00	00	—	00	00	—	—	—	0	—
29	—	—	—	—	—	—	00	00	00	00	00	—	—	00	—	—	—	—
30	—	—	—	—	—	—	00	00	00	00	00	00	0	—	00	—	—	—

—— indicates bond(s) outstanding for period designated.
00 indicates no bond outstanding for period designated.

independent variables obviously cannot explain the failure to achieve significant results.

Initially the flow variable was derived directly from the above as the rate of change in the stock variable. In this instance the constancy of the variable was marked as most changes of any consequence were due to maturity shifts; new issues were confined almost exclusively to intermediate (5 to 10 years) and very long term (25 to 35 years) maturities. Results were not significant. To make a further check of the hypothesis that flows are important determinants of the yield differential, independent variables were tried representing (1) the sum of new issues—public and private and (2) the ratio of Corporate new issues to Governments.[28]

---

[28] Source: *Federal Reserve Bulletin.*

Again results were not significant. The explanation probably lies not in the fact that new issues are unimportant but rather in the fact that new issues are floated with utmost care in order that they may be fitted into the existing interest rate structure with a minimum of upset. In the private sector investment bankers support new issues, i.e., support the price at the initial level until the new bonds are absorbed. If the bonds are not absorbed, the issue may even be withdrawn. In the government sector the Treasury Department chooses its time carefully. Except for one small cash issue in July 1955 when books were reopened for a 39-year 7-month bond, cash financing during the period under study was limited to maturities under five years until 1957. Only during the recessionary period from September 1957 to June 1958 when speculative demand for long term fixed interest securities ran high did the Treasury venture into the long term capital market. Even then when the market threatened to become disorderly following the June 1958 issue, the Federal Reserve and the Treasury stepped in to support the prices of Government Bonds. Statistical measure of the impact of these issues was made impossible by their random nature and also by the fact that psychological factors due to the high degree of uncertainty accompanying any decline in the economy overcame any consistent relation which might have existed.[29]

In short it was not possible to support the hypothesis that the stock *at specific maturities* along the yield curve or the flow variables have any important impact on the differential. One is able to conclude from this that the interest rate structure for long term bonds can be approximated by a series of smooth curves without the necessity of allowing for humps and/or discontinuities at various maturity points due to distinctly different proportions among outstandings. The long term bond market is relatively homogeneous (in this respect) subject only to general factors common to the over-all maturity range. The final equation thus includes two variables dealing only with gross volume and three variables bearing upon financial markets and the state of the economy. They are defined as follows:

1. The ratio of the total par value of Corporate Bonds listed on the New York Stock Exchange to the value of competing long term debt. Competing long term debt was defined as the sum of equity stocks outstanding plus mortage debt outstanding. The volume of equities was computed by dividing Dividends, as published under Personal Income and Disposition of Income in the Department of Commerce's National Income Accounts, by Moody's Stock Yields. The volume of municipal bonds was the total par value as published in the *Annual Report* of the Secretary

---

[29] For a similar conclusion based upon empirical analysis see Conard, p. 335 and especially p. 338 (top).

of the Treasury. For the last six months of 1959 it was necessary to estimate the figures through a conversion ratio utilizing Bond Buyer data based upon offer prices as published in the *Survey of Current Business*. Mortgage debt outstanding was taken from the quarterly figures published in the *Federal Reserve Bulletin* and the difference prorated over each quarter in order to have a monthly figure.

2. The ratio of the total par value of Government Bonds (as opposed to notes, certificates or bills), as published in the *Treasury Bulletin*, to the value of competing long term debt as defined above.

3. The interest rate on prime commercial paper (4 to 6 months) as published by the Federal Reserve Board.

4. The dividend yield on equities as measured by Moody's Stock Yields covering a sample of 200 stocks representing a cross section of industry.

5. The seasonally adjusted rate of unemployment in the civilian labor force as published now by the Bureau of Labor Statistics and formerly by the Bureau of Census. Prior to 1957 it was necessary to adjust the published data in accordance with the new seasonal adjustment factors in current use and to remove from total employed those on temporary layoff or waiting to start a new job or business. For 1954 the latter adjustment was estimated but should be very close to the actual figures (which were not available in published form at the time these computations were undertaken).

RESULTS

Table 3 and Figure 2 show the regression results for seventy-two monthly observations 1954 through 1959. Column one of Table 3 indicates the particular equation with, for example, A designating the dependent variable as Aaa Corporate minus Government yield and the number designating the specific maturity year at which the differential was measured: $A > 10$ indicates that the dependent variable was derived from the difference in mean yields for all Aaa and Government Bonds with more than ten years to maturity. Similarly B designates equations involving Baa Corporate Bonds. Values in the table are defined as follows:

a = the constant term

b_i = the slope of the ith independent variable; $i = 1, \ldots, 5$, in accordance with the above listing of independent variables

s_{b_i} = the estimated error of b_i and is indicated in parentheses below each coefficient; an asterisk indicates Student's t-Test (b_i/s_{b_i}) for testing b_i significant at the 0.05 level

R^2 = the coefficient of multiple determination

s_u = an unbiased estimate of the standard error of residuals

Table 3 Regression Results

	a	b_1	b_2	b_3	b_4	b_5	R^2	s_u
A-12	−0.24147 (0.21606)	0.08771 (0.06847)	−0.13825 (0.08278)	−0.06737* (0.02754)	0.24670* (0.04573)	0.00294 (0.01964)	.491	0.09381
A-16	−0.17883 (0.18907)	0.12900* (0.05991)	−0.21779* (0.07244)	−0.04936* (0.02410)	0.31698* (0.04002)	0.02665 (0.01718)	.694	0.08209
A-21	−0.30947 (0.17552)	0.17118* (0.05562)	−0.25325* (0.06725)	−0.02426 (0.02237)	0.26097* (0.03715)	0.02064 (0.01595)	.690	0.07621
A > 10	−0.31802 (0.17034)	−0.00303 (0.05398)	−0.10342 (0.06725)	−0.11668* (0.02171)	0.49525* (0.03606)	0.02997 (0.01548)	.819	0.07396
B-12	−0.96560* (0.30458)	0.22676* (0.11275)	−0.42824* (0.13797)	−0.22675* (0.04535)	1.0491* (0.07622)	0.12482* (0.03173)	.853	0.14864
B-16	−0.61794* (0.24998)	0.3320* (0.09253)	−0.55329* (0.11324)	−0.14803* (0.03722)	0.87254* (0.06256)	0.11497* (0.02604)	.877	0.12199
B-21	−0.86398* (0.27837)	0.32229* (0.10305)	−0.51053* (0.12610)	−0.06837 (0.04145)	0.75392* (0.06966)	0.11963* (0.02900)	.834	0.13585
B > 10	−0.23595 (0.20535)	0.14052 (0.07602)	−0.38585* (0.09302)	−0.21284* (0.03057)	1.1611* (0.05139)	0.13221* (0.02139)	.933	0.10021

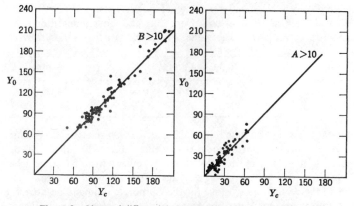

Figure 2 Observed differential plotted against computed differential.

F-Tests for each equation showed R^2 to be significant at the 0.01 level. To test the null hypothesis that there was no significant difference among equations A-12, A-16, and A-21, and similarly among B-12, B-16, and B-21, observations from each set of three equations were pooled and an F-Test made with:

$$F = \frac{(\sum u_j'^2 - \sum \sum u_j^2)/n}{\sum \sum u_j^2/N}$$

$\sum u_j'^2 =$ sum of the squared deviations (residuals) from the pooled equation

$\sum \sum u_j^2 =$ sum of the sum of the squared deviations from the individual equations

$n = 10$

$N = 201$

In both cases the F-Test indicated a significant difference at the 0.01 level among the individual equations: for the A equations $F = 17.326$; for the B equations $F = 9.684$; for 0.01 $F = 2.41$.

ANALYSIS OF THE RESULTS

Stock Variables

The first two independent variables, the ratios of Corporate and of Government Bonds to competing long term debt, are measures of the stock of bonds outstanding relative to major competitive instruments in the capital market. These variables serve as adjustment factors so that variables reflecting the more subjective elements in risk evaluation may be analyzed "given the relative volume of bonds outstanding." Between 1954 and 1959 the stock of both Corporate and Government Bonds fell relative to other assets. The values of the independent variables were:

	January 1954	December 1959
X_1	32.6	17.8
X_2	24.7	12.6

As the volume of Corporate Bonds fell relative to other assets, the original hypothesis was that prices would rise, yields fall and the differential decrease; as the Government ratio fell the hypothesis was that prices again would rise, yields fall but in this case the differential would increase. The signs of the coefficients, positive for the Corporate ratio and negative for the Government, supported the hypothesis. The values were significant, at least at the 0.10 level, except for equations A-12 and $A > 10$; the Government ratio exhibited the stronger impact throughout. Further the impact of these variables tended to be weaker at 12 than at 21 years. In view of the fact that two of the three expectational coefficients (b_3 and b_4) exhibit the opposite tendency, it may be concluded that subjective evaluation of risk based upon expected short run changes in financial markets dominates the more objective influence of the stock variables as the long term bond market (over ten years) becomes more nearly contiguous to the intermediate market (five to ten years).

Prime Rate on Commercial Paper

The prime rate on commercial paper (4 to 6 months) was chosen as an indicator of expectations of changes in the money market and of the availability of short term funds. The rediscount rate was not used since it is much more "sticky." Also it was desired to have a rate at least one step removed from the direct institutional control of the Federal Reserve Board yet strongly subject to its actions. At the other end of the spectrum the prime rate on bank loans might have been used, but, again, changes are relatively infrequent and more the result of institutional decisions than the free play of the money markets. The commercial paper rate was used as being the most responsive to changes in liquidity and as the best indicator of the general trend in interest rates—basically as the determinant of that portion of the risk premium demanded to compensate for the probability of a change in capital values due to changes in the interest rate structure. As interest rates fall, bond prices rise, the reward for undertaking the risk of capital loss is reduced and one expects the differential to increase if investors are to be induced to maintain approximately the current, over-all portfolio composition. The negative signs of the co-efficients support this hypothesis. Further, as maturity lengthens, the impact of the interest rate lessens; at 21 years the value is not significant. This is explained by the fact that the very long term market is more of a stable, investor's market not as subject to temporary fluctuations in the supply of funds nor as likely to attract speculators with short time horizons who are concerned with the possibility of capital gains from expected changes in interest rates.

For the A equations the interest rate was significant only when introduced with a lead of one month, i.e., at time period $t + 1$. The high quality bond market is by far the most sophisticated market—largely peopled by institutional investors. These professional investors keep themselves extremely well informed and are in a better position than most to anticipate changes in the interest rate structure. Generally liquidity changes in the banking sector prior to changes in the commercial paper rate, and these investors are well aware of the fact. This contention is supported by the results of a simple regression of the form:

$$r = f(\text{net free reserves})_{t-1}$$

The significant equation which resulted was:

$$Y = 2.9125 - 0.00216X$$
$$(0.057) \quad (0.00014)$$

The correlation coefficient, R, was equal to .88 and the computed change in the commercial paper rate (r) was approximately 20 basis points for every 100 million dollar change in net free reserves. This indicates considerable predictive value pertaining to the money market can be derived from a high degree of familiarity with the liquidity position of financial institutions. Substitution of net free reserves for the commercial paper rate as an independent variable in the equations showed some significant results but not the consistency of the variable adopted. For the B equations neither the commercial paper rate introduced with a lead nor the substitution of net free reserves proved significant—proving that in this less sophisticated market expectations are dominated by existing conditions. Sophisticated investors could easily enough invade the Baa market but part of sophistication is obtaining return while undertaking minimum risk. In perilous times high quality bonds offer the possibility of return with only limited risk; Baa Bonds offer a return but only with increasing risk of default as Corporate earnings drop. In favorable times the risk of holding alternative assets decreases, and the sophisticated investors, ensconced in high quality bonds, make the first move. In either case, it is the high quality market which sets the pace.

Equity Yield

The dividend yield on stocks is the best available measure of investor psychology—of expectations, uncertainty, and the relative attractiveness of monetary versus real assets. Since it is not a perfect measure, especially with respect to the bond market, there is a degree of uncertainty unaccounted for; but it still serves as an approximation for the determinant of that portion of the risk premium which is a function of the probability of capital loss or gain due to relative price changes between equities and bonds. The dividend yield was chosen rather than the earnings yield in this case since dividends are a much more stable element than are earnings. Thus, the variable is primarily a function of buying and selling pressures in the stock market rather than a combination of this desired factor and a cyclical element introduced by earnings fluctuations consonant with business conditions. With a buoyant stock market (falling yield), favorable expectations of business activity and a rising general price level, a preference for equity assets develops coupled with a willingness to expand the proportion of risk in portfolios. Between markets investors switch from bonds to stocks and bond prices fall; within the bond market the probability of capital gain increases and one expects the differential to decrease. The fact that the coefficients show a positive relationship bears out this hypothesis. It should also be noted that the values of the coefficients indicate that this variable is by far the most important of the expectational variables.

For the A equations no consistent trend in the coefficient values is evident. This high quality market is an institutional one dominated by those dealing primarily in bonds. For the B equations the coefficients show a tendency to decrease in value for the longer maturities indicating the pressure of offsetting evaluations of risk. Given a falling stock market (rising yield), investors seeking capital gain can reduce risk by switching from stocks to bonds. This action tends to bid Baa prices up, yields fall and the differential narrows. On the other hand, investors seeking safety within the bond market can reduce risk by switching to higher quality bonds. This action tends to depress Baa prices, yields increase, and the differential widens. In the very long term market it is evident that those seeking capital gains dominate, while the shorter term and Aaa markets are more strongly influenced by conservative investors who must balance liquidity against profits and risk.

Unemployment Rate

The percentage of the civilian labor force unemployed was designed to serve as a proxy for the subjective evaluation of default risk. It is a rough measure of the existing state of the economy upon which profits depend and ultimately debt coverage and default. As unemployment rises, profits normally fall, the risk of default increases, and one would expect the differential to increase. The positive signs of the coefficients support this hypothesis. The unemployment variable is basically weaker than those representing the financial markets. In addition, the coefficients proved not significant for the A equations. For both the A and the B equations the values of the coefficients were approximately equal for all points along the yield curves. This result might be expected. Aaa Bonds consist mainly of utilities plus some "blue chip" industrials and rails, e.g., General Motors, Standard Oil (N.J.), Texas Company, and Atchison, Topeka and Santa Fe Railroad. The possibility of default is remote barring another "Great Depression." Aaa is the top quality rating assigned by Moody applying as well to Government Bonds; the results indicate acceptance of the high degree of substitutability so indicated and further supports the view that, for a given stock, the most important functional relationship in determining bond yield differentials involves risk and expected changes in the capital values of monetary assets. In contrast the Baa bonds are mostly railroads, many of which have been experiencing a declining profit trend. The consistency of the values follows from the fact that maturity does not grant one a prior claim on the assets of a bankrupt corporation and further bears out the plausibility of a general quality rating for categories of bonds over the long term.

ALTERNATIVE HYPOTHESES

Upon plotting the residuals from the above equations against time, it was noted that the dispersion showed some tendency to increase during periods of business uncertainty. In an effort to explain this dispersion, it was decided to test the following hypotheses:

1. The rate of unemployment is not an adequate indicator of the economy.

2. The increased scatter is attributable to a change in the function during periods of business recession.

The latter hypothesis would be supported if it could be shown that either: (*a*) There was a change in the value of the coefficients, i.e., the slope; for example, reactions to the yield on equities might be greater in a recession than otherwise, or (*b*) The constant term was significantly different; for example, the risk premium might be greater in a recession than otherwise.

The independent variable (X_6), chosen as a substitute for the rate of unemployment (X_5), was the deviation from the trend of the Industrial Production Index (1957 = 100).[30] A trend line was fitted to the seasonally

---

[30] Source: Federal Reserve Board, *Industrial Production 1959 Revision* (Washington, 1960).

adjusted monthly index for the period July 1953 through June 1960 and the positive and negative deviations ($Y_0 - Y_c$) computed. This variable (X_6) was substituted for the rate of unemployment (X_5) in the regression. In addition, to test for changes in the slope, dummy variables of the form $d \cdot X_3$, $d \cdot X_4$, and $d \cdot X_6$ were introduced where $d = 0$ for a positive deviation and $d = 1$ for a negative deviation. (X_3 and X_4 refer respectively to the interest rate and equity yield variables as heretofore defined.) To test for changes in the constant term, a dummy variable, D_0, was introduced where $D_0 = 0$ for a positive deviation and $D_0 = 1$ for a negative deviation. The result was that of all the variables tested, separately and conjointly (including X_6), only $d \cdot X_6$, the product of the dummy and the computed deviation, was significant. The hypothesis that the constant term was significantly different under adverse business conditions as measured by the Industrial Production Index was not supported; the hypothesis that investor reactions to the interest rate or to equity yields differed significantly during recessions was not supported. The hypothesis that the rate of unemployment was an inadequate indicator of economic conditions was not supported (*a*) since the variable representing deviations from the trend of the Industrial Production Index (X_6) did not exhibit a statistically significant relationship and (*b*) although the coefficient for the variable $d \cdot X_6$ was significant, when substituted for the rate of unemployment (X_5), it did not materially improve R^2, the standard error of estimate, nor did it alter the trends in other coefficient values or the scatter of residuals. These results indicate that economic conditions, as measured by the Industrial Production Index, are only significant when adverse and that under adverse economic conditions there is no significant difference in the other coefficients (b_3 and b_4). It was concluded that improvement was insufficient to justify changing the original equation.

In passing, another relationship which might have bearing on this study should be mentioned, i.e., the relationship between bond yield differentials and the future course of the stock market. Each Monday *Barron's*, a financial weekly, publishes as a Confidence Index the ratio of the yield index on high quality bonds to its over-all bond index. Recently this Confidence Index has been presented as an instrument for predicting the trend in the stock market with a lead time of from sixty to ninety days.[31] To test this assertion various lead times were introduced into the original equations both with respect to equity yields and the rate of unemployment. At no time were significant results obtained. Admittedly the dependent variable in this case is the absolute differential rather than a ratio, but it is

[31] See J. E. Granville, "Market Forecaster?" *Barron's* (September 7, 1959), p. 9; also J. E. Granville, *A Strategy of Daily Stock Market Timing for Maximum Profit* (Englewood Cliffs, N.J.: Prentice-Hall, Inc., 1960), pp. 101–22.

dubious that this fact alone explains the lack of statistical significance in the above results. Certainly the high quality bond market is populated by sophisticated investors who often can and do anticipate changes in economic conditions and the financial markets, but there seems little indication that, in a world subject to great uncertainty concerning the future, bond yield differentials are other than coincident indicators when a consistent relationship over time is desired.

EXPECTATIONS

As mentioned above, when the residuals from the regressions are plotted against time, an increased dispersion is evident during periods of unfavorable business conditions such as the 1957–1958 recession (see Figure 3). Taking those deviations which exceed one standard error during 1957 and 1958, it is possible to discern a rough pattern (see Table 4). Since

Table 4 Pattern of Deviations Exceeding One Standard Error

		A-12	A-16	A-21	A-10	B-10	B-12	B-16	B-21
1957	J		+	+				+	+
	F	−					−		
	M								
	A			−	−			+	
	M			−		+			
	J		+	+	+	+			
	J			+	+	+			
	A			+	+				
	S	−	−				−	−	−
	O	−	−			−	−	−	−
	N	+	+	+	+	+	+	+	+
	D				−		+	+	
1958	J			−	−				
	F	+							
	M	+			+	+	+		
	A		−						
	M					+	+	+	+
	J								
	J								
	A	−	−	−	−	−	−	−	−
	S			−			−		
	O								
	N		+		+	+	+	+	−
	D	−	−	−	−				

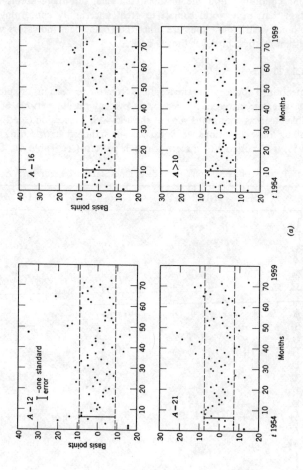

(a)

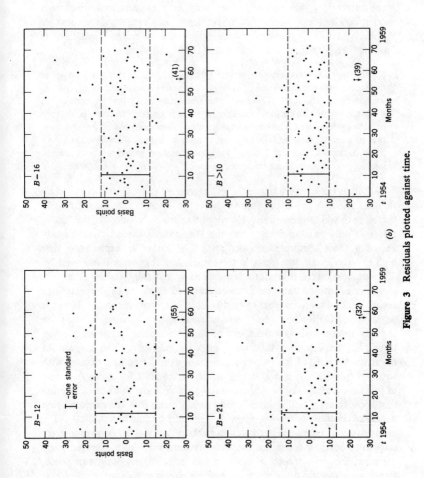

Figure 3 Residuals plotted against time.

statistical analysis has left this pattern inviolate, it seems pertinent to assume that the "goodness of fit" depends primarily upon the elasticity of expectations with respect to the interest rate. Especially in periods of great uncertainty there occur sudden changes in expectations which in a market lacking depth, breadth and resiliency may cause wide divergence of observed from computed values before the differential can find its "normal" equilibrium. As Hicks says,

> . . . the sort of variations in interest rates which are consistent with quiet times and with the maintenance of organized markets are quite small; for, as we have seen, the level of interest rates ultimately measures the intensity of a certain set of risk factors, and this intensity is unlikely to remain for long outside certain broad limits. Consequently, when the rate of interest (any rate of interest) rises or falls very far, there is a real presumption that it will come back to a "normal" level. This consideration would seem to prevent interest-expectations from being very elastic.[32]

Although Hicks refers to the "level" of interest rates, the context is such that his remarks are applicable to the entire interest rate structure and therefore to yield differentials. He goes on to say, in a footnote, the "short rate will only react quickly upon the long rate if there is immediately apparent some significant reason [and] this creates an expectation that high short rates are less likely in the future than they were in the past."[33] The implication is that during prosperous, basically stable times the structure of interest rates tends to be accepted as given, i.e., expectations are inelastic. Investors react to change only when convinced the change is permanent. Only when good and sufficient reason becomes evident are changes interpreted as harbingers of the culminating point of a given trend, i.e., expectations take on a negative elasticity. The concept of negative elasticity of interest rate expectations must be approached with some trepidation. It is a situation which cannot last for more than one or two time periods since otherwise one would be in the position of arguing that a continually falling interest rate would mean that the expected rate would be continually revised upward. This may be true in a cyclical swing as investors foresee a greater reaction back to "normal" the lower interest rates drop during a recession, but there are some limits as to the credibility of maintaining that such a position can exist in any long run sense. Expectations would more normally become elastic as a downtrend in rates is "recognized," tend to become only briefly negative as the turning point is anticipated and then tend to elasticity again as the turn is made and

---

[32] Hicks, p. 262.
[33] *Ibid.*

interest rates rise back to their "normal" level (at which inelastic expectations prevail). The more unexpected the changes are, the greater the elasticity of expectations as investors suddenly believe they can recognize a trend and, upon the basis of these expectations, revise their evaluations of the riskiness of competitive assets. Also, there is a decided degree of asymmetry in this process as expectations tend to exhibit more elasticity around the low points in business activity when uncertainty and bond market speculation are rampant. Such a point was reached in 1958, and, for this reason, analysis of the 1957–1958 recession may yield an explanation for the pattern of residuals.

THE 1957–1958 RECESSION[34]

The 1957–1958 recession differed from its predecessor in several important respects. Interest rates in the summer of 1957 were the highest in many years; Standard and Poor's Index of Stock Prices had more than tripled since 1946 with more than 70% of the rise having occurred since January 1954; the Consumer Price Index, except for pausing in 1953, 1954, and 1955, had risen ten points during the decade with the Wholesale Commodity Index following suit; the average maturity of the Government Debt had shrunk from five years and six months in 1954 to four years and nine months in 1957 and, much more important, the Treasury Department was determined to lengthen it; there had been a fortuitous tax cut in 1954; the financial community had expected the Federal Reserve to follow an easy money policy in 1954 and the monetary authorities had obliged—in 1958 the financial community expected the same policy only to be disappointed by an inital hesitation on the part of the "Fed" to take positive steps toward monetary ease followed by a cheerful readiness to take positive steps toward monetary restraint at the first sign of recovery; and finally, the 1957–1958 drop in economic activity was much sharper and of shorter duration than the 1953–1954 drop. Consequently, the pressures on the bond market were too strong and changing too swiftly to be accommodated without occasional, temporary deviations from the "normal" bond yield differentials.

The bond market was in a highly volatile condition entering 1957.

Events during the previous recession had provided ample evidence that market rates of interest could be expected to move downward with general

---

[34] For the ensuing analysis information concerning the general condition of the bond market has been gathered from: *The Commercial and Financial Chronicle, Barron's, Treasury-Federal Reserve Study of the Government Securities Market* (Washington, 1959), and Joint Economic Committee, *A Study of the Dealer Market for Federal Government Securities* (Washington: U.S. Government Printing Office, 1960).

economic conditions, as a result both of changes in private demands for funds and of shifts in monetary policy. Investor expectations were so sensitively attuned to these relationships that on earlier occasions during the cyclical advance of 1954–57—most notably in early 1957—interest rates had declined and bond prices had experienced a sharp temporary upward movement set off by transient indications of a slowdown or possible reversal in the pace of business activity.[35]

Normally inelastic expectations were experiencing some strain awaiting a signal which would indicate a turn in the bond market. This condition is evidenced in the pattern of residuals in January and February 1957 before the dip and, again, after the recovery in November and December 1958. In both instances there are indications of a plus, minus sequence as false starts result in overstated risk premiums subject to overcorrection as investors realize their mistake and confidence returns.

In the summer of 1957 there were scattered indications that the observed differential was tending to exceed the computed differential, i.e., there were signs that pessimism was building even though general business indicators remained high. Another factor was that the speculative excess of the long capital spending boom had not been corrected and a general desire to invest in competing long term assets prevailed. There were a few signs that the economy was weakening, but the demand for loanable funds was very strong and interest rates were high. Some banks and institutions were switching from long term Governments and Aaa Bonds to short term Governments due to rising uncertainty, while others were selling, especially longer term Aaa's, to obtain funds for loans.[36] Added to this was the selling pressure from investors who were moving from bonds to stocks.[37] The combined effect was a higher differential than "normal" between Corporates and Governments and a lower differential than "normal" between Aaa's and Baa's as selling pressures from all sides descended upon higher quality Corporate Bonds. By June the spread between Corporates and Governments was the highest in many years, and uncertainty concerning the economy was building up. In July some

---

[35] *Treasury-Federal Reserve Study*, Part II, p. 3.

[36] For example, in the second quarter of 1957 Commercial Banks sold 4.5 billion dollars of long term (*over one year*) Federal Obligations and increased short term holdings by 2.2 billion and loans by 2.1 billion. Source: Federal Reserve Board, *Flow of Funds/ Saving Estimates, Supplement No. 4* (Washington, 1961).

[37] This could be stated alternatively as the premium necessary to prevent bond holders from indulging in portfolio shifts. Consideration of this distinction would involve detailed microanalysis utilizing data not readily available at present. Moreover, it will later become clear that portfolio shifts among existing assets are far less important in the long term (*over 10 years*) bond market than the absorption rate for new Government Bonds.

buying appeared in bonds, but it was mostly of a professional nature. In August the stock market turned down and unemployment began a slow rise. At the same time the prime rate for bank loans and the rediscount rate were raised leading to a great deal of uncertainty and confusion. More money became available for bonds and the Government market stabilized; but the desire for liquidity was strong and selling of Corporates continued although trading volume fell off.

In September and October the situation changed. The computed differential basically exceeded the observed differential in these two months, indicating a high degree of confusion in the money market and supporting the contention that interest-expectations tend to be inelastic until "significant reason" is given for a change. Business conditions were worsening but without some specific confirmation of their fears investors were not evaluating risk accordingly. There had been false starts before (as in January), and investors weighed the risk of capital loss, should a sudden business upturn develop causing bond prices to fall, against the probability of capital gain should a true business downturn occur. There was some buying. Smaller commercial banks, experiencing a drop in the demand for loans, began buying Aaa Bonds for income purposes, and sophisticated investors started moving from stocks to bonds, particularly Baa's. The Government market remained relatively weak although a 4% twelve year bond issued for cash was readily absorbed during September.[38] During these two months, the professional who, in this thin market, carries out arbitrage transactions in accordance with his estimate of the proper interest rate structure was giving way to the investor throughout the market.

On November 14 the "significant reason" was given, and the elasticity of expectations with respect to the interest rate became immediately negative as a downturn in business was confirmed. On that date the rediscount rate was lowered by the Federal Reserve System.

> By far the most important single influence on interest rate expectations, therefore, is the outlook for general business conditions. Signs of changes in monetary policy are watched closely by participants in the Government securities market since such changes are often interpreted as confirmations of major turns in the business situation and suggest to observers possible shifts in the balance of pressures in the money and capital markets.[39]

---

[38] One would expect this new issue of Government Bonds to tend towards a narrowing of the differential. However, the lack of correlation between particular new issues and the dependent variable is indicated by the signs in the pattern of residuals in Table 2 at the time of this issue and of three other cash issues: minus, plus, plus, "normal" for 9/57, 11/57, 2/58 and 6/58 respectively.

[39] *Treasury-Federal Reserve Study*, Part II, p. 3.

The observed differential greatly exceeded the computed differential as the risk premium adjustment started with a rush. The basic yield adjusted first, falling markedly, with Aaa's close behind. Initially the lower quality yields rose; longer term Baa's were sold heavily as risk evaluation among monetary assets outweighed any evaluations based upon the choice between equities and fixed income bearing securities. Although the imperfect nature of the bond market precludes immediate adjustment, its tendency to maintain a "normal" differential soon re-asserted itself, and, by the beginning of 1958, most risk premiums reflected existing conditions.

During the Spring of 1958, as bond prices rose, expectations tended to have an elasticity greater than one, i.e., every change in interest rates was interpreted as indicating that the trend would continue. In January a second cut in the rediscount rate and a cut in margin requirements were reinforced by the more positive fact of a cut in the prime lending rate by commercial banks. Through the Spring the rediscount rate continued to fall, reserve requirements were cut and, again, the trend was confirmed by an April cut in the commercial banks' prime loan rate. All this caused investors to seek "certain" capital gains in the bond market as rising bond prices were extrapolated well into the future. A large speculative element arose aided and abetted by the determination of the Federal Government to lengthen the maturity structure of the national debt. As bond prices rose, the risk of capital loss due to a business upturn increased. The premium demanded for holding lower quality bonds showed a tendency to exceed that warranted by existing conditions. This tendency of the observed differential to exceed the computed differential for Baa Bonds became more pronounced as the stock market launched its recovery in March. Selling pressure from this source alone might have been absorbed within "normal" limits, but speculative buying was heavy in the high quality market encouraged in some instances by brokerage houses. Expectations were for an extended period of monetary ease and recommendations were being made for the purchase of long term Government Bonds for the recession and also of Aaa's if the yield spread were 50 basis points (0.5%) or more. Hypothecating at the bank was presented as a method of maintaining actual cash investment relative to the total value of holdings at a minimum thus enhancing profit potential.

Taking advantage of excess demand, suppliers provided new bond issues at a rapid pace. Since it is the Government yield curve which serves as the base from which risk premiums are calculated and indications are that differentials, except under stress, are predominantly a function of existing economic conditions, review of changes in Government Bonds outstanding during the 1957–1958 recession should provide some insight into factors affecting the over-all interest rate structure.[40] In February the Treasury sold six year and thirty-two year bonds in an exchange operation. This financing raised the amount of bonds (as opposed to bills, certificates and notes) represented in this fifteen billion dollar segment of Government debt from 1.5 to 4.5 billion dollars. There followed, in the same month, the sale of a nine year bond for cash. These issues, coupled with the twelve year bond of September and the seventeen year bond of November 1957, both for cash, increased the value of Government Bonds outstanding with over ten years to maturity by approximately 3 billion dollars. This set the stage for the speculative blow off which took place in conjunction with the final attempt of the Treasury to lengthen the debt with its June financing consisting of a 1.1 billion dollar twenty-seven year bond for cash and a 7.4. billion six year eight month bond in exchange for existing securities of predominantly shorter maturities. Of the 4.1 billion addition to Government Bonds of over ten years maturity between June 1957 and June 1958, 25% was absorbed by commercial banks and 50% by investors other than banking and financial institutions. In fact, absorption of new issues accounted for the only portfolio changes that occurred with respect to Government Bonds with maturities greater than ten years.

(billions)	Total	Federal Reserve	Commer-cial Banks	Savings Banks	Insurance	Other
June 1957	30.8	1.4	4.2	4.0	4.6	13.7
June 1958	34.9	1.4	5.2	4.1	5.1	15.9
Net change	4.1	(+0.03)	1.0	0.1	0.5	2.2

It has been stated that new issues have no statistical significance when included as an independent variable in the regression equation. The facts that the timing of new issues is carefully planned and, in the case of long term Treasury Bonds, restricted to periods when demand is high make this result credible. However, there is an impact to be reckoned with. New issues were absorbed by the more volatile elements in the market—commercial banks and "other" investors. Commercial banks expected to hold long term bonds only until loan demand revived and were anxious to take profits six months after purchase. "Other" investors were seeking an alternative source of capital gains—a "sure thing" with falling interest

---

[40] All data concerning Government Bonds have been taken from the *Treasury Bulletin*.

rates—until such time as an upturn in business was confirmed bringing with it a return to tight money policies. Up to May expectations were almost universally held (with "certainty") that interest rates would continue to fall as the monetary authorities attempted to stimulate a slowly recovering economy. In late Spring 1958 a sort of Damocles' sword overhung the market waiting for expectations to change before dropping.

> In the area of debt management, there is the problem as to whether, in periods when easy credit conditions lend investor favor to longer term, higher yielding issues, a large and rapid shift in the maturity structure of the debt may result in supply and demand distortions, which may later have upsetting and disruptive effects on the market.[41]

The Treasury's June financing attracted a large amount of speculative funds. The failure of this issue to provide immediate capital gains was strong evidence that expectations were outrunning the actual course of events. As distress selling occurred, the Treasury and the Federal Reserve found it necessary to support the long term market in June and July. Signs were growing that business recovery was underway. By May the stock market was well on the road to recovery, and the selling of Baa's is clearly reflected in the large differential between Baa's and Governments and between Baa's and Aaa's. Bank loans were picking up and selling pressure was building in the Corporate market. The Government market was in a technically weak position with speculators desiring to sell and institutional portfolios filled. In July it became evident that future Treasury financing would be short term, and this was taken as a clue that further cuts in the rediscount rate would not occur. Now, expectations reverted to their normal, inelastic state. Although it was fairly clear that interest rates would not fall further, it was unclear to many that they would reverse direction in the face of the continuing high level of unemployment and the anticipated slowness of the business recovery. Once again confirmation of a change was required before expectations exhibited negative elasticity.

In August the computed differential generally exceeded the observed differential as a congeries of factors added up to a "significant reason" for a change in expectations. The short term interest rate on prime commercial paper turned up indicating a reduction in liquidity; the stock market was rising. Margin requirements were raised, and it became clear that, in Washington, inflationary fears were taking precedence over concern with the economy. Those who had participated in the February Treasury financing had passed the six month barrier. The sword fell. To absorb the increased supply of Government Bonds a severe adjustment

---

[41] *Treasury-Federal Reserve Study*, Part II, p. 102.

in the basic yield was required. The bond market initially was unable to accommodate the rush of selling pressure.[42] Although professionals believed the market was overdiscounting any future change in credit conditions, institutions and dealers were unwilling to commit funds until the market had stabilized. Banks which had bought in June suddenly found themselves with short term capital losses which they were unwilling to realize until they became long term at the end of the year or early in 1959. Within the next two months the market did adjust, and the yield differentials reverted to "normal" limits. Just as November 1957 marked the beginning of the Recession Phase in the bond market as expectations of the "average" investor with respect to bonds turned bullish and everyone became a "buyer," so did August 1958 mark the end of this phase as expectations turned bearish and everyone became a "seller."

Basically both these periods of accelerated price adjustment were reflections of the high sensitivity of the Government securities market in recent years to shifts in the direction of economic activity and of the strategic role played in this pivotal market by the expectations of participants. In the summer of 1958, the timing of the economic upturn as well as the speed with which recovery in activity took hold was a surprise to the market. As evidence continued to pile up that recovery was proceeding, the impact on expectations was pronounced and the adjustment of Government securities prices severe.[43]

---

[42] It is interesting again to note that selling pressure can be stated equally well as that rise in interest necessary to make investors content with their existing portfolios. Ownership figures for Government Bonds indicate no portfolio shifts among existing securities during this entire adjustment period. Conard, p. 315, indicates this to be a somewhat normal condition as investors throughout the market adjust prices with respect to changes in expectations arising from any segment of the market without a great volume of shifting.

[43] *Treasury-Federal Reserve Study*, Part II, p. 78. The increasingly high sensitivity to the direction of economic activity may readily be explained by the secular shift in the composition of ownership of U.S. Securities. For example, between 1954 and 1959 total long term Government debt outstanding fell 22% with percentage holdings (other than Federal Reserve System, Government Agencies and Trust Funds) as follows:

	Commercial Banks	Savings Banks	Insurance Companies	Other
January 1954	15%	16%	20%	37%
December 1959	10%	8%	14%	54%

The more volatile elements—commercial banks and "other" investors—thus have become a much more important factor in the market. Particularly in 1958 this led to instability. Source: *Treasury Bulletin*.

Table 5ᵃ Differential Changes Attributed to Specific Independent Variables, July 1957 to February 1958

Change in Independent Variables	Estimated Net Change in Differential Due To:	Corporates Long Term Debt	Governments Long Term Debt (net) (1 and 2)	Interest Rate	Equity Yield	Unemployment
Change in Independent Variables		+ 3.0	+ 2.3	− 1.25	+ 0.61	+ 2.5
Basis Point Change (Y_e)						
A-12 =	+21.1	+28.4	− 31.5 (− 3.1)	+ 8.4	+15.1	+ 0.7
A-16 =	+24.0	+40.0	− 50.0 (−10.0)	+ 7.0	+17.0	+10.0
A-21 =	+17.0	+51.0	− 58.0 (− 7.0)	+ 3.0	+15.6	+ 5.4
B-12 =	+93.0	+68.0	− 98.5 (−30.5)	+28.0	+64.0	+31.5
B-16 =	+75.0	+95.0	−120.0 (−25.0)	+20.0	+50.0	+30.0
B-21 =	+63.0	+96.0	−118.0 (−22.0)	+ 8.0	+46.0	+31.0

ᵃ Actual differential changes, i.e., changes in the dependent variables were:

	A	B
12	+35	+110
16	+16	+ 79
21	+ 4	+ 61

In the cases of A-12 and A-21 the divergences between ΔY_e and ΔY_0 are marked. In the other cases the same general magnitude prevails. This is the result of choosing a single trading day in a particular month during a period in which an imperfect market is being subjected to the stress of highly volatile expectations. All the adjustments in evidence at any point in time will not be one hundred per cent successful. For example, A-12 through January 1958 showed $\Delta Y_e = +21$ and $\Delta Y_0 = +19$; A-21 through March 1958 showed $\Delta Y_e = +20$ and $\Delta Y_0 = +15$—discrepancies well within normal limits. On the other hand, choosing March 1958 as the terminal date would have shown for: B-12, $\Delta Y_e = +95$ and $\Delta Y_0 = +129$; B-21, $\Delta Y_e = +67$, and $\Delta Y_0 = +46$—discrepancies which appear rather large. In any case the general conclusions utilizing Table 5 do not appear to be invalidated by an argument to the effect that observed yields acted in any consistent manner differently than computed yields. As the preceding analysis has demonstrated, the differentials do maintain a "normal" relationship over time subject to occasional, temporary displacement. Therefore, use of the "normal" differential is justified.

CONCLUSIONS

There are three basic approaches to the explanation of the interest rate structure involving:

1. Institutions
2. Loanable Funds
3. Expectations

In this study of bond yield differentials the last approach has been favored with emphasis upon the subjective evaluation of risk under conditions of uncertainty. However, throughout the discussion frequent reference has been made to factors which may readily be classified under the general headings of either loanable funds or institutions. To justify the emphasis upon expectations and to provide clear cut conclusions, it is necessary to review the three possible approaches in the context of the results achieved. Since we are interested in the dynamics of interest rate structure, a period of maximum change in prices, yields, and differentials would seem to be best for illustrative purposes. Such a period was July 1957 through February 1958—the month preceding the stock market peak to the month preceding the stock market recovery.

Table 5 shows the change in basis points attributed to each independent variable by the regressions and the net estimated change of the differential over the period. It is evident from the table that:

(*a*) Differentials widened during this recessionary period.

(*b*) Lower quality differentials widened more.

(*c*) Changes in Corporate volume outstanding offset to a large extent, but not entirely, the impact of changes in Governments outstanding and both showed a slightly greater impact for longer maturities.

(*d*) Of the three remaining variables: changes in equity yields have by far the greatest impact; changes in short term interest rates have less impact as maturity lengthens; and economic conditions are much more important in the *B* than in the *A* equations.

Table 6 shows monthly prices, yields to maturity and differentials involving the three bond categories for means over ten years and the maturity year 1970. Only one maturity year is shown since the regression results all yield the same general trend with only variations in magnitude and since, for this maturity, there existed actual bonds outstanding in each category; checking the 1970 pattern against that for other points along the yield curves a high degree of similarity is found. In the case of the means (which do not have exactly the same average maturities) the adjustments in prices and yields are somewhat smoother, the recovery

Table 6[a] Patterns of Prices, Yields, and Differentials, July 1957 to June 1958

A. 1970 Maturity
Coupons: 3-3/8 Baa (adj.)
3 Aaa
2-1/2 Government

1957	Baa Yield	Baa Price	Aaa Yield	Aaa Price	Government Yield	Government Price	Differential *B* (Basis points)	Differential *A* (Basis points)
July	4.47	89-1/4	3.99	90	3.82	86-1/2	65	17
Aug	4.55	88-1/2	4.10	89	3.76	87	79	34
Sept	4.95	85	4.18	88-1/4	3.85	86-1/4	110	33
Oct	5.06	84-1/8	3.99	90	3.83	86-1/2	123	16
Nov	5.10	83-3/4	3.94	90-1/2	3.24	92-1/4	186	70
Dec	5.49	80-1/2	3.52	94-1/2	3.07	94	242	45
Jan	4.92	86	3.28	97-1/8	3.08	94-1/2	184	20
Feb	4.96	85-3/4	3.33	96-3/4	2.95	95-1/2	201	38
Mar	5.09	84-3/4	3.32	96-3/4	2.85	96-1/2	224	47
Apr	5.16	84-1/8	3.23	97-3/4	2.87	96-1/4	229	36
May	5.17	84	3.14	98-5/8	2.86	96-1/4	221	28
June	5.01	85-3/8	3.31	97	3.05	94-1/2	196	26

B. Means Over Ten Years
Average Coupon and Maturity:
4 1978 Baa (adj.)
3 1979 Aaa
2-5/8 1971 Government

1957	Baa Yield	Baa Price	Aaa Yield	Aaa Price	Government Yield	Government Price	Differential *B*	Differential *A*
July	4.90	88-1/4	4.12	84	3.66	88-7/8	124	56
Aug	4.99	87	4.18	83	3.68	88-3/4	131	50
Sept	5.09	86	4.16	83-3/8	3.65	89	144	51
Oct	5.20	84-3/4	4.12	84	3.70	88-5/8	150	42
Nov	5.27	83-1/2	4.02	85-1/4	3.41	91-3/8	186	61
Dec	5.13	85-1/2	3.68	89-7/8	3.24	93-1/8	189	44
Jan	4.92	88-3/8	3.60	91-1/4	3.09	95	183	51
Feb	4.93	88-1/4	3.61	91-1/8	2.99	96-1/8	194	62
Mar	4.99	87-1/2	3.65	90-1/2	2.90	97	209	75
Apr	4.97	87-3/4	3.51	92-1/8	2.89	97-1/8	208	62
May	4.96	87-7/8	3.53	92-1/8	2.88	97-1/4	208	65
June	4.86	89-1/8	3.59	91-3/8	3.06	95-3/8	180	53

[a] 1. All prices in this table have been approximated according to a standard bond value table.
2. In Section A the differentials shown are *not* those used as the dependent variable in the regression analysis. The dependent variables were calculated from pairs of curves fitted to yield scatters.* The above calculations are based upon actual yields utilizing the average of two Baa Bonds and single Aaa and Government Bonds.
3. In Section B yields are from the regression data for means over ten years.
4. In the case of Baa Bonds the yields are after adjustment as described in the Appendix to this chapter. (It is interesting to note that even without the adjustment the Baa data exhibit the same general price and yield pattern.)

* Actual Differentials Used as Dependent Variables for:

	B-12	*A*-12
July	86	20
Aug	106	24
Sept	117	17
Oct	129	15
Nov	195	67
Dec	201	38
Jan	175	39
Feb	196	55
Mar	215	55
Apr	208	33
May	211	35
June	181	28

of B bonds takes place one month earlier, and it is more complete. Since we are interested merely in illustrating the general trend, the data shown should be adequate. It is evident from this table that:

(*a*) A Bond and Government Bond prices rose considerably between July 1957 and February 1958.

(*b*) B Bond prices were not greatly changed by February 1958 due to an initial fall followed by a mild recovery toward the end of 1957.

(*c*) The greater change in the lower quality differential was associated with the relative stability of B Bond prices.

The implications of this experience with respect to debt management have been fairly well explored in the earlier analysis. Tables 5 and 6 confirm the previous assertion of the importance of Treasury financing and its potentially significant impact. The fact that all issuers of fixed interest bearing securities tend to follow the same borrowing pattern creates an offsetting situation in so far as the differential is concerned, albeit only as a result of the awareness of the protagonists. With respect to monetary policy Tables 5 and 6 do provide some additional insight. Table 5 shows that the commercial paper rate, the most sensitive to Federal Reserve action, dropped 125 basis points between July 1957 and February 1958. Section B of Table 6 shows that the mean yields for Governments, Aaa's and Baa's changed by −67, −51, and +3 basis points respectively. In other words, while high quality bond prices rose approximately $7, lower quality prices remained practically unchanged (following an initial drop). This fact would tend to support the argument that an easy money policy benefits primarily the larger corporations which enjoy the highest credit ratings as opposed to the more nearly marginal firms for which the need under adverse circumstances may actually be greater. The Aaa corporation can go to the market at a cost reduced from 4.12% to 3.61%; the Baa corporation, on the other hand, must still pay in the neighborhood of 5% to attract funds on the long-term bond market. It seems evident that quality, i.e., risk factors, outweigh factors bearing upon the structural inter-relationship of yield curves approached in a purely mechanistic manner. The above basis point changes indicate a relationship between the short and long term rates; the high quality short rate moved lower and with it the long but the latter to a much smaller extent as adverse risk evaluation weighed more heavily. Therefore, open market operations appear weak when judged upon the basis of their impact on long term rates. The data also indicate that they are weak upon an inter-quality basis, given the same maturities. The former problem can be met by extending the maturity range of Federal Reserve purchases, but, if expectations are adverse, the latter problem involving favored treatment for the best credit ratings remains—except in so far as Baa concerns might be able to benefit from a generally more effective lowering of long term borrowing costs. It seems that changes in yield differentials can affect the potency of monetary policy even barring any problems involving maturity. It is, therefore, important to understand what is behind them. If it is expectations, it seems dubious that the purchase and sale of Government Securities can, alone, provide an interest rate structure acceptable to all.

Can These Changes be Explained by Institutional Factors ?

Certainly the actions and statements of the Federal Reserve Board are among the most important influences in the bond market. Its actions can influence interest rates and the availability of credit thus having a decided impact upon bond prices, but there is no explanation here of how this impact is distributed among various bond categories especially in the long term market. As long as the Federal Reserve adhered to "bills only," it does not seem feasible to assign to it direct responsibility for changes in the interest rate structure for maturities greater than ten years. Only in June and July 1958 when direct support of the long term market was undertaken can direct responsibility be assigned. Otherwise, the influence of the monetary authorities is felt indirectly through its effect on expectations as to the future course of interest rates.

Another potentially important institutional argument hinges upon the fact that many financial institutions are restricted to Government, Aaa and some Aa Bonds. But if this explanation is used to explain the greater B bond differential, what is left to explain the fact that the A bond differential widens and narrows in accordance with changing conditions in the economy and in the financial market? For many investors there is no such restriction upon the quality of bond they may purchase. If these investors believed the yield differential so wide as to compensate for the additional estimated risk, there is no reason why arbitrage transactions would not take place.

Quality ratings in themselves constitute an institutional fact, but they merely indicate that a differential should exist, not how it may vary under changing conditions. The question to be considered is why the differential between two quality ratings is changed at various points in time, and this question comes down to the consideration of risk and the compensation demanded for undertaking it. Institutional factors may temporarily influence the results at any point in time but can hardly explain them.

Can These Changes be Explained by Supply of and Demand for Loanable Funds ?

The equation used in this study can be interpreted in the following manner. The first two independent variables, the ratios of Corporate and

Government Bonds to Long Term Debt, represent the supply of bonds (relative to competing assets). The last three variables can be interpreted in terms of the supply of and the demand for money. The short term interest rate (r) serves as an indicator of the supply of loanable funds or liquidity in the money market. The yield on equities (E) serves as an indicator of the demand for loanable funds or the demand for real assets, i.e., a proxy for investment demand. The rate of unemployment (U) serves over a short interval as an indicator of transactions demand due to changes in the level of national income. If we think of a three asset world having only money, bonds, and capital, we can represent a change in the amount of money (M) available either to be held as cash balances or to be exchanged for bonds as the algebraic sum of changes in the three uses and sources of funds outlined above. Let us designate them as follows:

(a) M_M = supply of loanable funds $= f(r)$
(b) M_E = net demand for loanable funds $= f(E)$
(c) M_T = demand for transactions funds $= f(U)$

A change in any of the parameters will either result in an increase or decrease in the amount of funds (M) available for holding as monetary assets, i.e., cash or bonds. The designation of M_E as "net" means that any change in demand for real assets resulting from changes in M_M or M_T is automatically adjusted for, leaving:

$$\Delta M_M - \Delta M_E - \Delta M_T = \Delta M$$

Between July 1957 and February 1958 r fell indicating an increase in the supply of loanable funds, E rose indicating a decrease in the demand for loanable funds, and U rose indicating a decrease in transactions demand. If we assume that a portion of the increased M funds will be used to purchase bonds, since all the above changes add to the supply of M, the demand for bonds must have risen. At the same time the volume of bonds outstanding rose, i.e., supply rose. There is no denying the importance of the supply side in analyzing the bond market. However, it is almost a passive element or a function of the demand for bonds; every effort is made to change the supply in such a manner as just to absorb the available funds without upsetting the existing rate structure. If the borrowers were absolutely successful, there would be no change in the interest rate at the time of increased supply. If demand falls back to its original level thereafter, an adjustment in interest rates (upward) will take place as illustrated in the diagram (as shown in next page).

The horizontal axis measures the volume of bonds in the conventional manner; the vertical axis, however, represents the rate of interest rising as it approaches the origin. A is the initial equilibrium; B is the equilibrium attained by an exact matching of supply to the increased demand; and C is the equilibrium following a return of the demand schedule to its original position.[44] The final equilibrium is at a higher rate of interest (lower price) than originally and illustrates in greatly simplified form the type of adjustment in the bond market which took place during 1957 to 1958.

What has the above analysis told us? It has told us that under circumstances similar to those between July 1957 and February 1958 people would increase their demand for monetary assets. But it has told us nothing of

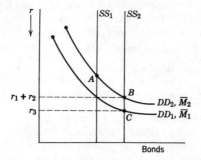

the choice among closely substitutable assets—between money and bonds, between different categories of bonds. We have slipped back to *the* interest rate and, more importantly, have had to assume that an increased demand for monetary assets is equivalent to an increased demand for bonds. This latter assumption is not necessarily true nor can it be expressed as some mechanical function of the funds available for monetary assets (although the assumption is usual enough to serve as a first approximation). To illustrate, assume an increase in funds available for aquisition of monetary assets under the following conditions:

1. (*a*) Investors expect equity prices to fall
   (*b*) Investors expect bond prices to rise
2. (*a*) Investors expect equity prices to fall
   (*b*) Investors expect bond prices to fall

In the first case the tendency would be to buy bonds and sell equities, but this may be tempered, or upset, by a tendency to shift into cash in the

---

[44] It may be argued that the supply schedule is less than perfectly inelastic due to the fact that a lower r (rising bond prices) tends to increase the "floating" supply of bonds actually for sale out of a given total stock outstanding. Allowing for this factor would not change the basic analysis although r_3 would be at a somewhat higher level than shown.

event overall expectations concerning general economic conditions are sufficiently pessimistic. In the second case, e.g., a panic following speculative excess, the tendency would be to buy neither bonds nor equities but to shift into cash. Thus, one cannot say whether or, more especially, how bond prices will be affected by an increase in funds available for monetary assets. In order to explain interest rate structure, one must be concerned with the allocation of funds among closely substitutable assets; and in order to explain this allocation, one must bring in expectations and the subjective evaluation of return and risk under conditions of uncertainty.

Can These Changes be Explained by Expectations?

Returning to case 1 above, expectations are that equity prices will fall and bond prices will rise. Implicit therein is the expectation that general economic conditions will worsen. Therefore, demand for different bond categories is not a simple arithmetic calculation of comparable returns for various qualities but depends also upon personal preferences and the subjective evaluation of risk. Bonds are preferred but not indiscriminately.

Looking at the period July 1957 to February 1958, probabilities favored a relatively short run recession as opposed to a depression of long duration. These expectations, however, were not held with certainty, and, therefore, there was an increase in estimated risk and a tendency toward bonds offering safety and liquidity. After cash, Government (G) Bonds come closest to having these characteristics, followed by A bonds with B bonds running a sorry last. Thus, we would expect the yield on B bonds to increase relative to A bonds and the yield on A bonds to increase relative to G bonds as reflected in the price and yield patterns of Table 6. The end result may even be a cumulative process accounting for speculation, particularly in the Government sector, such as occurred in 1958. The tendency to buy higher quality bonds in a period of uncertainty leads to relative price rises $G > A > B$. The pattern of price rises, in itself, indicates a potential for capital gains in $G > A > B$ and, therefore, attracts speculation in $G > A > B$. Table 6 shows the divergent price pattern for higher quality bonds (up) and B bonds (down then up) between July 1957 and February 1958. The following diagrams illustrate the manner in which, given individual preference patterns, changes in the subjective evaluation of risk and return can account for the patterns of prices, and, therefore, of yield differentials.[45]

---

[45] These diagrams are based on a model presented by James Tobin in "Liquidity Preference as Behavior Towards Risk," *The Review of Economic Studies*, XXV (February 1958) pp. 607–613, reprinted in Cowles Foundation Monograph 19, *Risk Aversion and Portfolio Choice* (New York: John Wiley and Sons, 1967), Chap. 1.

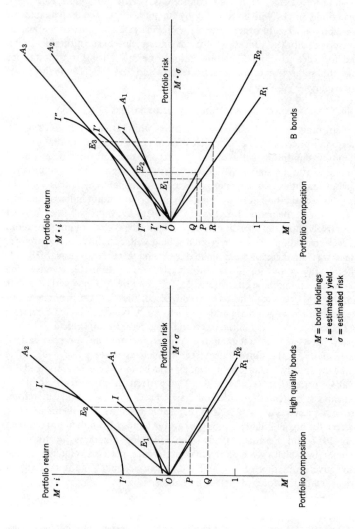

High quality bonds

B bonds

M = bond holdings
i = estimated yield
σ = estimated risk

The vertical axis in the first quadrant measures estimated return for various bond holdings, the horizontal axis measures estimated risk for various bond holdings and the vertical axis in the fourth quadrant measures bond holdings. OA is the opportunity locus representing all possible combinations of risk and return for the stock of bonds outstanding from zero risk and return for zero bond holdings to maximum risk and return for holdings equal to the total available supply of bonds. The slope is i/σ, or return per unit of risk, and is assumed constant for any combination. OR represents all possible combinations of bond holdings and risk with the slope equal to $1/\sigma$, again assumed constant. II represents one of a family of indifference curves between risk and return with the slope indicating that any increase in the risk content of portfolios must be accompanied by an increase in expected returns, i.e., the investor is a risk avoider. Equilibrium between investor preferences and return per unit of risk is indicated at a tangency of II and OA, with the bond content of the portfolio indicated in the fourth quadrant.

In July 1957 equilibrium exists in both the high quality[46] and Baa categories at E_1 with bond content of portfolios represented by OP. As the recession begins, estimated return rises as bond prices start to rise. In the high quality sector risk rises only slightly as the possibility of default is very small even if one expected a fairly widespread deterioration in economic conditions, and the marketability of these bonds remains good as investors attempt to acquire a return at minimum risk. With the increase in $i > \sigma$ the slope of OA (i/σ) rises and a new equilibrium is reached at E_2. The slope of OR ($1/\sigma$), on the other hand, does not change greatly. The proportion of bonds desired in the portfolio therefore rises to OQ with the result that the high quality bond prices are bid up. As indicated above, the increase in expected return may become cumulative, and as long as it does, prices should tend to rise.

In the B bond sector results are somewhat different. Estimated return has risen but so has estimated risk. The possibility of default is more real as indicated by the lower quality rating. Ratings are based upon such factors as greater fluctuations in earnings and less ample coverage of fixed charges by those earnings. This combination couples a lower tolerance for instability with a higher degree of it meaning that even taking safety alone into consideration the estimated risk would rise more for B bonds than for higher quality bonds. But in addition to less safety there is less liquidity. Between July 1957 and February 1958 investors were putting money into the bond market as a temporary measure. To them, liquidity may be defined as the expectation of a rising or at least a stable price during the

---

[46] Aaa and Government Bonds are here combined into a single category although the same analysis would hold for any combination of two categories.

investment period. The estimated risk on this score is also greater for B bonds. Thus, the slope of OA (i/σ) may increase if i increases more than σ but not by as much as in the high quality category. The slope of OR $(1/\sigma)$, on the other hand, falls more for the B bonds with the result that the new equilibrium at E_2 indicates a decrease in the desired proportion of B bonds held from OP to OQ. The tendency then is for B bond prices to fall. If estimated return thereafter rises sufficiently, equilibrium at E_3 may be reached with the portfolio content of B bonds rising to OR resulting in increasing bond prices. This type of demand analysis affords the only adequate explanation of the manner in which wider differentials were determined between July 1957 and February 1958.

We have now completed both a quantitative and qualitative analysis of bond yield differentials. The present and the preceding sections have supported the contention that an expectational approach to the theory of the interest rate structure is required. Although this qualitative analysis has been based almost exclusively upon the 1957–1958 recession, the relative emphasis should not be thought to detract from the generality of the conclusions. The period was chosen for expository purposes with the knowledge that the forces to be explained are in particular evidence during sharp changes in the level of economic activity and, therefore, more readily pinpointed. That such changes, whether more or less sharp, occur with sufficient frequency to allow generalization of these qualitative conclusions is self evident. Turning to the quantitative conclusions, a brief review may be in order.

Contrary to the original hypothesis it was found that independent variables representing the following were not significant:

1. The relative volume outstanding at specific maturities.
2. Changes in the relative volume outstanding at specific maturities.
3. New bond issues.

Within the general category of stock and flow variables the only significant results were obtained from the relative volumes of Government and Corporate Bonds, respectively, and competing long term debt. The broad conclusion is that the traditional representation of yield curves in the long term bond market as smooth, continuous functions is a close approximation of the real world. No support was evident for the hypothesis that the actual function is discontinuous and/or subject to humps depending upon conditions at specific maturities. The above must be qualified, as mentioned often in the previous discussions, by the fact that new issues are handled gingerly by both the private and public sectors. A sudden change in this condition might have material impact upon the yield curves—with present knowledge, of an imponderable magnitude.

Of the expectational variables the equity variable showed by far the strongest impact. Given the relative volume of bonds outstanding, conditions in the money market, capital market and the economy in general offer a basis for the explanation of a large percentage of the variation in bond yield differentials. The relationship is a consistent one not significantly altered by cyclical factors per se, although it cannot be gainsaid that cyclical elements are incorporated in the fluctuations of each of the expectational variables. More specifically, the money market variable (the rate on prime commercial paper) showed declining strength and an insignificant relationship as maturity lengthened. This result tends to support the traditional view that the impact of the short term interest rate upon the over-all structure weakens with maturity thus contributing to a greater stability in the very long term relative to the shorter terms. It is also interesting to note that in the high quality, highly sophisticated markets changes in the interest rate structure anticipate changes in the short term rate. The variable representing general economic conditions and at the same time serving as a proxy for the subjective measure of default risk (the unemployment rate) showed an insignificant relationship for the A equations and a significant, consistent one for the B's. Since Government and Aaa quality ratings are the same, such a result is easily credible. The consistency of the coefficient values for the B equations indicates that default risk looked upon as a function of general economic conditions (and therefore of corporate earnings) is not affected by maturity, i.e., the risk of default is no more nor less for an intermediate than for a long term bond. If a corporation defaults, all its bonds are equally affected. As mentioned above, the strongest expectational variable, and the one which exhibited significance throughout, was the capital market variable (equity yield). For the A equations, involving bonds of the same quality rating, there was no definite trend in the coefficient values. For the B equations a definite decrease in coefficient values was evident for longer maturities. Thus, there seem to be two elements in the decision as to the risk content of existing portfolios. When the investor seeks safety, for example, he tends to switch from physical, or capital, assets to monetary assets, but at the same time he tends to make a choice within the range of monetary assets with respect to quality and maturity. On the average, investors seeking safety attach somewhat higher priority to liquidity and the absence of default risk, i.e., there is a preference for higher quality, shorter term bonds as well as for bonds as such. The result is reflected in the pattern of coefficient values as maximum impact occurs at the short end of the maturity range.

This study has both quantitatively and qualitatively supported the contention that expectations are at the core of any adequate theory of the interest rate structure. Institutional factors play a role but primarily in slowing adjustments and in an indirect way through expectations. Supply comes out as an extremely strong influence tempered only by the wisdom of those issuing securities and their desire to place new issues with a minimum of upset to the existing market. This accounts for the significance and strength of the first two variables in the regression equation and for the failure to find any significant impact from new issues per se. However, it is the demand side which has accounted for most of the change in yield differentials, and it is when the demand for bonds is considered that we must turn away from simple monetary analysis involving changes in available funds to an expectational analysis based upon estimated risk and return. Yield differentials depend upon the allocation of funds among substitutable assets, and a theory which tells us only that the funds will increase under certain circumstances tells us nothing about how these funds will be used. It is for this reason that emphasis has been placed upon interpretation of the last three independent variables as expectational variables. It is conditions in the money market, the capital market and the economy in general that mold expectations, and it is the subjective evaluation of risk and return which serves as the basis for portfolio selection—the ultimate determinant of relative prices and therefore of yield differentials.

APPENDIX

Residuals from Baa Bond Adjustment Regression

Bond Number	December 1959		1958		1957		1956		1955		1954		Mean Adj.
	1	2	3	4	5	6	7	8	9	10	11	12	
1											+48	+47	+48
2											+72	+75	+59
3					−24	+7	+1	0	+26	+62	−4	−8	−5
4			+59	+63	+9	+16	−8	0	−8	0	+11	+9	+18
5	−4	−4	+10	+52	−76	−98	−78	+3	+5	+15	+29	+21	−7
6	+31	+22	+22	−7	−2	−20	−31	−17	+25	+33	−24	−31	−6
7	+29	+36	+19	+10	+5	−14	−40	−19	−6	−6	−11	−24	−2
8	+46	+19	+23	−12	+21	+10	+24	+27	−9	−9	+26	+13	+21
9	+19	+16	+60	+82	+26	+22	0	+8	+33	+27	−2	−3	+19
10	−81	−151	−191	−197	−139	−64	−35	−63	+4	0	−61	−61	−100
11	−41	−33	+2	−8	+5	−30	−12	+28	−74	−78	+40	+35	+5
12	−80	−22	−31	−61	−39	+12	+16	+12	+36	+41	+25	+26	−8
13	+6	0	−17	−37	−15	+15	−3	−21	+21	+22	−25	−19	−14
14	+49	+33	+35	+74	+38	+17	+7	−14	−18	−31	−30	−27	+11
15	−12	−42	+36	−9	+37	+3	+5	−41	−22	−30	−53	−54	−25
16	+25	+59	+52	−57	+4	+22	+27	+22	−45	−47	+23	+22	+22
17	−112	−92	−92	−39	+4	−6	+22	+30	+32	+31	+14	+9	−17
18	+9	+26	+16	−4	−26	−49	−9	+7	+33	+24	+9	+23	+2
19	+121	+105	+122	+139	+78	+36	+81	+59	+11	+10	+56	+66	+80
20	−72	−77	−77	−16	+11	−2	−8	−30	+54	+47	−44	−55	−37
21	+2	+9	+10	+17	−13	−6	−17	−24	−38	−41	−40	−39	−14
22	+27	+23	−5	−24	−8	+21	−6	−10	−29	−36	−12	−10	−2
23	−12	+10	+6	+18	+57	+52	+41	+16	−10	−11	+3	+12	+19
24	−12	+9	+13	+31	+15	+24	+40	+26	+11	+9	+37	+39	+23
25	+33	+16	+2	−11	+34	+29	+33	+31	+23	+31	+25	+28	+23
26	−9	−16	−39	−42	−10	−43	−26	−20	+24	+27	−31	−26	−26
27	+53	+29	+28	+4	+6	+28	+3	−11	−35	−25	−34	−16	+3
28	+10	+23	+17	+36	+10	+24	+11	+28	+23	+18	+27	+22	+21
29	+5	+3	+9	+9	+7	+1	−7	−23	−28	−32	−54	−60	−14
30	+43	+55	+54	+68	+48	+43	+28	+16	+9	+7	+13	+13	+33
31	−60	−53	−61	−69	−67	−43	−44	−30	−32	−20	−25	−21	−44

Residuals $(Y_s - Y_0)$ are calculated from the regression equation $Y = 5.0258 + 0.027769X_1 - 0.000503X_1^2$ with the constant term adjusted for each semi-annual period as shown in Table 1.

Final Baa Bond Adjustments

Bond Number	1959		1958		1957		1956		1955		1954	
	1	2	3	4	5	6	7	8	9	10	11	12
1			+61	+61	−24	+3	+3	+3			+48	+48
2					+4	+4	+4	+4	+59	+59	+59	+59
3					−84	−84	−84	−84	−5	−5	−5	−5
4					−15	−15	−15	−15	+10	+10	+10	+10
5	+14	+14	+14	+14	+20	+20	+20	+20	+22	+22	+22	+22
6	+25	+25	−15	−15	+21	+21	+21	+21	−17	−17	−17	−17
7	+20	+20	+20	+20	+1	+1	+1	+1	−13	−13	−13	−13
8	+19	+19	+19	+19	+1	+1	+1	+1	+25	+25	+25	+25
9	+44	+44	+44	+44	−54	−54	−54	−54	+1	+1	+1	+1
10	−152	−152	−152	−152	−12	−12	−12	−12	−69	−69	−69	−69
11	−20	−20	−20	−20	+13	+13	+13	+13	+36	+36	+36	+36
12	−47	−47	−47	−47	+13	+13	+13	+13	+24	+24	+24	+24
13	−12	−12	−12	−12	−9	−9	−9	−9	−23	−23	−23	−23
14	+48	+48	+48	+48	+21	+21	+21	+21	−25	−25	−25	−25
15	−25	−25	−25	−25	+15	+15	+15	+15	−48	−48	−48	−48
16	+45	+45	−57	−57	+19	+19	+19	+19	+27	+27	+27	+27
17	−84	−84	−84	−84	+13	+13	+13	+13	+20	+20	+20	+20
18	+17	+17	−22	−22	+12	+12	+12	+12	+12	+12	+12	+12
19	+122	+122	+122	+122	+64	+64	+64	+64	+56	+56	+56	+56
20	−75	−75	−4	−4	−4	−4	−4	−4	−42	−42	−42	−42
21	+10	+10	+10	+10	−15	−15	−15	−15	−36	−36	−36	−36
22	+24	+24	−11	−11	−11	−11	−11	−11	−11	−11	−11	−11
23	+6	+6	+6	+6	+42	+42	+42	+42	+9	+9	+9	+9
24	+10	+10	+10	+10	+26	+26	+26	+26	+33	+33	+33	+33
25	+10	+10	+10	+10	+32	+32	+32	+32	+26	+26	+26	+26
26	−27	−27	−27	−27	−25	−25	−25	−25	−26	−26	−26	−26
27	+29	+29	+29	+29	+12	+12	+12	+12	−24	−24	−24	−24
28	+22	+22	+22	+22	+18	+18	+18	+18	+23	+23	+23	+23
29	+6	+6	+6	+6	+6	+6	+6	+6	−44	−44	−44	−44
30	+55	+55	+55	+55	+34	+34	+34	+34	+11	+11	+11	+11
31	−61	−61	−61	−61	−46	−46	−46	−46	−25	−25	−25	−25

The Final Baa Bond Adjustments were calculated as the mean of the deviations shown on page 244 for periods exhibiting as nearly as possible stable market ratings. These periods were predominantly three two-year periods, as indicated, with variations of the middle period from 1956 to 1957 in accordance with the pattern on page 244. For a full discussion of the adjustment refer to the text, pp. 199–207.

Cumulative Author Index

This index includes names appearing in Monographs 19, 20, and 21 of the Cowles Foundation Monograph series. The boldface roman numerals indicate monograph numbers.

Cumulative Subject Index

This index includes subjects covered in Monographs 19, 20, and 21 of the Cowles Foundation Monograph series. The boldface roman numerals indicate monograph numbers.

COWLES FOUNDATION MONOGRAPHS

Orders for Monograph 8 should be sent to Principia Press of Trinity University, 715 Stadium Drive, San Antonio, Texas.

Orders for Monograph 3 should be sent to the Cowles Foundation, Box 2125 Yale Station, New Haven, Conn. 06520.

Orders for Monographs 12, 13, 14, 16, 17, 21, and 22 should be sent to Yale University Press, 92A Yale Station, New Haven, Conn. 06520.

Orders for Monographs 15, 18, 19, and 20 should be sent to John Wiley & Sons, Inc., 605 Third Avenue, New York, N.Y. 10016.